WHAT THEY'RE SAYING ABOUT *MARRIED TO MERLOT*:

"I am so thankful Martha shared her journey with me and with the world. I was excited, sad, angry, and I grieved and celebrated with her. That is the sign of a well written piece!"

—Michelle McDonald, Ph.D., Child and
Adolescent Psychologist

"Martha Louise's memoir about love, loss, family, and faith tells the heart-wrenching story of a war-damaged soul struggling to find peace and a wife and family trying to hold it all together. The narrative is full of Southern grit, pathos, and raw humor. Readers, especially those who have suffered the loss of a loved one to addiction, will find special meaning in these pages."

—GiGi Henry, Corporate Vice President

"Totally loved it! Martha's insight and thoughts are profound. She made me cry and laugh at times. A brilliant book!"

—Jacquie Reed, Real Estate Agent

"So well-written and poignant. It is simply beautiful. I cried and related to so many parts. This isn't one family's story but rather the story of what many, many families face. It isn't just about alcoholism. It is about any and every addiction. It is about betrayal, loss, grief, and facing the present moment and embracing life. *Married to Merlot* is a wake-up call!"

—Lorraine Cosgrove, Program Specialist for
School Libraries and Instructional Media

"Written with such honesty and power, every woman and man will be able to see themselves in elements of Martha's story and gain insight into the effects addiction has on others, and the ravaging aftermath war can inflict on relationships."

—Frances Keiser, Author

MARRIED TO MERLOT

A MEMOIR WITH A MESSAGE OF HOPE

Martha Louise

Frey House Publishing, LLC
Ponte Vedra Beach, Florida

Publisher's Note:
The details, events, and conclusions in this book are told from the author's perspective and reflect her opinions, views, and perceptions. The author has changed some names and personal details to protect the privacy and preserve the anonymity of a few select individuals mentioned in the book.

Cover art by Carol Watson
Book design by Frances Keiser

ISBNs
978-1-7329423-0-1 (softcover)
978-1-7329423-1-8 (hardcover)
978-1-7329423-2-5 (e-book)

Library of Congress Control Number: 2018964510

Summary:
A self-help memoir with a message of hope for those searching for healing as they deal with betrayal, divorce, PTSD, depression, emotional illness, addiction/alcoholism, tragedy, loss, and grief.

BIO026000 Biography & Autobiography/Personal Memoirs
OCC019000 Body, Mind & Spirit/Inspiration & Personal Growth
FAM014000 Family & Relationships/Death, Grief, Bereavement
SEL006000 Self-Help/Substance Abuse & Addictions/Alcohol
FAM015000 Family & Relationships/Divorce & Separation
SEL043000 Self-Help/Post-Traumatic Stress Disorder (PTSD)

Frey House Publishing, LLC
Ponte Vedra Beach, Florida

Printed and Bound in the USA
First Edition

To my three beautiful daughters,
Jamie, Alyson, and Lindsey—women of exceptional strength.

And a special thank you to the military
for all you have done for our country.
Thank you for all your sacrifices.
You are truly our heroes.

CONTENTS

PREFACE

I sit and watch the hours go by
Waiting and waiting—but for what?
Waiting to leave this prison of thoughts?
Or just waiting—a passing of the time?

I have been waiting. It seems I have been waiting all my life. Waiting for my husband's heavy drinking to reach the last stage of alcoholism, a stage in which the disease grips the drug user and does not let go. Waiting for my children to reach that next milestone in life—one that I believed would be easier or more fun or less stressful. Waiting for the future. I was never living in the present. I am sure there were fleeting moments of being present, but I was usually worried about something that had happened in the past or worried about what would happen in the future. I was not always this way. Living with an alcoholic and playing a part in the illness can do this to you.

I have learned so much since embarking on this unexpected journey, more than can be revealed in the writing of this book. I have learned the meaning behind "living in the moment." I have learned to rely on my higher being and my God to get me through the tragedy that found itself wielding its debacle on my family. I have found an inner peace that, while it may not be constant, it has branded its serene, quiet stillness on my heart and has enabled me to get through the days, one moment at a time.

My hope is that individuals who find themselves in similar situations or who find themselves wishing their lives away, thinking about the past or yearning for a better future, will read my story and be inspired to change their way of thinking and ultimately change their current way of living. I wish I had found Al-Anon when I was going through the stress of living with an alcoholic. My husband's problem became my problem. While I recognized that faulty thinking and knew his was a disease that required treatment for him to overcome the illness, I slowly let go of any factual knowledge. And I eventually replaced it with an emotional, bitter, angry reaction to behavior that I thought was within my husband's control. What that did to my self-image was deplorable.

Alcoholism is a pervasive disease whose execrable tentacles reach out and touch all socio-economic levels and all professions in our society. Ours is a drinking culture, and many people do not realize the nasty progression of this insidious disease. The statistics vary, but some reports indicate one out of ten who drink will end up with their drinking leading to serious problems for them and for their families. This statistic is especially germane to the military personnel who returned from the Vietnam War but also to some of those returning from the Iraq and Afghanistan wars. Many of these individuals find they are unable to acclimate to society and to "life." They have great difficulty adjusting to everyday life when they have been exposed to traumatic horrors in a land far from home.

My daughters and I have endless accounts of Vietnam veterans reiterating what my husband put into words, "I don't feel right. I don't belong in this world. I don't fit in. I never have." Many vets have uttered these same words to their family members. I think that maybe part of their perception is due to post-traumatic stress disorder (PTSD) from the traumatic events they witnessed or engaged in during wartime, but I also think the veteran who finds himself drinking increasingly finds he does not fit into the sober world. At some point he prefers the drunk world, and at some critical juncture he leaves his family for that world.

I have talked to war veteran counselors who tell me many service members find they simply cannot reintegrate into society, and they ultimately find a way to go back into military action. They are accustomed to feeling adrenaline rushes and being hypervigilant and fearful. Their homeland does not fit their "normal." If they are not able to reenlist, addiction to alcohol or other drugs may become their escape from a life that is not compatible with their altered world view.

The loss of control is the factor that transmutes the social or responsible drinker into the alcohol abuser. Some have the loss of control from the time they take their first drink. That was my husband. He could not have just one drink. He was unable to drink without going to the point of inebriation. As his tolerance changed over the course of time, the number of drinks increased. In his last few years, he was drinking a full one and a half-liter bottle of red wine a night. After many years of heavy drinking, he lost control of the ability to stay away from that first drink.

Others can drink socially for many years, and then they, too, develop loss of control. Once loss of control enters the dismal picture, the drinking only continues and proceeds incrementally. These drinkers find it virtually impossible to quit. They may make promises to quit or to slow down, but they cannot. My husband never promised he would quit, as he did not think he had a problem, and he always said he could quit if he wanted to. He simply did not want to quit drinking. If he had a night in which he lost all control because of his drinking, he would promise not to let his drinking get to that point again. However, he could not keep that promise nor could he keep the promise to slow down his drinking.

The love for one's family is not strong enough to break the cycle. It takes outside help and alcoholism treatment to stop the drinking and to achieve recovery. Unfortunately, the family member erroneously thinks, *If he loved me, he would quit.*

I have finally come to the realization that I was not responsible for my husband's drinking problem, and I was also not responsible for his recovery. Al-Anon has provided the support I should have accessed many years ago. That is one regret I have—not seeking Al-Anon sooner.

In addition, I realize my husband's drinking was a camouflage that kept his unresolved grief, perceived abandonment, and wartime trauma compartmentalized and outside of his awareness. He was carrying a heavy burden, and he was gradually sinking into a darkened abyss that not even he could understand. He reached out for the one floating life-preserver that could give him air and momentary relief, the one lifesaver that would enable him to escape from his depressed feelings and unending emotional torment: the bottle.

The initial prompting to write occurred the day my husband walked out of our family's life and our thirty-three-year marriage. Writing is cathartic, and I did not want to stockpile my emotions or bury them, as I saw my husband do. I did not want the divorce or the stress of my marriage to chip at and weaken the foundation of my emotional well-being. I had seen others go through divorce and had witnessed their embitterment, their resentfulness, and their inability to forgive. I saw how extremely unhappy these individuals were, and I decided I would not join their numbers and develop emotional or physical illnesses because I had internalized negative feelings. My purpose in writing was to explore the crisis and loss associated with divorce, to learn from mistakes made, and to move toward resolution of grief and ultimate healing. The course of my writing changed as other events occurred and as I continued to recognize the emotional struggles my ex-husband was enduring.

I hope my words reach the dear trooper who has lived or is living with a family member who has alcoholism or another addiction, PTSD, or any other overt manifestation of underlying emotional struggle. Whether you live it yourself or are living with someone who has depression, anxiety, or any other condition that we typically associate with poor emotional health, the ramifications are far-reaching and impact the entire family. I penned the words within these pages so that others could identify with and relate to the experience of living with someone who is mentally and emotionally fragile with the hope they can acknowledge their own loss and begin their own journey of healing. If you are that caregiver, supporter, or worrier, you are not alone. If you are that someone with fragile emotions, you, too, are not alone.

I truly believe we are given the opportunity to take what life has handed us, to learn from it, and to grow. Sometimes it takes a wild, bucking roller-coaster ride through the fear-provoking darkness before we can emerge at the end of it and see the light. When you find yourself on the roller coaster, however, taking that first step is extremely difficult, especially if you are careening around curves and are only trying to keep your family on board with you. You don't want to fall out. You don't want them to fall out. You don't want to jump and leave your family behind, either. It seems impossible for you to exert the amount of effort it would take to jump off and evaluate what is happening. You merely hang on for dear life and try not to lose your family.

When I was twenty years old, I wrote a number of poems and essays and titled the composite of writings, *Life and Love*. I subtitled it *Literary Reflections*. A friend had copied my literary attempts when he knew me in 1972, and he sent them to me during the time I was writing this book. I was astounded as I read the parallels between my thoughts then and the events of my life thirty-five years later. One of the poems is placed at the beginning of this preface; other poems and one prose selection are incorporated as introductions to the reflective sections that have the bear cloud emblem. Another poem follows the last chapter, and the final poem ends the postface. Perhaps you, too, will see the congruence and also wonder, as I have, whether we have preconceived knowledge or a prescient understanding of our life's path even before we reach the events that mark and define our journey. And incidentally, the introductory pieces were sent to me *after* I had written the passages they precede.

PROLOGUE

I sit here on the edge of the moss-laden, boulder-fringed bluff and look down at the speckled wooded sections of forest green that make a patchwork quilt of a segment of the Arkansas River Valley. Interspersed with those plots of forest trees are soft blankets of emerald green where the land is naked, but grass-covered and treeless. Lying to my left is the marvel of the three-pronged Lake Dardanelle. It covers an expansive area and beckons me. I know I am where I belong, however. I also know what lies between me and that expanse of land and water that hugs the valley below me. I breathe in the panoramic view: a kaleidoscope of color and wonder. It is breathtaking, and I sit above it, on the edge of my husband's beloved Mount Nebo. This is where it all began, and this is where it all ended.

I am here today to tell the story. It is a story that has to be told. I have driven one thousand miles to tell it. I hope I do it justice. I hope I do him justice.

～つ～つ

I was married to a Vietnam vet. My husband, Mike, could not talk about his time as a medic in the Vietnam War. I am sure he had experiences none of us can even remotely understand. Mike said those words to me when I asked him to tell me about Vietnam: "There is no way you can understand what we went through. It is something that you can't even talk about because no one could possibly understand." Sometimes there are things so far outside of what a person can imagine, so far out of human awareness, that the person knows he cannot talk about that unimaginable thing. The person who undergoes that experience can barely imagine it. He knows it is impossible for anyone else to comprehend. He can barely understand it himself.

Could I have possibly grasped the picture of my husband as a young boy of twenty in a crowded hospital room in the middle of a jungle with moaning, crying, pleading soldiers begging for their lives to be saved … or to be ended? Could I understand the young Mike's torment from day to day when he faced the crowded infirmary, filled with bloodied, writhing, half-torn bodies and heard the cries and smelled the stench of burnt flesh, fresh blood, and rotting body tissue? Not to mention the bodily fluids.

Could I have known that he handled a lot of patients whose bodies were covered with white phosphorus, which had left chemical burns that melted through their flesh and left horrible, seeping burns and large, gaping, bloodied flesh wounds? That he attempted to get the phosphorus out by lowering those torn bodies down into a water trough only to then hear the screaming when the water touched those open wounds? And that he had to keep the bodies submerged in the water even while the soldiers fought him? Could I have imagined all that he saw, what decisions he had to make—who to save and who to up the morphine on? Could I imagine a young boy in such a situation, a boy who should have been sitting in a clean, sterile university classroom, trying to keep from falling asleep while the professor droned on about western civilization?

How did he manage to keep his sanity after hearing the sounds, seeing the sights, and smelling the stench of the by-products of that awful war? Jack Smith, a famous ABC reporter who served in the U.S. Army from 1964 to 1967, wrote a personal account of an event in Vietnam for the January 28, 1967 edition of *The Saturday Evening Post*. His descriptive words in the article, "Death in the Ia Drang Valley," make me wonder what awful sounds my children's father heard daily as he went about trying to save lives:

> "I don't know why, but when a man is hit in the belly, he screams an unearthly scream. Something you cannot imagine; you actually have to hear it. When a man is hit in the chest or the belly, he keeps on screaming, sometimes until he dies. I just lay there, numb, listening to the bullets whining over me and the 15 or 20 men close to me screaming and screaming and screaming. They didn't ever stop for breath. They kept on until they were hoarse, then they would bleed through their mouths and pass out. They would wake up and start screaming again. Then they would die."

Is this what my husband endured day after day? The screaming … the never-ending screaming colliding with the cries, the moans, the hoarse voices, and the agonized pleas of the post-battle wounded warriors: *"Help me." "Oh God, help me." "The pain." "Somebody, help me." "God, help me."*

He had difficult choices to make—who would he treat first? He heard the pleas of his war brothers: "Save me. I have a wife and a baby. Please don't let me die." He did all he could do, but then they died. Maybe sometimes he aided their death. Maybe he knew they were going to die anyway, and he upped the morphine to speed their death and to put them out of their misery. Maybe my husband played God.

Mike told me one small bit about an abdominal injury. He told me how he had to push the entrails back into the soldier's abdomen and then suture the gaping hole. The abdominal injuries were the worst. He did not tell me about the screams. I now know they were also a part of his life-changing experience in that base hospital in Vietnam.

How does a young twenty-year-old deal with that mind torment? For that matter, how did any of the Vietnam vets manage to live even remotely normal lives? We know many of them did not. Many of them died by their own hand. Another number are homeless on our streets. Jack Smith describes the horror of Vietnam well in the following excerpt:

> "All afternoon there was smoke, artillery, screaming, moaning, fear, bullets, blood, and little yellow men running around screeching with glee when they found one of us alive, or screaming and moaning with fear when they ran into a grenade or a bullet. I suppose that all massacres in wars are a bloody mess, but this one seemed bloodier to me because I was caught in it.

> "All night long the Cong had been moving around killing the wounded. Every few minutes I heard some guy start screaming, 'No no no please,' and then a burst of bullets. When they found a guy who was wounded, they'd make an awful racket. They'd yell for their buddies and babble awhile, then turn the poor devil over and listen to him while they stuck a barrel in his face and squeezed.

> "We were all sprawled out in various stages of unconsciousness. My wounds had started bleeding again, and the heat was getting bad. The ants were getting to my legs. ... The medics at the L.Z. cut off my boots and put bandages on me. My wounds were in pretty bad shape. ... I was put in a MedEvac chopper and flown to Pleiku, where they changed dressings and stuck all sorts of tubes in my arms. ... I learned that Stern and Deschamps, close friends, had been found dead together, shot in the backs of their heads, executed by the Cong. ... Like most of the men in our battalion, I had lost all my Army friends."

How did they do it? How did Mike do it? I imagine he also had to cut off the boots of many soldiers and had to sew up the torn flesh and treat the burnt skin. He also had to bag soldiers' corpses and body parts and write the identifying information on a tag and attach it to the black, polyurethane, body bag. How did he do all of this as a young man of twenty? How did he later reinsert himself into society as though nothing had happened?

MARRIED TO MERLOT

Shadows on the Wall

Shadows on the wall
Memories of my past
Drifting out the window

Designs on my mind
Thinking of the present
Waiting for my turn

Time on my hands
Hoping for my future
Not knowing where to start

Stop.
And listen to your life passing by.

You go through stages, just as you do with any type of grief: the shock; the numbness; the denial; the sad, deep depression; the anger; and finally, the acceptance. How can you ever truly accept this event in your life? You can't. You can acknowledge it, but can you truly accept it?

He walks out of your life, and he has been a part of it for more than half of what you have lived. The emotional roller coaster is overwhelming.

You watch him pack. You even add things you think he will need. You care about him. But do you really love him? He is the father of your children. You love him as you love your mother, your brothers, your sisters, your friends. The relationship has taken a turn for which you were unprepared, and, while you care about him, you cannot let yourself feel the love you once had. Or maybe it is truly gone. Maybe the harrowing years of strife and stress have stripped you, layer by layer, until the love is no longer the essence.

You are married to an alcoholic.

You knew it all the years you were with him, and you tried to change the course of the inevitable future alcoholism was destined to take you. You worried when he started drinking alone. Then he started drinking all weekend. Then he added nights of the week.

Now he drinks every night, and you have not seen him for months without the alcohol. The only time he is sober is when he is at work. You are not there to see his sobriety. You are not there to see how easily he gets along with his coworkers. He does not drink around them. He drinks when he is with you and the children.

You have begged him to stop or at least limit the amount he is consuming. Your pleading falls on deaf ears. Literally. His hearing has declined as well, and that has added to your list of grievances. He has started making poetry with you. When you say, "How was today at work?" he replies, "Yeah, I think Jay's a jerk." You continue to plead, you sometimes cry, and you ask him again and again not to drink in front of the children. He occasionally complies, but the bad habits return.

He was the elephant in the living room. You and your children had to walk quietly around him. He may have had the television booming (he was going deaf, remember?), but he let you know when you were being too loud, and you were never as loud as that damn TV! You retreated when he became boorish and demanding. You slowly found other things to occupy your time, and you grew distant with each other.

The children grew up. You finally had the empty nest beckoning you. When you found yourself in it, however, you were alone. You had difficulty piecing together what had been ripped apart. What happened to your world as you knew it? You are incredulous, as you never dreamed of this happening. It is incomprehensible. The many times you wanted to leave him, you never did, and you never could have. You married for better or for worse, and when you commit, unfortunately, you really commit.

How many times had you thought you were happy everywhere in your life except for your husband's drinking? How many times had you considered your husband as a thorn in your side or your cross to bear? Too many to count. Sometimes you tried to overlook his inconsiderate ways, his apparent selfishness, his irritability, his impatience, but it always came back to smack you straight in the face. He may as well have hit you—the impact was just as hurtful. How could you love someone like him?

He continued to drink. His drinking remained an issue and was always a note of contention. You hated the look on his face when he was drinking. You could even tell when he had just one drink. His face changed. He was mean and crude, and he often wanted to pull you to him and have his way with you. Sometimes you went through the motions so you would not set him off. You did not like it when he was angry.

You might have even partied with him at times. After all, social drinking was an activity you did well—sometimes too well—and when you were both intoxicated, the lovemaking was exhilarating. That may have been what kept you involved with him.

Nonetheless, there were the ugly words exchanged between the two of you when he was drinking. You reacted to his irresponsibility and his apparent disrespect for you and for your children. You overlooked his evident disrespect for himself. You likely said horrible things to hurt him or to wake him up. You threatened to leave him, and, finally after an explosive evening when he was belligerent and cursed one of your children, you threatened to leave him if he ever became that drunk again. This time you meant it. He had heard it from you before, but he knew you now meant it. He had crossed the line. You could take it, but you would not let him hurt your child. You do not consider that she is his child as well.

After that, he managed to keep the drinking at bay, but he did continue to imbibe. He just never became reeling drunk. He never again stumbled through the house or knocked into walls or broke items as he bumped into them on his way from one room to the next.

You recall your harsh words … your loss of respect for him … your dismal feeling that he would continue down the alcoholic's path, and you would be left to pick up the pieces.

You threatened him with that as well. "You are hurting yourself," you say to him. "I will not be there to take care of you when you are debilitated because of what you are doing to yourself." He listens. You don't think he does, but he does. You also tell him you want him to lose weight. In your anger at his apparent self-destruction, you spat at him, "I didn't marry a fat man, and you need to think about your health." His fat is deplorable to you. He lays on you with his alcoholic breath passing over your neck, your face, your lips. He is drunk, and his fat belly presses on yours and overlaps it, and feelings of disgust rise from deep within you. You are turned off completely, and you wonder what has happened to your life. You ask yourself what this fat, drunk, old man is doing on top of you. You know he will get angry, so you don't push him off you. You go through the motions … and you hate it.

You hate his drinking, his behavior when he drinks, his "stupid" demeanor when he drinks, and you hate the stress his alcoholism does to your life.

You are happy everywhere else, but you feel strained when he enters the room. He does not make conversation—his comments are brief. He does not engage in the activities of the household. He is aloof ... distant ... withdrawn. He wants to watch TV, drink his Merlot, and be left alone.

The change in him is incomprehensible to you. The alcohol has gradually and surreptitiously taken over the man you loved, the man you married, the man with whom you had started making "growing old" plans. The transmutation leaves you baffled. You have a desire to look back and see your marriage as it truly was and not as you had dreamed it: the fantasy world in which you have always resided.

CHAPTER 1

THE BEGINNING

It all started with a simple introduction. I had a good friend in college who told me he wanted to introduce me to his brother.

"John, you never told me you had a brother!" John and I had become good friends in the three years I had known him. We cheered together on the cheering squad, and he was a "Cavalier." The Cavaliers was the first established social organization on our small college campus. I had been a Cavalier Sweetheart. In all that time John had never indicated he had a brother.

"Why have you never mentioned him?" I asked him, the surprise still showing in my voice.

"Well," John replied, "he's kind of retarded."

"Oh," I answered slowly, "so you want me to go out with your handicapped brother?"

John laughed. "No, he's not really retarded—the family just talks about him like that."

"That's terrible," I said. "What's wrong with him?"

"He's just always screwing up. He was always getting into trouble with Mother and Dad. He went off to Vietnam, and he has been in Lake Tahoe for the past year. He is coming in this weekend, and he is going to the football game. I told him I would find a date for him."

I already had a date for the post-game partying, so I declined John's offer. I had him point his brother out to me, though, while we were cheering at the game, and I looked at the tousle-haired, young man sitting in the bleachers. He was wearing an Air Force jacket. He saw us and waved at his brother. He was a doll … an absolute doll. I could see his great smile from where I was standing. He had beautiful, cerulean blue eyes, a set of engaging dimples—and that smile. I started giving the date idea a little more thought.

"Hey, John," I called to him, as he walked away from me. The captain had given the signal for the next cheer. "I may take a rain check on that date with your brother!"

That was in the fall of 1972. Mike enrolled in Arkansas Tech in Russellville and started there the following January. It was my final semester, as I was graduating in May. Not long after the semester started, John called me on a Friday night and asked if I could pick up his brother and him. They were at a party, and they were "shit-faced," as he so eloquently articulated. After some grumbling on my part, I finally agreed.

I drove to the house where the party had taken place, and Mike stumbled out of the front door first. He could barely walk. He climbed into the back seat and had trouble closing the car door, and he started laughing. John entered the front passenger door and said, "Please excuse my brother," and then he started laughing. Drunks are not that funny when you are sober. John made small talk, and Mike laughed at everything he said. At times they both burst into laughter. Okay, so they were not just drunk. They had apparently been smoking pot. I peered into the rearview mirror. Even in his drunken, stoned stupor, I found myself very interested in this guy. The Air Force jacket appealed to me as well.

The next day I went to the Catholic Church mass service and stopped by Mike and John's trailer afterward. Yes, a lot of the college students lived in an off-campus trailer park. It was a big party scene, and the park accommodated over two hundred students. My roommate, Frances, and I had decided to try it out our senior year. My family laughed at me and said I was "trailer trash," but I don't like that label, nor do I like the label "white trash" or for that matter "Caucasian garbage." I would not accept their description.

Mike and John were just getting up when I arrived. I had dressed up for church and, of course, I wanted Mike to see me at my best. Several days later he told me he did notice me that morning and liked what he saw. He told me many months later that he had looked up my dress when I sat down and saw my "beaver." Eeew! By the time he told me that, however, I was completely smitten with him and although I did not like what he said, I tried to overlook it. Besides, I did not believe him. I was always very careful when seating myself while wearing a short skirt. I dismissed it entirely. I wanted to. I liked him.

The following weekend there was a party at one of the Cavaliers' apartments. Mike was there, and I tried all night to get his attention. He was drinking and well on his way toward getting inebriated. I walked outside and found him and my roommate throwing snowballs at each other. She knew I liked him, and she asked me to join her in the snowball battle she was having with him. He was laughing and thoroughly enjoying himself. He did not seem to notice me but finally smacked me with a snowball and rubbed it into the back of my jacket. That was it. That was all I got. He turned back to Frances. I was devastated. He did not appear interested.

I gave Mike and John rides into campus two days a week, and my fondness for Mike grew. I found myself in small groups with Mike sporadically. A group of us would go to a concert or some other college function, or we would all travel to Morrilton in Conway County, the closest wet county, and gather at one of the bars there. Our college town, Russellville, was in a dry county. How archaic.

After a group of us had gone to Morrilton one Friday night, Mike, John, and I prepared breakfast. Mike made the best scrambled eggs, and I was happy he could cook. The attraction I felt for him seemed to grow more every time I saw him.

Two months into the semester, Frances and I had a party at our trailer. We invited our sorority and Cavalier friends, and the party went well. Girls were coming on to Mike, and I noticed. He paid me bits and pieces of attention during the evening, but not as much as I would have liked. There was a lot of drinking, and the night eventually began to wind down. I picked up a trash bag and started picking up beer bottles. Mike took the trash bag from me and started helping me. I was thrilled. One of us made an engaging comment, and we simultaneously and spontaneously gave each other a quick, unassuming but tender kiss. We separated as rapidly as we kissed and looked at each other and exclaimed in unison, "That was our first kiss!" It seemed special to both of us, and we both appeared to expect it was the first of many.

We carried the trash out to the dumpster and met a neighbor on the way. Mike's friendliness struck me at that moment. He put out his hand and introduced himself and invited the man to come in to the party. He did not seem to have any trouble talking to this veritable stranger. That was one of the many characteristics that attracted me to him, along with his good looks.

Mike and I were inseparable after that. Within the next few weeks he drove me up to his beloved Mount Nebo and showed me his great-uncle's cabin. We parked behind the cabin and looked out over the rock-strewn bluff that was behind it. It was a spectacular view. The orange and white lights twinkled and smiled up at us from the valley below. He held me close to him and told me he had visited here every summer when he was a boy. He appeared wistful for a brief moment, then he kissed me—a warm and lingering kiss that hinted at all kinds of possibilities, a kiss that left me with the feeling we had found each other.

Love Can Be Lonely

Love me like I love you
Take me as I am.
Fear not the voice of others
By this, we only can.

Near, but yet so far away
In my memories you will stay.
All those times we had together
All those times now passed away.

Our summer days we spent together
The winter months were filled with warmth.
You showed to me what love could bring
And then you left me in the spring.

Nevermore to taste your kiss
Or feel your warm embrace.
Nevermore to hold your hand
And try to keep your pace.

All these lonely nights I spend
Wondering where you are.
In my heart you'll always stay
Near, but yet so far.

Why can't you remember
*   as I remember?*

You have high standards. You always have. You see the potential in someone, and you want to push them toward being the best they can be. You have tried to edify your husband and lead him to grow with you. He balks for some reason. He does not grow. He does the opposite—he regresses. He feels you pull away, and he turns to his first love, the bottle. You do not fit into that scenario, so he finds someone else, someone who serves him the wine, someone who listens to his woeful tale of neglected home life. He thinks he has fallen in love with this someone. You know better. He is in love with the bottle—the someone only goes with the bottle. You don't go with the bottle.

He does not mean to fall in love. He tries to reach out to you, but you have already left him. You no longer respect him, and you realize he has chosen the bottle over you.

When he tells you he is leaving, you are in shock. He tells you he remembers when you were going out of state five years ago to visit your family, you told him you were sick of him and his fat body, and you wanted him to consider your absence as a separation.

What you recall saying is that you could not take it anymore. You are always upset, the children are always upset, and you want him to think about what he is doing to himself and to his family. You want him to think about how important his family is to him. You tell him he needs to make a choice. Stop drinking or lose his family. Little did you know he was already in the throes of alcoholism, and at this stage he would not be able to stop drinking without lengthy, extensive treatment.

You had worried about his path all your life with him. "Please don't drink tonight. ... I am afraid you are going to become an alcoholic. ... Please don't drink so much." How many times had you repeated these statements or made these pleas during your marriage?

Now, he says he is leaving you. You had never worried about that. That was inconceivable. You remember just a few months ago trying to get your relationship back, trying to add pizzazz to it. It had soured, and you wanted to make it better. It was empty-nest time after all, a chance to be with each other. He never wanted to go anywhere with you unless it involved drinking, so you set up "bar" meetings and flirted with him at the bar. He seemed to enjoy it, and you had a great sexual encounter afterward. He seemed happy, but you have always acknowledged he appears happy whenever he is able to drink. Vacations, parties, dinners—he enjoyed these because drinking was involved. You want to tear your hair out. The alcohol progression continues, but now he is leaving.

He is packing. You help him with toileting items you think he might need. You had spent the previous four nights talking, venting, sorting it out so you could understand it. He was never sober during those nights, but he was sober in the morning, and you lay with him each morning. You wanted the security, the safety of the known. The unknown was frightening. He plans to move out tomorrow, and you are scared. You have never been alone—ever.

You tell your husband of thirty-three years everything you need to say. Your feelings are tumultuous, and you feel the need to get them out. He reveals he has known this other woman (wine server, in your mind) for five years. He was mad at you for what you said before you left to go visit your family, and he says he "banged" her that night. You cannot bear hearing those words. At the same time, you realize you have at times wished he would find someone who would sweep him off his feet and take him away from you. You had wished he would find someone who would care about him the way you had before the alcohol had taken him. Of course, you never dreamed it could really happen. You are not prepared for this.

During the first night of shock, you are not yourself. You become detached as your insides churn and your anxiety level heightens. He tells you all the sordid details. He leaves nothing out, and you wonder at his judgment and common sense. You had previously started seeing signs of pre-senile dementia, and you now question his cognitive ability. He tells you how he has fallen out of love with you, and he is in love with someone else. Someone who loves him for who he is. Someone who doesn't care if he is fat. (Yet, he has lost thirty-five pounds over the past five months.) "She loves me for myself and lets me be who I am." He goes on to say that she does not beat him down for what he is doing. (After all, you consider, she comes with the bottle.) He tells you he is happy when he is with her, and he wants a few years of happiness before he dies.

You remind him alcohol was always the issue. It came between the two of you and robbed you both of a wonderful life together. It also came between him and his children. He does not think so. "Maybe," he says. You see that he is still in denial. Denial and defensiveness, you muse, the alcoholic's primary defense mechanisms.

You fear for him—for what he is about to do without you in his life. He is not himself. You can see a pronounced change in him, and you wonder what has happened to your husband. He says he loves you and always will. You do not know what has happened, but you know he is not well. You can see it in his eyes.

You recall his recent downhill spiral and what appeared to be a nervous breakdown one month ago. You worried about him then, and you worry about him now, especially since you know he has found someone who accompanies the bottle. You are afraid his drinking will worsen, and you worry about the path he is taking. You figure it is okay to worry about him as the father of your children. You don't have to worry about him anymore as your husband.

What are some of the things he tells you over the past four days, prior to his leaving you? He tells you, "This is too big for me." He is referring to his surroundings, his nice lifestyle, and all the "stuff" around him. He sweeps his arm around the room. "I don't want all of this." He refers to you as well. He tells you, "You are smart. You have a vision, and you are going somewhere. I have held you back." You have felt that way at times—that he has held you back. You are active and ambitious. He is passive and complacent.

He tells you, "You are beautiful and wonderful and have raised our daughters to be great people, and you have done that by yourself." You tell him, "No, you had a hand in that." He says, "No, not really." You realize there is some truth in that. He never seemed comfortable with them. He did not know how to interact with them. You were always telling him what to do with them, how to do it, how to be. He did not seem to know how to be a father. You wanted him to be a good father. You wanted to be a good mother. Family is very important to you.

CHAPTER 2

THE ENGAGEMENT

Mike and I saw each other more frequently after he took me to Mount Nebo, and I was crazy about him. He was busy his first semester in college, and I was equally as busy my last. He became involved in the student senate, pledged Cavaliers, and was voted pledge president. "Bear" took the latter job very seriously. All the Cavalier pledges had nicknames, and Mike's was Bear. He was six foot one, and his brown hair was somewhat long (he grew it out after leaving the Air Force), and I guess he had a grizzly look about him. The other nicknames were not as favorable: Yard Ape, Buckwheat, and Mousetrap to name a few.

I was always trying to find out from Buckwheat and Mousetrap where they would be that weekend or what the pledges were doing, as some of their girlfriends and I liked to spy on them. Of course, I did not tell them that. We would drive up close to the site and walk to where the pledges were meeting. Sometimes we would see them, but usually they were inside a building, and we saw nothing. We had to ask the other pledges, as Mike would never tell the pledge secrets.

One day a pledge told me something I was not supposed to know. I saw Mike later at his trailer and teased him.

"I know something about what you all are doing," I called out gaily as I entered his meagerly furnished abode.

"What do you mean? What are you talking about?" he asked disinterestedly. He was lying on the sofa, looking at his class notes. He was studying for an upcoming test.

"Oh, don't worry about what I may know. I just know something about what you and the pledges are planning," I said lightly in a teasing tone.

He looked up brusquely. His previously composed face transmitted irritation and then anger. Apparently, something big was being planned, and I was not supposed to know anything about it. He could tell I knew something. He glared at me. "Who told you?"

I did not know what to say. He looked so angry.

"Who told you?" he insisted.

He jumped up from the sofa and walked over to me and took my forearm and twisted it behind my back. Ouch, that hurt!

"Tell me who told you, and what do you know?"

I cried out, "I'm just kidding; I don't know anything."

He bent my arm back even more. "Tell me," he hissed.

"Mike, you are hurting me!"

"*Tell me*," he yelled.

"Ow! You are hurting me! Please stop," I pleaded. I never dreamed Mike could be so mean. He was hurting me, and I could feel tears welling up in my eyes.

"Please stop, Mike, that really hurts." By this point I was crying.

He finally released me, but my arm was killing me. I lay down on the sofa and sobbed. That was so hurtful, and he did not appear to care. He stayed angry and just looked at me with a blank look. His reaction to the pledges' secret went far beyond what I might have anticipated. His aggressiveness scared me. I had already committed myself to him, and I was afraid. Yet, I loved him, and he said he loved me. I chalked his behavior up to stress—he had a lot going on with pledge leader responsibilities, concurrent school work, and impending tests.

By this time Mike had already professed his love to me. He seemed infatuated with me, and I was smitten with him. He was like a little boy the day we talked about our feelings. He was excited and was restlessly pacing around his miniscule living room in his small trailer. I was standing in the kitchen area, smiling at his boyish antics.

"I have never felt like this about anyone before! *I love you!*" he shouted. "*I love you!*" he yelled again as though he was incredulous that this could be so.

I was laughing. I had never seen him so animated. "I love you too," I said.

"I want to marry you," he said.

We had only known each other four months, and we were talking marriage. I was in the last semester of my senior year. I knew there was a life sequence: go to college, get married, buy a house, and have children. I knew this was the guy I was going to marry. He was the only man I had ever dated that I could envision standing at the altar when I imagined my wedding day. Of course, we would marry. It was the order of things. I knew he was the one.

Mike sent me roses the day after he professed his love to me. We were talking of marriage and making plans for our future. I was on top of the world, and I thought he was there with me.

Mike courted me and took me to dinner at nice restaurants. He showed me how to eat steamed artichokes. He watched chick flicks with me and let me cry at the sad endings. He met my parents and charmed them, as he had a propensity for enchanting older people. I had frequently witnessed his captivating the heart of an elderly individual, whether it was a store clerk or a family friend or a parent of a college buddy. He possessed charisma, and he had a twinkle in his eye when he greeted others. His admission to me of his love was unremitting, and I basked in the unity I felt with him.

Then little things started to happen. One of the Cavaliers told me at a Cavalier party that Mike was a jerk, and he thought I deserved better. He told me to be careful. He did not like how Mike was talking about me. Mike was going around saying he could "get it whenever" he wanted it. I was hurt. I loved Mike, and our chemistry was amazing. I could not help myself. I had waited a long time for this part of life, and we were going to get married—that was certain. But I did not like what I was hearing.

I confronted Mike that night. He laughed, "No, Marti, it's not like that. Guys just say things."

He hugged me to reassure me, but my feelings were hurt. He kissed me, and I responded. "Really," he murmured close to my ear, "Guys just say things. It did not mean a thing. You know I love you."

Then there was the Julie Hunt incident. We were at a semi-formal Cavalier party, and Mike kept looking up Julie's dress. Each time he went by her, he would pull her dress up and laugh. He did that right in front of me. She would fuss at him each time, but I could tell she was not that upset. I was very upset, however. He was drinking and possibly near drunk, but that was no excuse for his behavior. I was slowly becoming tormented, as I loved him and was starting to question his love for me. I wanted his love in return. The big fight we had that night was simply a prelude to an amazing make-up sexual encounter.

Our engagement was short. We met in January, and by May we had set a wedding date for October 27. We were separated over the summer months, as I started working in Little Rock, and he worked as a life guard in Fort Smith, where his parents lived. I had met his parents, Deenie and Cecil, in early May—I always thought it strange that Mike and his brother called their parents by their names and not the traditional titles associated with mother and father. At that time his mother had not appeared happy about his decision to get married.

"How are you going to live?" she had asked. He had told her I would be working, and he had the GI Bill. I had witnessed her reaction and asked about it later, and he said, "That's just my mother. She has never been happy with anything I have done. It's okay, Marti. I want us to get married."

The summer months passed, and I wrote him letters. He did not like talking on the phone, so I wrote to him. He hitchhiked to Little Rock on the few weekends he did not have to work. When he did have to work on the weekends, I drove to Fort Smith. I was planning our wedding, so I had to consult with my mother, and I made frequent stops in the town of Morrilton where I grew up and where my parents still lived. I also consulted Mike's mother regarding our gift registry selections and the rehearsal dinner, so my trips to Fort Smith were multi-purposed. It was a very busy summer.

I was so happy on my wedding day. It was truly all about me! I remember my cheerleading partner, Johnny "Bones," picking me up and holding me up high, laughing with me during the wedding reception. I was exhilarated. I also remember how the night before I wanted to call it off.

Mike was grumbling during the wedding rehearsal the previous evening, as it was taking longer than he thought it should.

"I am ready to get this over with!" he whispered to me in a growl. His impatience was obvious.

We had practiced the entrance several times, and the priest was telling us what to expect when we stated our vows and when we placed the wedding rings on each other's fingers. Mike's irritation grew. "Let's go … let's go," he said to me.

Finally, I snapped at him and started walking away from the church altar down the aisle toward the front entrance. We were finished, anyway, and most of the bridal party had walked out ahead of us. We had stayed behind to talk to the priest. I felt tears stinging my eyes, and I did not want anyone to see me crying the night before my wedding, so I made a quick detour and walked up the stairs to the choir loft. Mike's father, who was Mike's best man, followed me and showed concern.

"I can't marry him," I said to my fiancée's father.

"You're just having cold feet," he offered.

"No, I think it is more than that. You saw how he acted. I can't marry him."

"Really, Marti, you're just having cold feet. It is normal for the bride the night before her wedding."

"Is it normal for the groom to act that way? I don't think so, Cecil. I cannot marry him," I said emphatically. "I don't like him."

I knew my emotions were in shambles. It was the night before my wedding, and my husband-to-be was acting like the jerk I had been warned about. "Why does he do that?" I sniffled.

"He is probably just nervous, and both of you are wound tight right now. It will be better in the morning. I know you both will be fine." He added, "Really, you will be okay."

I was not convinced, but I knew the wedding party and rehearsal dinner were waiting for us. I took a deep breath and exhaled with a heavy sigh. I looked at Cecil and grinned slyly and said, "My feet are not cold. They are actually rather hot and sweaty in these shoes." I smiled ruefully. "Let's go to the rehearsal dinner."

Mike was oblivious to how I was feeling, and I told myself it would be okay. He drank a lot at the rehearsal dinner, he laughed, he responded to the toasts, and he went out with the groomsmen afterward. I spent the evening packing for the honeymoon with my maid of honor's assistance and tried to shake off what I saw as a glimpse of my future husband. I had seen other markers, which seemed to surface more and more as familiarity set in with the man I adored. However, I was not yet accustomed to his apparent impatience and irritability, so I charged these negative attributes as situational.

A note from Mike's mother had come in the mail a few days before, and I had set it aside. I wanted to read it on the night before my wedding. I was expecting encouraging words and unparalleled mother-in-law wisdom. I opened the envelope after I fell into bed before I fell into sleep. Mike's mother had written a two-page letter, but two of her sentences stood apart from the rest and left me with a feeling of unease. They appeared simple and straightforward at first glance, but I suspected there was something more behind the stark words. She had made references to Mike throughout the body of her note, and her closing remarks left me with a feeling of sadness for him.

"I have tried all of these years. Maybe you will have better luck and will be able to do something with him."

What Is It?

What's weighing so heavily
on your mind?
Like a tiny, whipped puppy
you pout and stare.
I'm only wondering if you
really do care.

What is it you want?
Love,
affection,
companionship?

You know that I'll always be here.
Waiting
for what?
(For you to finish your beer?)

What is it you need?
Consolation,
advice,
or is it only love?

If it's love you need,
why can't I be yours?
Or is there some hidden secret
tearing up your breast?
A thought being pondered upon
from your recent past.

Loving you
is like taking a roller-coaster ride
with its ups and downs,
turns and lurching curves,
and at the end …
a dizzy swooning.

As you look back over the years, you remember the great times, the passion, the heat, the roller-coaster love you had for him. He is a kind, sweet, almost shy man when he is sober. He is distant, aloof, and sometimes offensive when he drinks. You love that sweet man, and you always have. You initially tolerated the drunk, and now you hate the drunk. After he started on an antidepressant, he became more subdued and withdrawn.

You think back to his rising anxiety and the panic attacks he had been having at work the last few months. He was worried about the panic attacks and thought at times he was having a heart attack. He bought a blood pressure measurement kit, and he became even more anxious each time he saw how high his blood pressure had risen. He went on an antidepressant. He was miserable. You tried to console him. You went on long walks with him, and he held your hand. He was going through something frightening, and you wanted to help him. You had no idea he was getting ready to tell you he was leaving you.

"I never thought I would feel like this," he said while on a long walk with you through the neighborhood.

"What do you mean? Feel like what?" you asked.

"Like this. This is not me. This is not me at all. I don't feel anything."

You think, maybe that is what antidepressants do. They numb your feeling, so you don't have to feel depressed.

You later realize the antidepressant may have helped him leave you. He was unable to feel anything, which made his decision easier to follow through. It was obvious that he was more subdued. He never raised his voice. He seemed even-keeled. He did not show irritability, impatience, aggression. He had shown those often in the past. He seemed to withdraw further away from you and into himself.

He did not seem to care about anything. Yet, he was nervous, his hands trembled, and he told you he felt he was going insane.

When he finally tells you what he is up to, he lets you know he is in love with another woman, and he needs to leave you for his own happiness. He tells you he knows you will be okay. "You're strong. My dad always said you were a rock." He has even said that to you himself.

You wonder if he was ever truly comfortable with you—your high standards, your expectations, your confidence, your success. He even tells you he is going from a "Level A to a Level C" with this woman. You grasp his meaning. He is in love with a woman who does not have a college education, who is ordinary, "a little plump," as he puts it and adds, "She adores me." He says you should get your doctorate. "I always thought you should be a doctor. You are such a smart woman." You look at him. Does he really think this talk will lessen the blow?

You think about the time when the two of you adored each other. "You are wonderful." "You are awesome." "I love you." "I love you more." "I love you much more." "I love you much, much more." "I love you much, much, much more … more than infinity." One of you would start it, and the interchange would continue until the final "more than infinity." It had been a nightly ritual for many years—the good years, the years when you had felt happy, secure, safe in that fantasy world you had created.

But that was before the bottle. You know you still love each other. Even before he walked out the door when he left, he held you and he started to cry. You held him, and you both cried in each other's arms. He tried to leave you, and you said, "I will let you go … but wait …" You held each other. You both sobbed … hard. Then he left.

Somehow you both seemed to know it had to happen this way. Even when he first told you, your voice from deep within said, *Let this happen. This is the only way it can happen. Let him go. This is the way it is supposed to be.* "It is what it is," he said.

So many thoughts go through your head after he leaves. *Did I do this? Was he never happy with me, with our life together?* He had packed only a few things, and you saw how you had taken over his life. The house was filled with your things, although several furniture pieces had been in his family's possession. He did not seem to care about any of it. He was a small part in the house, as he was a small part in the home, in the family. But he played a large part in all of it.

Before he left, he did say you had brought him to a level he had never thought he could reach on his own. He thanked you for that. He said he appreciated it. "If not for you, who knows where I would have ended up. Down some drug lane, possibly. I really appreciate what you have done for me."

You recall he wanted a simple life. He wanted a boat dock and a low-key lifestyle. What pressure he must have felt to be that successful businessman, that provider for his family, that suave and sophisticated guy his wife idealized him as being.

The true person won out. He is not that sophisticated, debonair man his wife had deluded herself into creating. He found someone who does not have those kinds of standards or expectations. He feels comfortable, safe. You feel scared and out of control.

CHAPTER 3

THE FIRST YEAR

Mike appeared nervous during the wedding mass service. He had a hangover, and it was a long hour for him. Following the ceremony, he had an unaccounted number of drinks at the reception, and so did his grandfather and my father. Both relatives passed out before the day ended. Mike's mother must have noticed Mike's drinking, as she started giving him cups of coffee. His fraternity brothers followed him and switched his cup out each time for one filled with beer. His mother kept giving him more coffee. His frat brothers gave him more beer. By the time we left for our honeymoon, he had more than enough—beer, not coffee.

Mike was drunk as we drove away from the wedding reception. The picture in the wedding book shows it. We drove north on scenic Highway 7 toward Branson, Missouri. As we sped around curves, the jagged bluff bordering the drop to the valley below was sometimes too close to my side of the car, and I begged him to slow down.

"I'm okay, Marti," he said in an exasperated tone.

"No, you are not, Mike! You have been drinking, and your driving is scaring me. Please slow down."

This was my wedding night. I had dreamed of this night, and this was not going as I had envisioned. I was imagining the headline, "New bride is killed in car crash the night of her wedding." I guess Mike had survived, as he was not mentioned in the headline. My thoughts were interrupted by the screaming of the tires as he took another curve too fast. I was really scared for my life.

"Mike, please slow down. You are really scaring me."

He again refused, and this time his tone was sarcastic and mean. I prayed for my life not to end that night.

We made it safely to Branson and had plans to stay a couple of nights there and then drive on to the Lake of the Ozarks further north. We enjoyed each other in our honeymoon bed, but he initially seemed preoccupied and distant. I did not want to provoke him, so I said nothing more about the harrowing drive up the mountain. Besides, this was a time when I felt his love for me, a time when I enjoyed him the most. Our chemistry was electric and explosive. It never failed us. After he fell asleep, and after I was over my disappointment that we were not going to talk before sleep, I lay there thinking, *This is my husband.* I felt so much love for him. I kept whispering it over and over as I gazed at him, "*My husband.*"

We woke up early the next morning and drove over to Silver Dollar City, but Mike was not interested in the activities in the park. He did not want to do the things I wanted to do, and again he seemed preoccupied. He finally said, "Let's go," and we headed back to the hotel. We stayed one more day, then he was ready to go back. We had only been there two days. He said he needed to get back to school and to his classes. He had already missed one day.

"What about the Lake of the Ozarks?"

"We can do that another time, Marti. I really don't want to get behind in my classes."

"Well, you could have at least warned me. I was planning on a longer honeymoon."

He gave me his sweetest smile. "We can continue the honeymoon back home."

He called his good friend Scott to see if he wanted to meet us at a winery and a restaurant that were on our way home. I thought it strange that he wanted Scott to join us the last night of our official honeymoon, but I liked Scott. He had been my friend first, and I went along with it.

I looked at Mike as we drove toward Altus. He was acting differently. Before our wedding day, he had been attentive and eager to go along with what I wanted to do. Now, he was acting as though what I wanted did not matter. He did not look at me with the interest he had previously shown. *I am imagining this,* I thought. *Maybe he is really worried about school.* He had flunked out of two colleges before he went to Vietnam. He partied too much at each school, flunked out of both, and signed up for the Air Force. *He wants to be successful this time.* With that, I dismissed all other thoughts.

I had found my prince, and I eagerly awaited his arrival each afternoon after he had finished his classes. I was home early, as I was teaching special education at an elementary school that was ten miles away. He liked to eat early, so I attempted the wifely duties. He loved to eat, and I was able to prepare the meals he liked. He usually came in from class, asked what was for dinner, and plopped down on the couch in front of the television set. Wait, what happened to my prince? Where is the hello kiss? This was not what I had imagined.

He seemed to only attend to me when we were in bed together. He seemed to want to have sex that first year more than my body could tolerate, and he was not always loving and tender. He was almost vicious in his lovemaking, and he did not seem to care how I was responding. It was all about him. I was becoming more and more disillusioned … and sore. I was also becoming a nag. I did not like how he was ignoring me, and I let him know. The more I nagged, the more he ignored me.

He started staying on campus later and later. I called the student center one day to see if he was there, and, of course, he was. I had been expecting him to come home, and I was missing him. I had not seen him all day. I could hear the person on the other end of the line call out to him. I could then hear loud guffaws and male voices saying in sing-song fashion, "Oh Mikey, your wife is calling." "Oh, the wife's looking for you." I could hear the clatter of the phone as he dropped it and picked it up, and I was prepared to hear him say, "Hello." All I heard was a rough voice saying, "Don't ever call me here again! Ever! Do you hear me?!" I was stunned. It was Mike's voice, but the tone was harsh and malicious.

I sat down on the garage-sale sofa in our scantily furnished apartment and was nonplussed. I wondered what I had done. Then I recalled something Mike had said to me shortly after we were married: "I will never do anything to look 'pussy whipped' in front of any guy, and I want you to know that. I won't ever do anything that will make me look that way."

I had ignored what he had said, as I did not think it would be an issue. I was easygoing. I would not push him to appear "henpecked," as I preferred to call it.

I leaned back on the sofa cushion and closed my eyes. I thought back to the first few months of our marriage and recalled how difficult it had been. The guy before marriage was fun (though usually drunk) and liked being with me. He had said nice things to me. Now, he was starting to criticize me in front of others, he was starting to belittle me, and he was often getting irritated with me.

One of our mutual friends, Kay, admonished Mike one night when he flung a sarcastic remark at me, and I told her, "It's okay, I really do not care about him." It scared me that I could say that so easily, and it frightened me even more because I knew I meant it in that moment. However, I was married to this man, and I was here for better or for worse. Little did I know.

Three Little Words

When I say "I love you"
I say it with conviction
I commit myself to your will
With no fears of breaking the ties.

When you say you love me
I feel it with conviction
I commit myself to your will
With no wish for the ties to break.

Then why all this pain,
This bitter agony,
This feeling of rejection
When I don't hear those three little words?

Should I not be able to see your love
As I <u>feel</u> mine
Without having to express it in words?
You know how I feel
I don't have to say it ...

What is scary to you is that he is pushing aside thirty-three years and going toward the unknown. He is rejecting all the hard work, stress, strife, successes, and defeats—all the effort put into those thirty-three years. He is running from the tired woman who was with him through the child-rearing years, the problems associated with those years, and all the ups and downs. Now, he has found someone who did not have to go through any of that with him. How do you throw all of that away?

You described how you felt one night during that last week with him with an analogy. "Listen," you say, "you and I are pulling a wagon up a hill. In the wagon are precious rocks, valuable rocks. We climb up the hill with our collected items, and I slip and stumble. You pick me up. You fall, and I hold you back up. You slip, and a pebble flits out from under your shoe and accidentally strikes me in the face. I think it was intentional and throw a pebble back at you and try to hurt you. We keep pulling and pushing, wearing ourselves out, struggling the last few miles of it, until we finally reach the top. We are both panting, completely frazzled. You are worn out. I am complaining about the rocks you hit me with, about how tired I am, and you try to reach for me, but I am too tired and exhausted to reciprocate.

"You look over and see a woman standing on top of the hill without a care in the world. She didn't just go through that uphill struggle. She looks at you with pity because of that nagging wife beside you—that wife that had just gone through the struggles with you, the one that is now breathing heavily and trying to catch her breath.

"You and your wife are looking at the beautiful scenery in front of you, the rolling hills of green carpet, the pleasures you face on your downhill ride. You look at the wagon and the valuable rocks you collected that will buy you financial independence. You look at your wife. She is still panting and upset. You look at the other woman. She smiles at you and offers her hand. You hesitate. You look at your wife. You look at the other woman. You kick your wife off the hill and take the other woman's hand and lead her to sit beside you on the wagon bench. The wagon slowly slides down through the captivating landscape, and you feel the wind brushing through and lifting your hair, as you breathe in the refreshing air and enjoy the effortless, descending ride after that stressful, tumultuous ascent. The wife struggles to her feet and watches you both go and cries."

Divorce is not a word you thought would ever apply to you. It is damaging to your self-esteem and your sense of who you are. Divorce seizes your identity, and it tosses it around in a whirlwind of emotion and lost dreams. Adapting to the change that is taking place in your life seems insurmountable, as everything as you know it is no more. Even your day-to-day routine changes, and you will have to reestablish a routine without your husband as a part of it. If you are fortunate, you may have already done that to some degree. Everything that was familiar is lost, to be replaced with the unfamiliar: living alone, the single life, new activities, new friends, an unforeseen and altered future, a new identity. It is impossible to believe at the outset that this unfamiliarity will one day also be familiar.

You married with forever in mind. Now you wonder how much of what your husband says to you can be believed. He will say things to assuage his guilt. He will say things to make you feel better, as he is the one who is breaking up this "forever" marriage. He does not want you to be angry and vindictive, as he knows you could probably hurt him financially. What can you believe?

Can you believe his tears? His words when he left you, "I love you, I have always loved you, and I will always love you"? His complimentary attitude toward you and how he knows you will be okay? What can you believe from a man who has been living a lie? He says he met her five years ago, and the relationship developed over time. He realized he was in love with her and wanted to be with her three months ago. After all, he loves the bottle, and she has the bottle, you remind yourself.

Despite all that he is doing to you, you are worried about him. You are fearful about his mental stability, and you feel apprehensive when you are with him. His eyes are empty when he looks at you. After he moved out, you met him in public restaurants to give him mail, to talk to him. You see his distant look, the emptiness in his eyes, the lost soul. You want him to come back home. This is where he belongs—not in a bar, drinking with her every night. You want to be friends with him; you want this to be civilized. You want to eventually forgive him. Your spirit directs you. You know you can be friends with him. You can be mad at your friend, you can be hurt by your friend, and you can love your friend. So, you can be friends with him. There is no law that says you cannot. You are going through a divorce, and you are faced with settling financial matters with him, so you want him to be a friend. You don't want him to hurt you more than he already has, and you know he could do that financially.

You write him an email and thank him for a picture he sent to you of some of his fraternity brothers. You ask in your email, "Who are all these old men? I recognize most, but a few throw me off." You then write in the email, "I just wanted to tell you that I know that this financial part is difficult for both of us—heck, this whole thing is difficult, but I don't want us to be pulled further apart. Let's try to work through this amicably. I know I sometimes say things to you because I want you to hurt like I do. I guess that is only natural … but let's both try to remember what we had for thirty-something years. We were partners, we were lovers, we were best friends. Let's try to remember what we shared and try to keep that in mind so we can salvage the good part of that relationship. If we handle this the right way, hopefully we can remain on good terms as we go our separate ways. You said you always loved me and always will. I have always and will always love you too."

You push "send" and wonder how he will react. You want him to think about his marriage and what the two of you had together. You want him to love you and not hurt you in the divorce settlement.

CHAPTER 4

HIS COLLEGE YEARS

After the first year of our marriage and Mike no longer felt the need to use me up, our sexual relationship improved. We were more spontaneous, I was not as sore, and he was not quite as forceful. I always looked forward to our passionate lovemaking. It was the one part of our relationship I could count on. He told me he loved me again and again while we were in bed. And I reveled in it.

I never felt his love at any other time, however. I wondered what had happened to him that he could not care for me in the way I wanted and needed. I asked John what Mike was like before he went to Vietnam, and John did not see much of a difference.

"He was pretty much like he is now. I never liked him when we were growing up. I hated him in fact. He was awful to me."

"What do you mean? What did he do to you?"

"For one thing, he gave me the tart part of the pecan and made me eat it. It was nasty, and I have never eaten pecans since."

"That was pretty low," I teased. I did not see the harm in it. Didn't brothers do that? Engage in horseplay and get each other's goat … or pecan in this case?

"One time he spread honey all over his arm and let bees sit on the honey. His arm was covered with bees. The other boys in the neighborhood and I thought it was great. We put honey on our arms, and we tried to attract bees. We were all stung! He forgot to tell us he had pulled the stingers out first. The neighborhood moms were calling Mother for a week. She was not happy!"

Again, I wondered at the seriousness of these boyish pranks. "But, does he seem changed from the Vietnam War?"

"I don't see anything that different," John replied. "He drinks more and smokes a lot of dope, but he was always an asshole." He laughed as though he felt a need to lessen the harshness of his declaration.

I tried talking to Mike about the war.

"I can't talk about it, Marti. You have no idea what it is like over there, though. You can't possibly imagine. I don't even like to think about it. I can't talk about it."

At least he was not having flashbacks and waking up in the middle of the night, reenacting a battle with his wife as a target. I had heard about some of the returning vets and how they woke up in the middle of the night to the sound of an airplane flying overhead and thought they were back on the battlefield. They would startle at their wife's presence in their bed and start to fight with her. At least I did not have to contend with that. Yet, I knew he had seen things I could not possibly comprehend, and I knew it had to be affecting him.

"Don't you think you should talk to someone about what happened over there? A counselor, maybe?"

"No, I can't, and I won't. Drop it!"

He was angry with me, and I did just as he directed. I dropped it … for the time being.

Mike was taking a full load of courses, as he was trying to graduate within three years. He thought he could transfer some of the coursework from his previous college experiences. He had not flunked out of all those classes. He also planned to attend summer school. He asked for my help with book reports, and while I resisted (I told him I had already done college), he was forceful and would sometimes get angry with me. It was easier to help him than to deal with his irritability. He was working hard and maintaining A's. How could I not help him? He went a little too far once when he asked me to read the book and write the report. Helping him was one thing, but doing it all was totally different.

He pleaded, "I don't have time. I'm not good at writing anyway. Can't you do that for me?"

"No, Mike. That is your book report—your work assignment. I am through with college."

"Marti, I am really terrible at writing. You're good at it. You're great at it. Won't you do this for me?"

I had such a hard time resisting him. "Oh well, I guess I can." What else did I have to do?

Mike and I made friends with other couples, and we frequently spent time with them. We would have a get-together and cook out, or we would go to a Cavalier function. He was always great in social arenas, and I was always proud to be by his side. However, he was also flirtatious, and he seemed to like to push my jealousy buttons. He would pay compliments to the other women, and he was always charming and attentive to them. He would neglect me while we were at large gatherings, and while I had learned how to mingle, I would eventually start to seethe. He was far too inattentive. It seemed to work in his favor, as my jealousy feelings made me want him even more. I could feel insecurity creeping up into my being, and the more insecure I felt, the more I wanted to cling to him. When these feelings arose in me, we would have a big fight, and the making up was always intense and passionate.

After a night of passionate lovemaking, I assumed he would treat me the next day with that same loving attitude. Not so much. It was enough, however, to get me through the rough times.

One evening Mike surprised me with a confession.

"Marti, I need to tell you about something." He sounded serious, and he looked sad, so he had my attention immediately.

"I was at one of the guy's house a few nights ago, and we were all drinking, and there was this girl ..."

My heart sank. What was he about to tell me?

"They were all taking their turns with her. I'm sorry, Marti, I was drunk, and they were all doing it, and I just did it."

She apparently was giving them all head, his words not mine. I was crushed. "I am so sorry, Marti. I keep messing up. I always mess up. I am so sorry," he repeated. He cried. He kept saying he was sorry. I was hurt ... extremely hurt, but I did not leave him.

For better or for worse.

Changes in My Mind

Time and time again
I find my mind drifting
    to new fields
    to rolling plains
    to endless bliss.
I drop all that I've had
And take up new horizons
Wishing away my old memories
Gaining the experience of the new.

Finding myself like I have
I become disgusted with my actions.
My thoughts have changed from optimistic
    to pessimistic within a short time
And my actions quickly followed.

My life has seen many changes.
Changes within myself,
Changes which have caused hatred,
    pain,
    suffering.
Changes which have brought about
    new love,
    joy,
    and happiness.

Will these changes ever cease and
Leave me a solitary soul with that one?
Or will I only have a varied, saddened life?

Now he is leaving you. You are both looking at an amicable divorce settlement. You hope to achieve this without undue attorney costs. He asks you why you have not filed for divorce yet. You have resisted, as you are not ready to undo what you had with him. You do not want to do this.

You go through a grief process when your spouse of thirty-plus years decides he wants out of the marriage. Not only do you grieve the loss of your marriage, but you also mourn lost love, a lost relationship, albeit a bad relationship. You feel the hurt, the pain, the rejection. You struggle through your feelings, and you let them work through you. You know you must feel the pain before you can reach the healing point. You acknowledge your tears, your frustration, your anger, your disappointment, your heart-wrenching sobs, your out-of-control apprehension, your fretfulness, your fearfulness, your terror, your worry, your anxiety, your dread, your angst. This is a crisis in your life, and the finality of this tragedy in your life must be accepted.

For you to accept what has happened to you and for you to survive it, you will have to go through radical changes. You will never be the same. You are already not the same. Your life will never be as it was. You will need to change yourself and your world and view it differently. The world, as you know it, has changed. You will make sense of it all and find new meaning. You may never get over it, but you will get through it, and you will accept that this has happened in your life.

Your husband described you as a rock and reminded you that is what his father called you. What is a rock? A protector? A problem solver for the family? Being strong, capable, in control? If yes, then you are a rock. But now you realize that should have been your husband's role. How and when did you two switch roles? More importantly, what did that do to his self-esteem?

You may not be able to understand how he can now be so cold, so distant. Yet, you know men try to block out their grief. He has no trouble avoiding thinking about the impending divorce or the feelings associated with it. After all, he is a master of avoidance. He has engaged in this practice all his life. He has never had the language for sad feelings, and he has always been without words when it comes to his emotional pain. He does not need the words; he avoids any thoughts that remind him of his inner discomfort. He has always fought to be a true man, strong and without cowardice. True men do not express feelings of sadness.

However, you know better.

You have had difficulty understanding how he has been able to function at work. Oh yes, the master at work. To keep intrusive negative and painful thoughts away, he has thrown himself into his work. He is focused when he is at work; he single-tasks, and by getting involved in his work, he can keep disturbing thoughts and distressing feelings at bay. He feels in control. It gives him emotional relief.

You, on the other hand, are having great difficulty concentrating at work. Your mind obsesses about this tragedy in your life. You think about what he is doing, where he is, and why he is doing this to you. You obsess endlessly, and you are in crisis. You have always obsessed—about him, his whereabouts, his drinking, the stress he was bringing into your life. You continue to obsess about him. Where are you? What about *you*?

You seem to know rationally that this is the best thing for you in the long run, but first you must let your emotions and feelings catch up to what your mind is telling you. And the anxiety is overwhelming. Your emotions are spiraling, and you feel as though you may take off and corkscrew uncontrollably out of this planet. You no longer feel safe and secure and that fosters an anxiety that is overwhelming. You have been hit hard, and your trust is shaken. The betrayal alone leaves an acrid aftertaste in your mouth that has you gasping for air and leaves you thirsting for a gulp of sweet solace.

When security is taken away, you lose your confidence. You no longer feel whole. You feel broken. Your trust in people is disturbed. You withdraw from others, and you feel fearful. You do not know what the future has in store for you. You fear being alone, and you fear life itself. You apply these words to yourself, but you cannot help but see the parallel between these utterances and your husband's way of life. Isn't this what happened to him so many years ago?

The negative feelings find a way of overpowering you. You do not want to deal with the feelings. You never have. You pushed them aside for years. He was not the only one involved in avoidance behavior. You were never still when he was in your home. You were always busy. Keeping busy kept your mind occupied. You did not want to feel. You became a perfectionist about certain things—how the house looked, how the children looked, how you entertained. You became bogged down with projects and years later became obsessed with fitness activities such as walking, yoga, and weight lifting. You spent time outside of your nonexistent relationship doing onerous activities, so you could avoid the knowledge of what was lacking in your life: a satisfying, fulfilled relationship with the man you had married.

You avoided the man who was no longer married to you. You did not want to see that he had already left you and was now married to Merlot. You had thought you were the one married to Merlot, but then you realize he was the one in that particular marriage—not you.

CHAPTER 5

GLIMPSES OF THE PAST

After Mike's confession, he showed such remorse. He attended to me, sat with me on the sofa, and held me. He caressed me and whispered his love to me. He had me, all of me, and I continued to love him. By this time, I was starting to piece together some of what I felt may have affected his early emotional development. I had majored in psychology, and I had a need to understand this man with whom I had fallen in love and had committed myself to being with for the rest of my life. I knew he loved me, but I was not convinced. I could not see it in his eyes, and his behavior said otherwise.

"Tell me about growing up. What was it like in your family?" I asked Mike one Saturday afternoon. We were sitting on the sofa, making plans for the evening. I had been thinking about what John had told me a few months earlier about his growing up years with Mike, and I wanted to hear Mike's side of it. He had popped the tops on two beers and handed me one.

"Oh, the usual," he replied, as he took a sip. "You know the basic stuff—playing baseball, mowing lawns, getting into trouble."

"What kind of trouble?"

"Just little stuff," he replied. "I put a frog in my first-grade teacher's desk," he announced proudly.

"Did you really?" It may have been an innocent prank, but I knew teachers would react vehemently to such an act. "I guess that was better than putting a snake in your teacher's desk."

"I did that too!" he grinned slyly.

"Mike, that is outrageous! The teacher could have had a heart attack!"

"Do you think I thought that far ahead? Gosh, Marti, I was only six!" He continued, "Yep, my mother paid lots of visits to my school. She was called several times a year."

"You sound proud." I could not even imagine, as I was such a goody-goody.

"So, how was it with John?"

"John and I never got along. We did not like each other. He was always crying to Mother, and he was always getting me into trouble."

"Again? It sounds like you were getting into trouble everywhere."

"Pretty much," he said. He started moving restlessly.

I noticed his movements, and I said casually, "Were you that kid that walked by the teacher's desk and touched everything as you walked by?"

He stopped moving and looked at me. "Maybe ... listen, I don't want to talk about this anymore."

I knew that Mike and his brother had not had a good relationship growing up, but I also knew they were getting along well as adults. Mike was genuinely fond of John, and I sensed John's reciprocal affection. Mike did not like talking about his past, and this concerned me. He did not have much to say about either his mother or his father.

Mike's mother had told me she had lost both of her parents when she was in her mid-twenties. They were killed by a drunk driver late one night when they were on their way home from a social event. She had apparently been very close to her father. Mike was two years old when his grandparents died.

If Mike's mother had such a significant loss in her life when he was two years of age, her resulting grief had to have affected him. He never mentioned his maternal grandparents, but I knew he was close to his paternal grandmother. He called her Mimi and talked about her a lot. I knew he had spent many hours, days, and even weeks with his grandmother, but I wanted to know more. All he ever told me was that his Mimi loved him, and he was her favorite.

"Really? You were her favorite? Didn't John care?"

"John was usually with Mother or with our great-aunt. He was taken care of," he said disdainfully. "Marti, I don't know. Mimi just took me everywhere and kept me a lot. She liked taking me places."

"You stayed with her too?"

"Yeah, I probably spent weeks at a time with her."

"Did your Mother see you during that time?"

"No," he answered in a matter of fact tone. "I never saw my mother when I stayed with Mimi."

I loved Mike's Mimi. I did not have any grandparents—they died before I turned fourteen—and I adopted her as my Mimi as well. Mimi and I liked each other instantly the moment we met, and I thought we were a lot alike. Men usually marry their mothers. Mike had married his Mimi. Mimi was warm and affectionate with Mike, and he took care of her. He offered to pick her up for family get-togethers, and he checked on her often. "You okay, Mimi?" "You need anything, Mimi?" He was so sweet to her. I did not witness this type of interaction between Mike and his mother, however. His mother seemed critical and seemed to find fault with him. I did not sense warmth from her, but I did observe a better connection between her and John.

I did not come up with that on my own. A mutual friend of Mike and John's had noticed the family interaction during a visit to the family home. He was one of several college students who had spent a couple of nights at Mike's parents' house the weekend of the pep rally and football game annually scheduled in Fort Smith. We had thought we were just having a place to lay our heads, but Mike's father had grilled hamburgers on that Friday evening, and his parents treated us as their guests. They had been wonderful to us, and they had been gracious hosts.

"Don't you hate the way Mike's parents show favoritism to John?" Greg asked me a week later while we were sitting on a large flower-print sofa at a Cavalier party.

"What?" I set my drink down on the coffee table. "What do you mean?" I asked as I turned toward him.

"How could you not have noticed? They were so excited to see John and had very little to say to Mike. Don't you see how they dote on John and ignore Mike?"

"Don't you think Mike had something to do with that?" I asked. "He didn't have much to say to them while we were there. He always walked in when we came in from elsewhere and said a few things, then walked straight to the sofa and parked himself in front of the TV."

That I had noticed. Mike did not interact with his parents the same way John did. John was gregarious and was never at a loss for words, and while Mike seemed friendly enough, he did not have the same social ease that John displayed. I did not give it much thought. I saw it as the difference in their personalities.

"Well, I don't like it," Greg said. "I like Mike, and I don't like how his family treats him. I like John, too, and it's not his fault. He can't help how his parents are."

I shrugged. I really did not know what he was talking about. I did know, however, that when Mike and John were growing up, his father coached John's baseball team but did not attend any of Mike's baseball games. "Not one," Mike had told me. "He did not see me play one time." He said it in a matter of fact tone, without feeling. I felt a stirring of compassion when he told me that.

I found out many years later that Mike's dad did coach Mike's Peewee team but was unable to coach any of Mike's other teams. Mike either did not remember his father coaching, or he chose to discount that experience for some reason. Either way, I wondered how much pain this man had suffered—Vietnam may have only been a small part of it.

Where Am I?

As the clouds float in yonder sky
I wonder also where am I?
I float too
Drifting
To God knows where.

The seagulls breeze over the purple sea
But I ask where soon will I be?
I fly too
Drifting
To God knows where.

Two chipmunks play amongst the trees
As mine own heart yearns for peace.
For where is mine?
Is he drifting too?

Now he was taking his pain with him and leaving you physically. He had already left you a long time ago, the first time he left you for Merlot. The first time he was with her. It was the night after you left to go to Arkansas to visit family. You wanted him to consider what his drinking was doing to the family. You wanted him to choose the family and relinquish the alcohol. You told him you were considering the next week as a week of separation, so you and he could both think about what was important.

You left him with a letter you had written two years earlier. You had never given it to him. You had written it in July 1998 but had talked to him instead. After you wrote it, you talked to him, you cried, and you begged him to not drink so much. His drinking was affecting you, the children, and your home life. He said he would try.

After your talk, things improved. You and he celebrated your twenty-fifth wedding anniversary with a trip to Cumberland Island that fall. He bought you a shimmering diamond and emerald ring that you knew was too expensive, but you accepted his desire to please you. You threw a big party for him the following December for his fiftieth birthday, and while he appeared to enjoy the party, he seemed subdued and a little sad. His brother came to the party and noticed the melancholy as well. You slipped further away from each other the next year and a half. And when you gave him the letter in July 2000, you told him what you wrote in the letter two years earlier remained true:

> "While I am in Arkansas I am going to seriously think about us, and I hope you will do the same. You know I have not been happy, and I know you are not happy. Right now, I think we have no relationship—and I think you would agree. I have thought about this all week, considering myself separated from you, and trying to see what it is that I want.

> "I know what I want. I want to live with a man who enjoys being with his family—not sitting in front of a television set ninety-nine percent of his waking time but really interacting with his family. I want my children to have a father who is excited when he sees his children and wants to know what's going on with them, what they did at camp, what they did that day, etc. I want my children to brag about their father and what he does with them, whether it is taking them bowling, putt-putt golfing, or just to the club to hit putts, drives, etc. I don't expect a full-time devotion, just moments of simple pleasures that will leave indelible memories—an hour here and there, maybe a couple of hours once in a while, or an entire afternoon. I want to never again see the hurt in one of my children's eyes when they ask a simple request to "do something with me," whether it's play a game, take me to the pool, etc. I am so tired of defending ... "Well, he's tired ... he works hard all week and needs to relax ..." I am especially tired of hearing I cut my husband down in front of my children—I defend you more than you will ever know, and that is what I am most tired of.

"I want a man who wants to go on an outing with his family, a one-day trip, a weekend trip, whatever it takes to just enjoy being with his family and showing he likes being with them. Children do not understand. I don't expect every trip to be accompanied by the father, but occasional trips would be great.

"I don't think what I want is extreme. I expect a man could have a balance—he works, plays golf, socializes with the guys, and has time to spend with his family (not just be in the same house) and engage with them.

"My perception of what you want is that you want to be left alone when you are at home, you want to relax in front of the TV without any of us interrupting your view, you don't want the kids talking to you when you are watching TV, and you don't appear to want to spend any time with any of us. The kids never get good-night kisses. On the weekends it appears you want to be at the Club bar on Friday night, at golf all day Saturday until five or six p.m., you nap, and you'd like for us to go out maybe, but you don't consider the kids during these two days at all. Sunday is not much better. If we are lucky, we might get to go to church with you, but even that has decreased, and we don't even go to church as a family. What do we do as a family? I am sorry, but family is important to me, and that includes Mother, Father, and children. I realize I am a little late with this, or maybe it has just gotten worse over the last two years, but I can't continue this way. If we are not going to be a family, then let's quit the pretenses. If you want to be left alone …

"The family is one part of it, but the most important issue here is our relationship. We have none. If you think differently, maybe you could tell me, but I think you will agree. We are almost to the point of hating each other, and neither of us needs that. You are tired of my demands, and I am tired of making them. You can't change your habits, and I can't seem to stop harping on them. Sometimes I'm afraid you are on a self-destructive path—with all the drinking, overeating, "chewing," etc.—and I'm probably pushing you down that path. So, it doesn't seem good for us to be together. We are not good for each other right now. I think we used to be, but I stay too mad at you for things I think you can control.

"As I have said, I know what I want, and I know what I don't want. While we are away, I really want you to think about what you want. Words will no longer sustain this relationship. Actions will have to accompany the words, but if not, maybe what you want and what I want are not the same thing after all.

"I would like to have a balance—time with friends at bridge or tennis, etc., work time, time with the kids, time with you and the kids, and time with you. I want to have time at home between six and eight p.m. with no TV and have you join us in the kitchen or wherever we are and talk to us for more than just five minutes and not at the dinner table only. I want to not worry about how much you are drinking on a Saturday and what your mood will be like when you get home (though this has improved; you used to be a lot meaner than you have been). I want you to show an interest in Aly's soccer or Lindsey's gymnastics, etc., and be there for them—and not just sporadically or begrudgingly. I don't want you to grumble, even if you are teasing—they hear the grumbling and think you really don't want to watch them. I want you to be kind and considerate, and I want to be kind and considerate, which is something I am having great difficulty being."

You remember signing the letter and feeling frustrated and resentful. His drinking had become your problem. It was not his problem. He did not seem to be having a problem with it at all.

CHAPTER 6

BEFORE CHILDREN

Mike and I spent the summer before his senior year on Mount Nebo. Our friends, Jack and Donna, stayed with us. Donna and I rode into Russellville together to work at our respective jobs each morning, while Mike and Jack stayed behind to work on the cabin. Mike's great-uncle had owned the cabin and had left it to Mike's family when he died the previous fall. Mike volunteered to strip the outside walls and repaint it. He was not taking summer classes, and he was excited at the prospect of staying on the mountain a good part of the summer. I was a little leery, as I had to go into work each day, and the snaking mountain highway was a bit wearisome to manage. The twists and curves seemed endless. I agreed though, and it ended up being the most wonderful summer.

Mike was in his hiatus. He was through with classes temporarily, and he loved being on the mountain. He loved my being there with him. He enjoyed the refurbishing work and tore into it with his heart and soul. I had never seen him so energetic. I fell in love with him all over again. We got along beautifully with Jack and Donna, and the friendship with them lasted as long as the couple lasted. (They would break up two years later, and each move away from the area.) Mike was fun and affectionate, and his conviviality on the mountain, along with his wit and sense of humor, kept all of us content and amused.

Times on Mount Nebo were always good times. No stress, no worries.

During his senior year we took weekend breaks and went camping and fishing. These were the best of times. He had a small flat-bottom fishing boat, and he would fish all day out on Lake Ouachita while I lazed in the boat and soaked up sun rays. He would have his beer, and I joined him frequently. A cold beer on a hot summer day—nothing quenched the thirst better. I had to be quiet, though, when we were out on the water, and that was difficult for me. "*Shh*," he would often warn me when a thought came to me that I started to share with him. He caught lots of fish, and we hosted several fish fries that year.

On other weekends Mike hunted. He was an avid duck hunter, and I liked these weekends the least. I was alone. Most of my friends were still around, but I felt my place was at home with my husband, and I did not sustain contact with them. I would see them when he and I were out at parties, and we would catch up then, but that was it. I did not like being alone. I was so excited each time he returned from his hunting trip.

Mike graduated with honors in May 1976. *Hurray!* It was a joyous occasion. He had maintained an A-B status most of his coursework, and he had worked hard to obtain his degree. Granted, I worked hard as well. I was proud of him. His parents came to the graduating ceremony, and we celebrated at the cabin on Mount Nebo. Lots of friends celebrated with us. His parents stayed for a brief time and returned to their home.

Mike and I partied into the night, and we each had quite the hangover the next morning. We had given lots of parties at the cabin during his senior year, and a lot of his friends had crashed in whatever space they could claim. This night was no different. I woke up to beer bottles, homemade foil ash trays filled with cigarette butts, and sleeping bodies scattered throughout the cabin. It had been a great celebration!

Mike's father sold him his Ford LTD, and we prepared to move to Pine Bluff. Mike had moved from Fort Smith to Pine Bluff just before his junior year in high school. He graduated from Pine Bluff High School in 1966, and he had always planned to move there after college. I was skeptical. I had cheered at a basketball game at the University of Arkansas at Pine Bluff (UAPB), and my impression was not a good one.

I told Mike what had happened. After the ball game, another cheerleader, Paulette, and I and a couple of guy friends exited the gymnasium and walked toward the parking lot. On our way to our parked vehicle, we were accosted by some of the UAPB students. It was frightening, as one of the men taunted our driver and swung a punch at him. Our driver did get hit but kept yelling at us to get to the car. Paulette and I ran to the car, toward what we hoped was safety. Our two friends were right behind us, although I could hear the continuing altercation. We all jumped into the car, and the stalkers threw rocks at the windows. I heard the rear windshield crack and shatter. Paulette and I lay down in the back seat and covered our heads. Fortunately, our driver was able to get away without further mishap. His lip was bleeding. Paulette and I were shaking.

After hearing this story, Mike convinced me the area of town in which we would reside would be far away from the UAPB campus. He really wanted to move to Pine Bluff, and when he found a job with a bank there, I had no further argument.

Mike started out as a bank teller, then loan officer, and moved quickly to branch manager. He was finding success at work, and we made lots of friends in Pine Bluff. Our social life was filled, and we were meeting new people all the time through his work or through our club association. He played golf at the country club, and I played tennis. We both played bridge. It was a good life. We worked during the week and partied hard on the weekends. I became restless after several years.

"What about kids?" I asked him one lazy Sunday afternoon.

"What about them?" he asked.

"I am thinking we should have a baby. I think it's time." A lot of our friends had young children, and I felt something was missing in my life.

"I don't know, Marti. I don't know if I am ready to take that step. We are having fun. We don't have that much responsibility right now. I don't know. I can see us traveling and enjoying ourselves for a while."

That's funny. He had lived in Lake Tahoe and had promised to take me there one day, but whenever I brought it up, he said, "Someday." So far, we had only traveled from Russellville to Pine Bluff with an occasional excursion to a nearby lake so he could fish.

"I am ready," I said simply.

"Well." He sighed and thought for a moment. Finally, he said, "Why don't you get off the pill and let's just see what happens."

So I did. My doctor told me it could take months for my body to adjust after getting off the pill, and I would not likely get pregnant for six months to a year. Three months later I found myself buying a pregnancy test on a Saturday morning. Mike was playing golf. The test showed positive. I was nervous. Mike planned on my getting pregnant in a year, and it had only been three months. I fretted and anxiously awaited his return home.

"Oh, Marti." He sounded upset when I told him. "We weren't expecting this for another six months," he lamented.

"I know, Mike. I guess the doctor was wrong." I looked at him with tears in my eyes. I really did not want him to be upset by this news.

He thought for a moment, looked at me for what seemed an eternity, and finally reached out for me. I walked into his outstretched arms. "It's okay," he said softly. He pulled me to him and wrapped his arms around me. "It's just sooner than we expected. We can adjust." Then he was quiet. He continued to hold me. After a moment he put space between us and looked down at me.

"We are having a baby," he said in wonderment, as though trying out the words and feeling their import.

"We are having a baby," he said again but louder and with emphasis on each word. He was grinning. I smiled back at him. We both became exhilarated.

"We are having a baby!" he shouted happily. He grabbed me again and hugged me tightly, squeezing his arms around me and pressing my body close to his. "Oh," he said as if he just remembered something. He released me and separated his body from mine. He touched my stomach. "I don't want to hurt the baby."

What Happened to the Good Times?

I wanted to remember the good times
the ramblings in the yard
the tumblings
the sparkling laughter
our happiness.

Not a hand slashing at me across the seat
words thrown at me due to spite
for the misery I had caused
the worries I had mustered up
the tears I had conjectured.

You realize after you reread the letter you gave him, that you did not want him to be who he was. He wanted to sit in front of the television set and ignore his family. He wanted to be left alone. Why else would he do what he did? That was what he wanted to do. You would not let him be who he was, as that was not a person you would have liked or would have married.

You had a vision in your imagination of that perfect guy for you: sophisticated, handsome, but also humorous, kind, considerate, and compassionate. If you saw any hint that these were not his characteristics, you avoided that knowledge. You looked the other way. When he exhibited behavior contrary to your ideal, you excused it. *That's not him.* Little did you realize that the very same defense mechanisms he employed were the same ones you used. You denied him from being who he was, and you constantly defended him.

You start to look at how you treated him. You recall pushing him away with your comments or your anger, then you would see his rejection of you, and the fear of losing him or having his attention placed elsewhere was the catalyst for your next move. You would then manipulate the situation and him and regain his "love." Your relationship was a volatile one, full of drama. You are now realizing how big a part you played in that. You never let him be. You always attacked him with what he should be doing, how he should be acting, what you needed from him, and how you were not getting it. You wanted a relationship with him, but you did not have it. You are beginning to see that you are part of the reason you did not have it. It takes two, you tell yourself.

What was life like for him? You were never satisfied with him. Only during sexual activity with him did you feel satisfied, content, even fulfilled. You now realize that was the only time you were truly present with each other. At other times you resented past behavior—his transgressions. And you resented present behavior—his not giving you the attention you craved from him. But, what if he had? You probably would not have liked it. You also resented the future, as you were worried he was on a self-destructive path. You saw alcoholism developing, and you did not want to have an alcoholic for a husband. You had an alcoholic father.

Additionally, you now realize he could never show you the love you needed from him. You never felt truly loved by your alcoholic father, whom you saw as inaccessible and unavailable. You never felt his approval. You always tried to seek it, but you never gained it.

Maybe now you don't feel you deserve a man's love.

So, you found a partner who would not give you the love you so desperately needed, and so the pattern continued. You were in your comfort zone. It felt familiar. It was what you knew. You wanted love but could not feel sure you had it. You had never felt sure of it. Your sexual relationship was a specific manifestation of your love for each other. That is when you felt he loved you, and the passion and excitement were heightened because of your continual striving to attain the love whenever you could get it. But you would never really have it. Somehow you must have known that. You felt during your lovemaking that you did have his heart, and you wanted it so desperately.

But you never had his heart. You never felt secure in his love. Within just a few years of your marriage, you started looking for attention from other men. It was harmless enough—just flirtation. You wanted to be noticed. You wanted to be loved. However, one night you were left by a female friend at a local night club, and your single, male tennis instructor took you home. Nothing happened—you were merely given a ride home. When you answered your husband's question the next day about who drove you home, he looked at you and commented, "Well, if you are going to do something, you could at least do it away from our town." That had not even been a possibility. That was not something you would do. You looked at your husband in astonishment. Did he not care about you at all? He did not appear the least bit concerned. You figure that since he had already crossed that line, he assumed you would. You would not ever cross that line, and you wince at his comment.

You become more obsessed with him because of his distance, and you slowly become more addicted to him. You want him, and you want his love. You are beginning to see more and more that you do not get along with him in any other arena but the bedroom. You wonder how you could be so obsessed with him when your personalities are so different.

You start to see that somehow all this discord and your discomfort serve a purpose. You look inward. You see that so long as you can focus on him, you don't have to look at yourself. So long as he tries to control you with his comments, his moodiness, or his drinking, he does not have to look inside at himself. You are both engaged in a struggle of avoidance.

Knowing this, you take a longer peek inside and observe what it is you are attempting to avoid. You take a deep look inside your being and allow yourself to feel the insecurity, trace it to its origin, and make discovery. You realize you received little nurturing in your growing up years, and you see how you may have tried to meet this need vicariously by trying to care for your husband, hoping he would reciprocate.

You saw his "wounded puppy" appeal early in your relationship. As a medic, he had seen horrendous injuries in the Vietnam War, and he had his own emotional pain from his growing up years. You were not yet sure what all of that entailed, but you knew it was there because of the acting out behavior he had exhibited in his youth. He had continued to act out with you. You wanted to rescue him and make his life better. You wanted to fix him and make him whole again.

You were unable to change your emotionally unavailable, alcoholic father into the loving parent you wanted him to be, and you now see that you were attracted to your emotionally unavailable husband with the hopes of changing him. You were being given a second chance. You knew your love was strong enough, and he would be able to change. You married him with that intent. You told yourself you only wanted to improve him. What you really wanted to do was to control him.

You thought he had abandonment issues. Yours are even stronger. You did everything you could possibly do to keep your marriage together and to keep your husband with you. You were accustomed to a lack of love in your personal relationships. So you waited, and you hoped, and you placated, and you tried harder to please.

The longer you stayed with this insecure man, the more insecure he tried to make you. On some level he knew that if you were insecure, you could not leave him, and he could keep you at arm's length and control you. You notice how low your self-esteem has plunged over the years. You notice your feelings of insecurity. Maybe you never believed you deserved to be happy. Maybe you had to have the drama and the emotional pain, as they were comfortable, and they kept you from peering inside and kept you from taking responsibility for yourself.

You never faced the reality of your marriage while you were in it. You were always caught up in the fantasy of how you wanted it to be. You became more addicted to him and more addicted to emotional pain. It became a part of you. It became your identity. So long as you were able to focus on him, you did not have to focus on yourself. You recall when a psychologist friend talked to you about self-hypnosis twenty years earlier and about focusing inward. The very idea of it scared you beyond words.

CHAPTER 7

STARTING A FAMILY

Mike was very attentive to me while I was pregnant. We spent quiet moments talking about our imaginings of our child—our expectations, our dreams, what he or she would be like. We could not wait to meet this new person coming into our lives. In those still, peaceful times, I would ask him about Vietnam. I knew he had seen some gruesome sights. I knew they were buried deep inside of him, and I felt it important that he talk. He was always reluctant, but he opened up one lazy afternoon.

"Marti, you cannot possibly imagine. It was awful. I remember trying to keep these guys alive, and it was all I could do. I kept trying, but they kept dying on me. It was killing me. This one soldier came in, and he was so messed up. Half of his body was missing. I could not believe he was even alive. He begged me to save him. He had a wife and a baby back home, and he wanted to return to them. He had no idea what shape he was in."

He stopped for a moment, remembering the horrendous unspeakable where he had dwelled for what must have seemed a lifetime. I was still. I did not want to interrupt his thoughts. I knew he needed to get some of this out.

"I did everything, Marti." Was he trying to convince me or himself? "I worked my ass off to keep this man alive. I stayed up with him all night. I couldn't save him. He died on me."

He hesitated for a few seconds, his face solemn. Then he continued, "When he died, I remember backing up against the wall and sliding down it. I was crying. By the time my butt reached the floor, I was laughing. I laughed, and I laughed, and I laughed. I laughed my head off. I could not stop laughing."

He stopped and looked directly at me, and said flatly, "That is what I remember about Vietnam."

I looked back at him and thought to myself, *And that is when Vietnam broke you.*

Our Jamie was born seven months later. Mike was a wonderful Lamaze coach in the practice sessions, but when I found myself in labor pain in the middle of the night, he became frantic and nervous. I was calm and packed my things slowly. He was not so calm. He wanted me to hurry. I knew I had plenty of time. When the labor pains later intensified at the hospital, he looked at me with all the love he had in his heart and told me he wished he could take some of the pain for me. That was one of the few times I felt his love outside of our bed, and I held onto it.

My doctor ordered Pitocin to speed up the labor process, and I questioned his recommendation. Mike and I both knew Lamaze did not prepare us for this procedure, and Mike and I both became angry. We tried to resist, but the nurse was adamant that it was necessary. We were never given a valid reason.

My contractions were coming one after the other without any restful intervals, but I was determined to outlast my doctor. My doctor had not wanted me to deliver naturally; he had told me several times during the prenatal care visits that he did not agree with my decision. "Why feel the pain when you don't have to feel it?" I reminded him these were contractions, not pains. I had been a good Lamaze student.

Somehow, Mike coached me through it, and our little girl was delivered. My parents had arrived during the delivery, and Mike ran excitedly out to the waiting room to tell them, "We have a girl!" My mother later told me she had never seen him so excited. She also told me that when he drove them to our home that day, he kept exclaiming, "We have a girl!" while throwing up his hands. She was worried, as he was supposed to be holding on to the steering wheel. He could not help himself. He was thrilled. We had a healthy, beautiful baby girl.

My parents returned to their home the day after Jamie was born, and Mike's parents and his Mimi arrived the day before I left the hospital. They were all enthralled with their family's first grandchild. "She comes from good stock!" Cecil declared as he gazed upon her.

Cecil and Mimi returned to Fort Smith, and Deenie stayed behind to help me at home. The delivery had required a triple episiotomy, and

I had to undergo several sitz bath treatments daily to aid the healing process. Deenie was such a wonderful help, and she took care of Jamie while I was involved in the treatments. I took pleasure in how she held Jamie and talked to her. I had never seen this side of her. Deenie had not ever shown me affection. I had not seen fondness directed toward Mike, and it warmed my heart to see the care and love she showed for her first grandchild.

I took to motherhood as though I had done it all my life. I loved this little infant, our creation, and held her all her waking moments and most of her sleeping ones as well—during the daytime at least. Mike would walk in from work, and I would be holding her. "Come look at her," I would call out to him. He would take her from me. "Isn't she just adorable?" I crooned at her as he held her. I had never felt such intense love as I did for this beautiful little child of ours.

We had lots of visitors those first few weeks, and I was usually in a euphoric state. I think my close friends were worried about my eventual let down and "crash" they were predicting. I was determined not to accede to their forecast, and I eventually emerged from my elated phase. I had been too excited to sleep at night, and I finally surrendered my sleep deprivation and caught up with my rest. Mike was a big help. I was breastfeeding, so he could not take care of all of Jamie's needs, but he would change her diaper in the middle of the night when she woke up with her cat-like cry and then place her in my arms.

As time passed and my adoration grew for this little baby, I noticed Mike becoming less enthused. I was getting completely wrapped up in our infant, and I thought I detected jealousy in Mike. I knew I was not being as attentive to him, but the baby required my attention to survive. He did not. He and I had occasional babysitters and went out, but my heart was not in it. When we did go out, I talked about Jamie most of the time, and my mind was back home with her. I tried to remember the days before Jamie and made an effort to treat Mike as I had in those days. It seemed to work. We had fun. Yet, I would catch a wistful look sometimes when we were home, and I was playing with and openly loving our little girl.

I had to return to work three months after Jamie was born and found myself traveling a lot more on the job. I was then working as a regional representative for Mental Retardation-Developmental Disabilities Services, a division of the state Department of Human Resources. (Thank goodness the division's title was later shortened to Developmental Disabilities Services.) My job required one-day travel all over Southeast Arkansas, and, luckily, I was able to avoid any longer stays away from home.

After Jamie turned one year of age, I started attending three-day conferences in Little Rock or in various resorts in northern Arkansas. During these times I left Jamie in Mike's care, and he was a wonderful father. He clearly loved his little girl. The travel was hard on me, but it was a part of my job. I also knew it was good for her father to occasionally do the sole caretaking. He was good with her. Now it was my turn to get jealous, as she did not always respond immediately to me when I returned home after a three-to-four-day absence. I was happy to see their bonding, however.

When Jamie was two and a half years old, I stopped working for the state department and stopped traveling. I concentrated on course work needed for a master's degree in counselor education and attended off-campus classes in Little Rock, which was a forty-five-minute drive away. At the same time, I was helping two gentlemen write a grant for monies to start a combined halfway house and treatment center for alcoholics. I had put a lot of time into the grant writing, and after the two directors received the award, we hired an individual to start the program. The newly hired program administrator was charged with developing the overall program, planning the course of treatment for each client, and maintaining the halfway house. He had previously worked in a treatment center, and he was very knowledgeable. He was a recovering alcoholic.

Although I had been told by the directors that they and their secretary would be available to work at the center, they were infrequently seen, as they had their hands in other businesses and projects. Subsequently, the staff at the center was always shorthanded. I started spending extra time at the facility and found myself doing more of the secretarial work. When I complained to the directors, they sent their secretary from another business to assist me—for an hour at most. I felt I was being used, and I regretted I was not getting to apply the counseling skills I knew I had inside me.

I had words with one of the directors one afternoon, and his responding statements were an assurance that the secretarial aspect would continue so long as I would allow it. There were clerical tasks that needed to be done, and there was no one else available to do them. The director asked me to do what I could; he promised it would get better.

I was at home later that afternoon lying on our bed when Mike walked in from work. He saw me looking distraught, and he immediately started a conversation with me. I thought he was going to ask me what was wrong and offer his support.

"Marti, I need to talk to you." I did not like his tone. It did not sound supportive, and I knew he saw I was upset. What could he possibly need to tell me when my gloomy mood was so obvious?

"I was at a party a few weeks ago, and the guys were taking their turn with a girl …"

No, not this again.

"I had intercourse with her."

Now, I was really crying.

I sat up and stared miserably at him. "Why, Mike?" I said through the torrent streaming down my face. "How could you? How could you do this to me? To us? To Jamie?"

I was bawling. I could not stop. I was heartbroken. I felt as though he had reached through my ribs with his bare hand and had punched my heart, sending it banging around haphazardly inside of my ribcage.

"I'm sorry, Marti. I'm so sorry. Please forgive me. I am such a fuck-up. I don't know why I did it. I was drunk. I shouldn't have done it. I am so sorry. I wish I could take it back. I wish it had never happened. I feel awful, and I am scared you won't be able to forgive me."

Forgive him. How could I ever forgive him? This was his second transgression, at least that I knew of. How could I ever trust him? I felt sick. "I don't know, Mike." The torrential downpour on my face slowed to a steady stream. "You've done this before. How can I forgive you again? I don't know if I can." I turned away from him and lay my head back down on my pillow. I turned my back to him.

"I know … I know … I know," he said despondently, "and I am so sorry."

"You will need to take some medication," he added.

"What?" I lifted my head from the pillow and turned abruptly. I looked at him sharply. "I need to take medicine? For what?" I looked at my husband incredulously. Is this why he was telling me? Would he have confessed had he not walked in with the prescription in hand? I wondered, and I never knew the answer. I forgave him after several days of his apologetic, sad-faced, dogged tug at my sympathy and compassion. I loved this man, and I was in a "forever" marriage.

Solitude

The wonder of thy self
The contemplation of one's thoughts
The wisdom of the mind
and loneliness.

The fear of being left
The want of companionship
The yearn of inner peace
and loneliness.

The loneness in a crowd
The withdrawing of one's self
The never ceaseless tears
and loneliness.

Solitude
Loneliness
A part of human existence.

I was in a forever marriage, but now he wants a divorce. He is now married to Merlot, and he found a woman who would get drunk with him and … you don't even want to think about the rest. You understand his leaving you. The drunk world is not your world. It is your husband's world, and you need to let him go to it. He has found a playmate who shares his same world. You would no longer play with him. Somewhere along the way he had crossed the line, and he was no longer fun. He had told you before he left, "You all took a right, and I took a left." He was referring to you and to your daughters. His daughters. He did not mean to leave them, too, but he was now married to Merlot, and his girls did not fit into that world either.

You tell the daughter that is home from college that summer, and she cries. She had been the sports player in elementary and high school and had wanted to win his approval by being his little athlete. She had made frequent comments over the summer months about his drinking—she saw the significant increase—and she becomes enraged that he would leave you.

You call the eldest and tell her you and he are getting a divorce, and she replies, "It's about time, Mom. You should have left him a long time ago." She is stunned when she hears it was his doing, not yours.

You cannot tell the youngest daughter, because she is in summer school away at college and will be taking her final exam in one week. You do not want her to be distracted by this sad event in the family, and so you keep it a secret from your friends for one week. You do not want the word to get back to your youngest.

You call your college roommate. She lives far away, and she will not be telling anyone—it will not get back to your youngest child who is studying for her exam and who is oblivious about the family upheaval. Besides, you know that your college roommate will give you the support you need and will be able to help you get through the next few days.

You go back to work the Monday after he leaves you on Saturday. You cannot bear it at work. Your world has been turned upside down, you cannot tell anyone, and you are miserable.

You do not see how you are going to get through the rest of your life alone, without him. Your lives are intertwined, and you do not know how you are going to become disentangled from him. The financial part cannot be separated out. It is too burdensome. You sink deeper into despair. You cannot see how you are going to survive this. The hurt is so deep.

You reflect that life with him has always been a roller-coaster ride, but now you find yourself on the longest roller-coaster ride you have ever experienced. You cycle—you go through the ups and downs. You secretly hope he will see the evil of his ways and return home to you. You feel some relief with that thought. Yet, you are not sure you want him home with you. You do not want that drunk world brought back into your life. He tells you something that indicates the finality of the separation, and you get slammed again. You are so confused, and you are so sad. The emotional roller coaster becomes too much.

You call him often when he is at work in the first few weeks after his leaving. You don't mean to, but you call and ask innocuous questions about the household, the bills, and by the end of the conversation you are angry, and you ask him how he can live with himself.

You continue to hope for his change of heart. You set things in motion to leave the door open for him. You do not file for divorce. You are not the one who wants a divorce; you seek consultation with attorneys to protect yourself, but you do not file the petition. He waits. You wait.

You kill him with kindness as you wait. You offer to pick up a specific eye contact solution that is only sold at a store that is fifteen miles away. You are going to the store to get the solution for yourself, and you call him. He says he just picked up a bottle a few days earlier. Your voice is pleasant. You say, "Okay," and hang up after a friendly goodbye. You take him his favorite dessert; unfortunately, you must take it to the bar where he now spends most of his waking time outside of work.

You talk to him on the phone intermittently during the two months after he leaves your home. You tell him he is a good guy, but his family was not good to him. You have lots you want to say.

"I tried to get you to be that person I thought you were. I know you are at the bar all the time—that's who I guess you want to be. It's not my problem anymore. I took it on as my problem. I did not want you drinking. That was always the issue."

He interrupts, "You think that, but it really wasn't."

You continue, "I am trying to understand it. I didn't like your drinking, and you chose the drinking over your family. I'm trying to accept that."

He replies, "That's not it. We just brought out the worst in each other."

You had said those same words to him the previous week. Now he uses them against you.

You go on, "I know you are in denial, and if you are not drinking right now, then I am wrong."

He says nothing.

You tell him you want this to be amicable—he had said the same thing. You tell him you are trying and that you are reading a book on God's grace and forgiveness. "I am trying to forgive you and accept this. It has been hard on me the past two months."

"I know it has been," he says. "I know."

You say more about wanting to forgive him. "If we can forgive each other, we can have a better relationship for our children's sake." You know you also played a part in all of this.

"I care about you," you say. "I always have and always will. I sent you an email …"

He interjects, "That was sweet. I also thought that was sweet you were picking up the eye stuff and would get some for me."

You reiterate your goodwill gesture. "I know I've said hurtful things to you and hurtful things about what other people were saying." You recall how you told him how his golf buddies were talking about him and how they were disgusted with him. "I was hurting, and I wanted you to hurt too. I guess that's only natural. I didn't think you were hurting." He has heard these words before from you.

He acknowledges that he understands.

"But I'm not going to do that anymore," you continue. "I am trying to get over it and move on. I am trying to accept it."

You talk about the division of the finances. He says he cannot pay the alimony you are asking. You tell him you need a lot more, and you are asking for less. He says, "I need to live too." You remind him that he did this. "We were barely managing in one household. How do you expect us to manage in two?"

He ignores that and says, "I can't afford to pay you that." He then asks, "Have you filed?"

"Filed what?" you ask innocently.

"Filed a petition."

"No," you answer.

"Who's your attorney?"

"I don't know yet.

"Yes, you do. You have one."

"No, I really don't. I thought I did, but then someone told me something, and I'm not sure. I should know today or tomorrow."

He thought you had probably already tied up several attorneys, and he wanted to know who you were going to take as counsel. He had not made contact yet. You wonder who had been talking to him. You had indeed consulted with four attorneys, the top four in the area. You did not want him consulting with any of them. You know that prevented him from securing them, as your consultation established a conflict of interest.

CHAPTER 8

PARTY TIME

Forgiveness. It is not easy to forgive someone for the unpardonable, but I somehow forgave my husband for his second transgression. He became contrite, and he tried to please me.

Mike's peccadillo occurred in March 1982, and I found myself pregnant three months later. I carried the fetus for two months and had a miscarriage, which was a very sad occasion in our lives. I did not know this little one, but I felt the loss intensely. I had been put on bed rest for several weeks because of the threatening miscarriage, and during that time I had been studying for a licensure board exam. I had previously completed the coursework for my master's degree, and after taking several additional post-graduate psychology classes, I was ready to pursue my license so I could work as a psychological examiner. While I was on bed rest, little Jamie would come to my bed and show me the clothes she had selected for her day's outfit. She had just turned three, and she was already coordinating pieces of clothing. She had an innate sense of style.

I passed the board exam, and my score was acceptable for the PhD level. It was a bittersweet victory, as the miscarriage was still fresh on my mind. Yet, I knew I would never have to take that exam again. I did hope to obtain my PhD one day, and I already had a high enough score for that license. Mike and I celebrated.

During those few years when I had returned to the college academic world, my friends were constantly telling me how Mike had bragged on me, how he talked about the grades I was making when taking the courses, how smart he said I was, and how he bragged about my high score on the licensure exam. Their disclosures always surprised me. I did not get this affirmation from him directly.

When I was not studying during those years, I was playing with Jamie, playing tennis, or playing bridge with a group of women. Mike and I also attended parties or played couples' bridge. Sometimes we had Jamie with us, and she played with the hosts' children. Other times we had babysitters. During those events Mike drank more than I would have liked, and I usually drove home. I was noticing that Mike did not appear able to drink one or two drinks. When he drank, he drank enough to get drunk. He drank that much on both Friday and Saturday nights. He did not drink during the week unless he played poker with his friends, then he would come stumbling in late on those nights.

I had a scare one night when we attended a Razorback football game in Little Rock with four other friends. Mike took an ice chest into the game and had been drinking most of the afternoon before the game. During the game he became belligerent with one of the fans, and I was embarrassed. No amount of shushing could quieten him. The game finally ended, and Mike picked up the ice chest and walked ahead of us. I was mad at him, so I let him get ahead. I would deal with him at our vehicle.

He was not there. He was nowhere to be seen. He was not in the parking lot. We called for him. We looked everywhere in the vicinity near the stadium, and he was not in the area. We started driving away from the area. I had no hope of finding him, and I pictured him lost, lying in a ditch someplace. I knew he was drunk, and I was mad at him, but I still cared about him. We drove up one street and down another. By this time, we were all mad at him. We finally saw a man walking haphazardly down one of the streets, weaving back and forth, and carrying an ice chest. It was Mike. We stopped, and he and the ice chest were pulled into the van. No one spoke to him during the hour-long drive back to Pine Bluff.

When our friends let us out at our home, Mike fell in the yard before he got into the house, and I left him there. I thought about turning on the sprinkler system. I thought about leaving him there all night. I couldn't do it. I went out and tried to pull him through the yard and through the doorway. I discovered the meaning of dead weight. I don't know how, but I got him into the house. He threw up on the living room carpet. I left him lying in his vomit. He put me through hell that night.

We continued to spend time with friends, and there was always lots of drinking. Mike started buying six packs, then half cases of beer, and he started drinking quite a bit of beer at home. I could only imagine what he was doing when he was away from home. He sometimes attended banking conferences. At one point he told me he and a friend were drunk at a convention, and they streaked down the hotel hall. He laughed as he related the story. He thought it was funny. I wondered what would have happened if his boss had known.

I found myself getting restless during this time. After I had received my license, I had started working at the Southeast Arkansas Mental Health Center as a therapist in the Children's Services Department, and I was having difficulty seeing "normalcy" in the world. I found myself sinking into low moods and taking my frustration out on my child. I felt burdened with the household chores on top of the full-time job, and I was not getting any help from Mike. I was in the kitchen one evening, cleaning up after dinner, and I called out to my husband who was lying on the living room sofa, watching television.

"I could use some help in here." I was exhausted from the day's events at work—I had been called in to handle a mental health emergency, and I was drained.

He did not respond. "Mike," I called again. "I need some help with the dishes." He still did not respond. I waited. I seethed. Finally, I exploded. I ran into the living room and jumped up and straddled him. I beat my fists into his chest. I had let my frustration fester for too long. He had not been helping with the household chores, and I lost it. He grabbed my wrists, stopping the attack, and I shouted, *"I just need your help! I can't do all of this by myself, Mike. I need you to help me! I work too!"* I started crying. I felt out of control and weak, and I hated what I was feeling.

"Marti, get ahold of yourself. You are crazy!"

"You are driving me crazy," I shouted. *"Mike, why in the hell do I have to do everything! I just need your help!"* I screamed. *"You are so frustrating!"*

I was so angry and continued to spit venom and expletives at him. Finally, I cried, "Just help me! Why won't you help me?" He got up from the couch and walked into the kitchen and washed the remainder of the dishes. I was too mad; I flounced off to the bedroom.

I felt anxious and out of control, and I did not like the imbalance of job-sharing in our household. I was even the one mowing the yard—an exercise I actually preferred over housework. He was doing nothing.

It's Not Fair

It's not fair, is it?
It's not fair that we couldn't
spend our last days together with only
happiness at our disposal
instead of the heart-breaking,
grief-tormented words pitting at each other.

It's not fair—that we have no
better memories than the
anguish, tears, pains, and
unhappiness that we caused
for those last days.

He is now badgering you about the identity of your attorney, and all you can wonder is how it got to this point. You cannot believe this is the man you have been married to for nearly thirty-three years.

You think back to the times when he seemed distant, preoccupied. You get flashes of events that denote his moving farther away from you. There were times when you did not think he loved you like you loved him, and you felt your self-esteem getting lower and lower. The more distant he became, the less confident you felt. You clung to him. You only wanted his love. He pushed you away at times, claiming you were too hot. He did not want you next to him. Your body heat was too stifling. Your self-esteem was what was getting burned. You felt his rejection. Was he pushing you away, so that you would reject him— *his* normal? You only wanted his attention. You started to look for it elsewhere.

You realized his retreat from you was the result of unresolved grief, but you were not always sensitive to that excuse. You knew you would never abandon him. You thought he must have felt abandoned when he was younger, when his grandparents died and were no longer in his life. You vowed you would never do that to him. He had lost his beloved grandparents, and he had never been encouraged to express his grief.

At that traumatic time in his young life, you could imagine him looking around in bewilderment, wondering where everyone went. You had to know more, so you consulted his mother one month before he moved out. You did not know he was planning to move out; you were only trying to find answers and help him with the heightened anxiety he was experiencing that summer.

You learned that his maternal grandfather had taught him to walk. You saw a picture in your mind of the doting grandparent who spent many hours with him. You felt the close attachment between the little boy and his loving grandfather who showed his excitement when the little one took his first step. Suddenly his grandfather was out of the picture. He never again crossed the threshold of the home. His maternal grandmother never visited again either. No one talked about them. They were never mentioned. He saw his mother upset and angry, but he did not know why. He wondered what he had done. You recall his words when you relayed to him how traumatic that time of his life must have been. He had said in response, "I remember being happy and never being happy again."

You know the profound impact the sudden death of a close family member can have on a child. You know a child cannot possibly comprehend or process the unexpected, sad event or the change in the interactions in the adults around him. The child often believes he is the reason for the change in the adult's actions or reactions. You know if a trusted adult becomes withdrawn and appears neglectful because of their own trauma, this can create anxiety and apprehension in a young child and can be traumatic to the child. You also know a child who experiences trauma will either withdraw or become defiant. You consider that he not only lost his grandparents' love through their death, but he may have also lost his mother's love through her loss.

If his mother reacted to her parents' death in a way that led him to feel rejected by her, he may have perceived her reaction as a withdrawal of her love. He may have wondered, *What did I do wrong?* He may have tried to win back her love, but when his efforts were thwarted, he may have become defiant and may have acted out his own depression. You know how important the first three to five years are in the attachment/ bonding process and in the personality's development. You also know that a child's level of comfort is in his home—that is what he knows. If that is compromised, and he perceives aversive reactions to his being, the less healthy he is as an adult.

You recall his words when you again brought up the topic of the early loss in his life. You knew Mimi had taken him on numerous occasions; she probably saw his mother's grief and took him away to give his mother time to herself. He had told you the week he was leaving you, "I remember my Mimi walking up to the screen door to get me one day, and Mother took me to the door and shoved me at her, yelling, 'I am so glad you are here. Take him! I don't care what you do with him—just take him. Throw him away! I don't care!'" You winced then, and you cringe now, recalling his words. You wondered at the reality of it, yet you knew this was his perception.

He did not know his mother was angry that her parents were taken from her, and he was unaware of her sadness and grieving. He did not understand what had happened, nor why she was always upset with him. As time passed, he became more and more oppositional, and he tried to get her attention in a way he was learning was the best way. He was not able to get her attention otherwise.

As you consider the possibilities surrounding the loss of his grandparents, you remind yourself that when trauma occurs in a young child whose brain is developing, the part of the brain dealing with the trauma takes over, and the part of the brain dealing with happy, healthy functioning does not develop. You also remind yourself that increased vulnerability to ailments and diseases over the course of life can result.

You had tried to understand that his unresolved anger, sadness, and confusion were contributing to his attitude toward you. You had taken into consideration his post-traumatic reaction to Vietnam and how that experience had affected his psyche, his mood, his very being. However, you have needs as well, and it was difficult for you to continue to see through his behavior and understand the pain behind his actions, his infidelity, his escape with the heavy drinking. You only wanted his love and affection.

Unfortunately, over time you had forgotten about Vietnam. You had forgotten about his early loss. You had forgotten about his relationship with his mother. You had forgotten that he was depressed. You only saw his drinking and blamed him for not loving his family enough to quit. You gave him ultimatums: "Quit drinking so much and be with your family" or "If you keep drinking like this, you will have to leave." How many times did you tell him you could not take it anymore?

You could no longer take his incessant drinking, his lack of involvement in family matters, or his reticence. You could no longer see the connections between his present behavior and his past experiences. You only judged him and found fault with him. He did not share the household tasks or the parenting responsibilities, and your resentment grew. The more responsibility you took on, the less he claimed. Eventually you found yourself over-functioning—taking care of the household as well as financial and family matters.

You were doing it all, and you were growing tired and weary.

CHAPTER 9

DICTATOR

Our marriage was rocky during the next few years. Mike began to drink more, and I was experiencing fatigue with all I found myself doing. I would get Jamie ready in the early morning and drop her off at daycare on my way into work. I would leave work just in time to pick her up before the daycare closed and get dinner going as soon as I arrived home. Mike was attempting to further his career with the savings and loan industry, and he usually arrived home just in time for dinner. While I continued to play tennis and bridge, he played golf on the weekends and poker on Monday nights.

He was usually inebriated when he arrived home on Saturday afternoons after eighteen holes of golf at the country club. This was becoming a problem for me, as I needed him to babysit Jamie after he got home so I could play tennis. I did not like leaving her with him when he had been drinking. He usually took a nap, and she was only four years old at the time.

Mike came home one Saturday afternoon while Jamie and I were in the shower. I was holding her, and we were both laughing in the shower. I heard Mike come into the bathroom, and then I heard the shower curtain hooks scrape along the shower rod. I turned toward the sound. Mike was standing there, holding the shower curtain back and holding his penis while making a growling noise, acting like he was going to pee on us. I shielded Jamie's eyes and screamed at him to go away.

"Mike, stop it! What are you doing? Go to the toilet. What are you doing?" He continued to wave his penis at us. It scared me. What was happening to him? I started shaking. "Mike, please stop." I started crying. Jamie started crying. He finally left us alone. I consoled Jamie and told her it was okay.

"What was he doing, Mama?"

"Oh, he was acting silly. I am sorry I scared you."

"But you were crying."

"I was being silly."

She did not ask any more questions, and I pretended nothing had happened. After the shower, we got dressed and found her daddy asleep on the sofa.

A few months later, Mike and I were invited to a Halloween party at the country club. He had played golf that Saturday, and he came home drunk. I told him to take a nap, but he was ready to go. I donned the Daisy Mae outfit I had planned to wear, and he was wearing overalls to complete our Dogpatch theme. He handed me a lemon tied to a rope.

"What's this?" I asked him. I then looked at him and saw a rope tied around his waist. The rope was tied in front, and the end of it was tied around a potato. The potato was hanging in front of his crotch.

"Mike, what is this?"

He sneered in his drunken stupor, "I am going as a dick tater, and you are going as a sour puss."

"Mike, that is not funny. No, I am not doing it. That is stupid."

"No, Marti," he said, attempting to sound serious. "Really, I got the idea from a guy at golf today, and I think it is hilarious."

"Well, I don't. I am not going to wear that lemon. That is disgusting."

"Yes, you are. I want you to wear it. C'mon, Marti, it's funny. Where is your sense of humor?"

"Mike, there is nothing funny about it. Please don't make me do this."

"I promise you it will bring lots of laughs. We all laughed at the idea when we heard about it."

I did not think so, but I begrudgingly gave in to him. He was as persistent as he was drunk, and I did not want to make him mad. Besides, I could not think of a good argument.

We went to the party, and he declared himself the dictator and me the sour puss to everyone we saw. He continued to drink, and I don't know how he was standing on his two feet. I finally moved away from him. I had not heard any loud exclamations of laughter when he identified what we were, as he pointed to the produce hanging in front of our crotches. I was mortified to say the least. Some of these people were mere acquaintances. This was the country club crowd. Most of these people were not our close friends.

I stayed away from Mike most of the night and enjoyed myself despite him. I also discarded the lemon. As the party was winding down, I realized I had not seen Mike in a while. I started asking people if they had seen him. No one had. He apparently had left. I could not believe he had left me there. I finally was able to get a ride with one of the guys he worked with, and he and his wife seemed sympathetic and concerned. By that time, though, I was mad, and I had plenty to say about how awful and what a jerk Mike was. I launched into a litany of his bad traits.

When I arrived home, he was asleep in the bed. I was furious. I took the babysitter home, but I had to take Jamie with me. I apologized to the babysitter—I could only imagine the shape my husband had been in when he walked into our home. I was embarrassed. The entire night was embarrassing.

Mike got up the next morning and was off to play golf before Jamie and I were up. I felt sad and depressed but wanted to get out of the house before he came home. I told Jamie we would go shopping. She was excited. There were not too many shops open on Sunday, however, so we went to a drug store. I let her pick out a toy, and I opened my wallet. I saw immediately that my credit cards were gone. I was sick. I knew Mike had taken them, as my purse had not been anyplace but home.

I paid with cash, and Jamie and I went home. Mike came in later, and I ignored his entrance. I was paying bills at the kitchen counter, and I did not speak to him. He did not speak to me either. I was sick to my stomach. I did not know what he was thinking, but I assumed he suspected I would leave him, and he wanted to protect his credit and limit my access to the credit cards.

That is exactly what he was thinking. He thought I would leave him.

"Mike, do you want a divorce?"

"No, but I was afraid you might."

"I should," I told him. "I don't know what's wrong with me that I don't walk out right now." My insides churned, as I realized I did not want him out of my life.

"Mike, I know you were drunk last night. Why did you leave me there?"

"I couldn't find you," he answered, "and I was ready to go."

I looked at him in disbelief. My voice rose an octave, "*So, you left me there?*"

"I knew somebody would give you a ride home."

I do not know how he turned on the charm, but he did, and I gave in to him. I knew I did not want to lose him. The making-up was frenzied and passionate, and it erased any unease I had been feeling.

He gave me back my credit cards.

Taking for Granted?

Taking for granted?
That's not your thing
Now you realize
What's meant by that ring.

You both are so good
So true and great!
That's the word—
You really rate!

She does all she can
To prove her love,
The one you chose
To cherish, to love.

He tries so hard
To prove to you
That you're the one
And his past is through.

This is your test
To show each other
For you're husband and wife,
Now father and mother.

The real question is why has he not talked to an attorney? You ask him, and he tells you he is not there yet. You ask him why not? He tells you he is just taking one day at a time. You tell him he should get himself together and stop listening to someone else. You tell him women are so different now and the woman he is with thinks he has money, and she is after it. She does not have any. You say, "She is probably telling you, 'You need to do this ... you need to do that ... why aren't you doing this.' She's probably trying to tell you what you should be doing."

You add, "You did that with me. You'd come home and ask me about things, and I guess I tried to tell you what to do. Now, you have someone else telling you what to do."

He says nothing. You think you have struck a chord. Of course, she is telling him what to do. He had quit thinking for himself a long time ago. You are convinced she wants to get as much money out of him as she can.

It does not seem fair that someone else could reap the financial benefits of what you had helped develop. Over the years your roles had changed. At the beginning of the marriage, he took care of all the bills, the financial matters, the living expenses. As time progressed, you found yourself with increasing responsibility.

He had wondered why you were not as responsive to him as you used to be. He was wearing you down. Your obligations were wearing you down. He did not witness you feeding all three children breakfast and getting them off to school, then getting yourself ready, fed, and off to work. He did not see your frazzled rush to get each child to her after-school activity, your rush to start dinner, and have dinner ready for him when he came home from work. He did not see your making sure homework was done, baths were taken, lunches were packed, backpacks were searched, school field trip paperwork was completed—the tasks were endless. He did not understand your shortness with him, your moodiness, your fatigue, your resentment.

You had asked for help in the past. You had given up a long time ago. Even when he did try to comply with your wishes, he had exerted little effort and did the least he could. The result was not satisfactory, and he knew it. He did not want you asking again. You did not want to have to ask. You simply wanted him to join in and help with dinner preparation and clean-up, laundry needs, and children's lunches. He would do some of it begrudgingly when you asked, but you were tired of asking.

He went to work. He came home, and he sat in front of the television set with a cold beer. He was not an equal partner, and you became angrier and even depressed. The distance grew between you, as you chose silence and ignored him. You recall deciding not to expect anything from him so that you could get through the day without anguish. You had complained about his lack of assistance, his lack of involvement, but he did not change his passive existence. Once you released your expectation of him, you were able to cope better for a while, at least until the tension mounted, and you eventually blew up at him.

As the years passed, your expectations lessened even further, and you took care of everything. You discussed house maintenance with the roofers, the window cleaners, and the air conditioning technicians. You cleaned the house and took care of all the bills and financial needs. You would have continued to mow the yard, but you hurt your shoulder through progressive tennis playing, and you had to relinquish that duty.

The silence grew between you when you were at home. You were civil when you were at social events. He could drink, and he could charm. You felt you were living in the same house, but you had no relationship with him. You were coexisting. You did nothing together. You felt emotionally divorced. You started doing more activities. Even though your shoulder was hurting, you started playing more tennis as well as bridge, and you started going out to dinner with girlfriends.

As your children became teenagers, their activities seemed to multiply. The older one was involved in drama and had to be taken to play practices. The second one participated on a soccer travel team as well as on high school soccer and volleyball teams. The youngest competed on an all-star cheerleading squad and later participated in high school cheerleading. They all took singing lessons during their high school years. The voice teacher was forty minutes away.

You asked him to help with transporting the girls to their activities, but he always had an excuse. You were particularly miffed when the activity location was on his way to his own destination. You continued to ask him to accompany you to one of their sports events, and he went occasionally but not nearly enough. You hated to see the look in your daughter's eyes when the realization seemed to hit her that daddy was not coming. It was only when his second child was goalie for her high school soccer team and en route with her team toward a state championship did he become heartily involved. Even then, he had to have a few drinks before each game, and he continued to drink after the game ended. You were scared. You knew where he was headed, and you did not want to live with an alcoholic. You had already done that.

Your father was an alcoholic, and you saw your husband entering the first stages of alcoholism. You knew where this could lead, and you chastised him and warned him even more that he was becoming an alcoholic. You now wonder if you contributed because of your hyper-focus. His drinking had been your focus for years. Did you bring this upon yourself? What if you had focused upon his positive traits, his goodness, his success in the business world? What if you had praised him and focused on what you wanted to expand instead of what you feared? You now wonder, and you beat yourself up. Did you create your world?

CHAPTER 10

THEN THERE WERE THREE

I wanted to have another baby. It had been a year since the miscarriage. Mike agreed. I became pregnant, and Mike and I were thrilled to tell Jamie she was going to have a brother or a sister.

Jamie turned five in July, and Alyson was born two months later. Jamie was a blonde, and Alyson had fiery red hair. Mike was thrilled he had a redheaded child. I was not so sure; I did not think redheads could be out in the sun, and I loved the outdoors. She was beautiful, however, and I had never seen such big, striking blue eyes as this precious one bestowed upon me when I first held her. Yet, I felt a familiarity I could not quite put my finger on. I knew her, just as I had known my first child.

Mike wanted me to get a tubal ligation, and the doctor agreed during the delivery to leave the IV hookup in place in preparation for the next day's procedure. I was unsure that I wanted the permanence of pregnancy prevention, and the next morning my doctor sensed my reluctance. He made the decision for me and advised against the procedure. Mike was not happy, but he went along with it.

Mike and I could not agree on our second child's name. We had tossed names back and forth during the pregnancy and again during the labor and delivery, and by the second day in the hospital I was worried she would remain nameless. I was still working at the community mental health facility, and I decided to have a "Name the Baby" contest for my coworkers. I received lots of suggestions, but Mike and I still could not agree on a name, and now we had too many options from which to choose.

Alyson Marie was named moments before we left the hospital with birth certificate in hand. The director of Children's Services had offered it, and when I tried the name on my newborn, it seemed to fit. No other name had. I was very happy with her middle name, as I had been suggesting it all along. My mother's name was Marie. Mike wanted to call her Helen after his great-aunt who had been married to his great-uncle Joe, the owner of the Mount Nebo cabin. But our first child had a name from his side of the family, and it was my side's turn.

Jamie was in kindergarten, and I had lots of quality time to spend with Aly. I loved the tiny infant stage, and I spent hours holding her while Jamie was in school. Aly nestled easily in the crook of my neck, and she was a perfect fit. We had lots of visitors, and I was touched by all the mental health center employees who dropped by to visit. They always commented on Aly's big blue eyes as well as on her alertness and her strength. While a visitor talked with me, Aly would arise from the crook in my neck and hold her head up for brief instances. They were amazed. She was only two weeks old. I did not realize it then, but her athleticism was already on display.

As I watched Aly's personality develop, I was amazed at how alert she was. She seemed so aware of her surroundings, as she would often turn and gaze with a piercing look at a colorful object nearby. She seemed to notice everything. She showed excitement when toys were brought into her line of vision, and at two months she was batting objects as she attempted to grab and hold onto them. She was constantly moving her legs and arms, and she was quite strong. Again, I did not realize I was seeing her athletic potential. It was there at the beginning.

Unfortunately, I had to return to work after three months, and I hired a day nanny. I was jealous of the amount of time she was able to spend with Aly. It was extremely difficult to carry on my duties as a mental health therapist, as I tended to pour myself into my interactions with my clients. I was always spent when I arrived home.

One day a therapist in the adult services section approached me and asked if he could interview me. He was doing a project for community mental health and was sending his findings to the local newspaper. No names would be mentioned. We decided to do the interview over our lunch break. His questions were related to stress and what I did to relieve my stress. It was harmless. After the interview was completed, he asked if he could interview my husband. He wanted to interview a Vietnam veteran, so I gave him Mike's office phone number.

Three days later the therapist saw me in the hall and asked if he could talk to me. I was free for a few minutes, so he accompanied me to my office.

"Your husband is in trouble. He is in big, big trouble. He needs help," he blurted before I could close the door. I shut the door and turned around and looked at him.

"What do you mean?"

"Marti, I tried to talk to him about his experience in Vietnam, and he broke down on me." He lowered himself into the client chair and continued. "He is carrying a lot of pain and, apparently, a lot of horrible memories, and he needs counseling."

"I know that, Paul." I walked to my desk chair and sat down. I looked directly at him. "He won't do it, however. We have been down this road before. He refuses to talk to anyone. Wait … did he talk to you?"

I was hoping he had, but Paul's answer told me he had not. "He wouldn't talk about it, but he was really torn up—he is holding a lot inside, Marti, and it will get him eventually." He looked at me and said soberly, "I am going to call him back and ask him if he will come in and see me."

"That would be wonderful," I said. I felt a smidgeon of hope. "The fact he cried with you is a good sign. He has always been very stoic when I have mentioned Vietnam, and he has never shown me any emotion. I have not brought it up in years." I did not want to say that I doubted Mike would talk to him. I could only hope. I continued, "I know how important it is that he talk to someone. Please call him."

I had not approached that subject in years, and I am sure Mike was not prepared for Paul's questioning. Paul had caught him off guard, and I could only imagine the flood of memories that must have surfaced after Mike had kept them at bay for so long.

Mike never mentioned his interaction with Paul, and he never made an appointment to see him. I knew there was nothing I could do or say, and I did and said nothing.

A part-time job became available at the Jenkins Memorial Center that spring, and I applied. Jenkins was next door to the Southeast Arkansas Mental Health Center, and I was ready for a change. My world was full of the mentally ill, and I was having a hard time seeing the world as normal. Being on call once every six weeks was particularly trying. I would get calls in the middle of the night, and sometimes I would have to go to the emergency room to evaluate what appeared to the ER nurses and doctors to be a mental health patient. Their suspicions were always correct.

Jenkins Memorial Center provided educational, therapeutic, interventive, and support services to children and adults with developmental disabilities. The center was looking for a licensed psychological examiner whose primary responsibility was to administer psychological evaluations for the center's school age population. Physicians in the area also made referrals to the center and requested complete psychological evaluations for their patients. The position was part-time, and I prayed I would get the job. I wanted to spend more time with Jamie and Aly.

I was hired, and I began working three days a week. I was exhilarated. I was at home when Aly took her first steps two months later. She was only ten months old, and I marveled at her physical prowess. She was constantly on the move after she started crawling, and now she really had a set of wheels. Busy little girl. Her doctor had always expressed concern that her weight was below average, and when she was younger I had told him, "If we moved our arms and legs as much as she did, we would be underweight as well!"

Before Aly turned nineteen months, I was pregnant with our third child. Mike was a little apprehensive.

"Marti, you don't even have Aly out of diapers. In another six months, it would be starting to get so much easier. A third child? I don't know."

I knew he was scared. It was quite the responsibility, but I also knew he would love this child as he had the other two. I felt it was meant to be. By this time, however, in addition to my part-time work at Jenkins Memorial Center, I was also working part-time with a private psychological group who contracted psychoeducational evaluations with public schools in Southeast Arkansas. I had started the second job six months earlier. I found myself now working fifty or more hours per week, as I had to do evaluation reports at home. What happened to my desire to spend more time with my children? I wanted a third child, even though I knew this pregnancy would be difficult for me. I would turn thirty-five half-way through it.

Jamie entered the second grade while I was pregnant with Lindsey. I had a beginning of the year conference with Jamie's teacher, and I looked forward to meeting her. Jamie had previously attended private school, and Mike and I had both eagerly anticipated her entry into public school. Jamie and I both attended the conference, and the teacher and I were in the process of having a pleasant conversation. She asked me what Jamie's father did. Before I could answer, Jamie spoke up.

"All my daddy does is drink beer."

I was astonished. I looked at Jamie. Is that what she thought of him? I had not noticed he was drinking all that much. Had I become accustomed to his drinking habit? I immediately considered the amount of beer he had been drinking, and I realized he was opening a beer every evening when he got home from work. He would have more than one. Maybe he was nervous about the upcoming birth of a third child. I wondered. I recovered quickly and laughed.

"Oh yes, I guess he does drink beer sometimes." I was embarrassed. My child was telling on him, and she did not even realize it. "What he actually does is work as a branch manager for First South, a savings and loan institution," I added without further delay. Jamie's teacher was familiar with First South, and I encouraged any forthcoming discussion. She had a friend that worked there, and I rattled on about Mike's branch and the number of employees he managed. I was hoping she would not take Jamie's comment too seriously, though I apparently was.

My third daughter was born the following December. The pregnancy had not been as difficult as I had anticipated. Mike was helpful with Jamie and Aly, especially during the last two months when I was at my largest. Jamie was reasonably self-sufficient at seven years of age, but Aly had just turned two in September. She was thankfully out of the diaper stage.

Lindsey's birth narrowly missed her DeeDee's birthday, and she missed her initial meeting with DeeDee and CeeCee (Jamie's names for Deenie and Cecil) by a narrow margin as well. Mike's parents had stayed with us the week she was due, but they had given up on my delivering any time soon. They packed up and left to return home, four hours away, the day before my contractions started.

This little one was born with very little hair, but her bright eyes and spryness were visible immediately. Her father was just as excited when she was delivered as he had been with the first two. She was the same miraculous composition as the others, and once again I found myself in love. Once again, I looked into deep blue eyes, and I felt a connection.

Lindsey was the happiest baby! Her father later claimed that every morning when she woke up it was as though she was experiencing the world for the first time. He said every day was a new day for his "happy-happy-joy-joy" Lindsey.

Even though Mike continued to drink, he did seem to settle down somewhat with the responsibility of being the father of three. We had started attending the Methodist church in Pine Bluff, and he accepted the nomination for president of our Sunday school class. No one else was interested in being president, and he won the unanimous vote. He wanted Jamie to have perfect attendance in her Sunday school class, and he was the first to arise on Sunday morning. He would dress the baby and the two-year-old while Jamie and I were getting ready.

Jamie did make perfect attendance that year, and I gave Mike full credit. He also made sure Jamie was able to attend the church's children's choir, as the choir teacher had a beautiful soprano voice, and he wanted Jamie to be able to sing. His wishes came true, as Jamie had a solo in one of the church's children's play productions. She had a beautiful voice. Aly would always attempt to sing the songs she practiced, and I could already tell Aly, too, would get involved in the children's choir. Lindsey just sat happily and smiled at their singing.

Then financial tragedy struck. Several of the First South directors were involved in a scandalous, fraudulent scam that made national news. First South stock plummeted to worthlessness, and many employees lost their life savings, their retirement, and their future financial security. When the FSLIC took over, Mike and numerous other employees were hired by them. Mike became agitated and was very nervous. I finally confronted him.

"Mike, what is going on with you?"

"Marti, I am just scared. There are a lot of people who had insider information, and I am afraid someone may think I did. People get killed over less than this."

"But if you didn't have insider information, they can't get to you."

"That's the problem—they could speculate that I did."

"But you didn't, and you lost money too."

He had taken Jamie's savings and had invested all of it in First South stock when the stock went public. He had also borrowed money and bought stock for us. At one point the stock quadrupled, and he sold enough to pay off the loan. He lost the rest when First South went under. I could not see how he could be accused of having insider information. He, on the other hand, was worried that since he had sold stock to pay off the loan, he would be questioned.

He was questioned, as were all the employees, but he was not one of the accused. He had a job with the FSLIC, but he knew it was temporary, and he was looking elsewhere.

Life and Love

Life is strange
Life is pure
We all live our lives
in unity with each other.
That is our point in common—
life and love.

Love is strange
Love is pure
We all can love
in unity with each other.
This is the mark of man—
life and love.

Happiness
peace
security
These virtues are those we strive for.
We live for
happiness
peace
security
As we love for these assets.

You have been looking elsewhere. In your search for support, you have looked toward family, friends, Bible studies, God, and toward books on grief related to divorce. You have been looking inside yourself as well. You know you will have to establish an identity without him, and you are taking steps to pursue your interests. You talk a girlfriend into accompanying you to North Carolina. You have always wanted to visit the mountains in the fall when the leaves are turning, and you had asked him numerous times over the years to make the trip with you. He never did. Now you can.

Neither of you have filed a petition for divorce. It has been two months. You know you can wait him out, so you do just that. You also await the change that is in your life.

Change can be very difficult. You know that to survive this significant life shift, you will have to adjust to it, accept it, and reestablish your sense of balance. You will have to gather together all your willpower to get through this and to feel whole again. You feel your life has been shattered, and you know you will have to pick up the broken pieces and mold them together with the glue of your soul's strength. The resulting mosaic will not resemble the life you had, your life before it was broken, but it will be pieced back together. But it will be strong and resilient, and it will be a colorful masterpiece.

You were not expecting this change, and you naturally feel helpless and unprepared for what lies ahead of you. One thing you must know is that you have to heal. You must also know you have to go on with your life. You have been told it takes time.

"It takes time." You hear these words from well-wishers who only want to see you happy again. It takes time—sometimes more time than you feel you have. You were married more than thirty years, and you feel you do not have that much time left. You sometimes feel panic and feel rushed to find another relationship. You do not want to be alone forever.

It takes time, but you know you must take your time. It is not the ticking of the clock and the passing of the hours, but it is what you do with that time. You know that. You know you must use it wisely. You must grieve the loss of your marriage, the loss of your mate, the loss of your life as you have known it. You will be in another relationship one day—you want to believe that. But for now, you will have to integrate the old self with the new you. Your life has changed, and *you* will need to change as you adapt to the new activities, people, even new friends that await you.

You have come so far. When he left, your total structure was knocked down. He pulled the rug out from under you, and you lay groveling on the floor. What once made sense no longer made any sense, and you found yourself in crisis mode. But look at yourself now. You are pulling yourself back together, and you are trying to examine your values and make sense of them.

People depend on their values to make sense of the world, but when something unexpected and tragic happens, their basic values fall by the wayside. They seem pointless and unimportant. You have lost your value structure for the time being. You feel numb and ineffective. You have lost your sense of control, and you feel helpless in the wave of emotion that seems to be sending you to your undoing. But you do not have to give in to that. You have a choice.

You can grow. You must believe it. You will find a sense of security again, but not without a lot of thought and a lot of soul searching. You will find that as your security becomes strengthened, you will have peace and happiness again. Your values will come to the forefront, and as you find that inner peace, you will find yourself being considerate, respectful, and full of love for others. You must believe this will happen.

As you heal and recognize your values, you will live as your values dictate. You will develop new relationships and will have friends you did not have before he walked out. People may even be drawn to you because of the love you demonstrate toward others. You will find inner peace, and it will show. You will have a keen appreciation for life, for nature, and for the friendship others will offer you. You will accept kindnesses, and you will want to be kind to others. You will express gratitude once again.

CHAPTER 11

LEAVING ARKANSAS

I was so grateful that Mike had paid off the loan and that we had not lost all our retirement. He told me he had sold more of the stock (not just the amount needed to pay off the loan) when it had quadrupled—long before the fraudulent activity came into question. He actively pursued employment elsewhere, and I supported his every move.

Having three children proved to be more than I had bargained, but I was so in love with these three little girls. Aly was not so sure about the newest addition to the family, and I sometimes caught her planting a firm kiss on top of Lindsey's head as Lindsey sat on the floor, playing with a toy. Lindsey would topple over, and pull herself back up to the sitting position, smiling up at her big sister. She thought it was a game.

I tried not to show Lindsey too much attention while Aly was around, so Aly was given plenty of my attention. She loved to complete puzzles or build things with magnetic blocks or Legos, and she and I played whenever Lindsey napped. Whenever I tried to turn on the television set and catch the news, she would pull me away and hand me a construction set or a puzzle. "No, Mommy, TV off."

Jamie was enjoying second grade, and she was a great big sister. She would frequently organize play time with her little sisters while I prepared dinner. She sometimes directed small plays but would become quickly frustrated because her sisters were not always cooperative. Lindsey was easy—she always played the part of the baby. Their dad was going through quite a bit of stress, and Jamie thought entertaining him was the solution to his feeling better. Her compassion showed at an early age.

Mike applied for a position with Computer Power Incorporated in Jacksonville, Florida. That company had been one of First South's clients, and he had consulted with some of the employees. He now hoped CPI might be able to use his consulting expertise for their customers. He was called for an interview, and he was excited but apprehensive. He wanted me to go with him, and I called his parents and arranged for them to stay with the children. We flew to Jacksonville in July 1987. While he interviewed, I toured the area with a local realtor.

After his interview, Mike and I explored the area by ourselves and at the end of the day drove to the Landing, a downtown boardwalk the realtor had suggested for a relaxing evening. We stood on the second-floor deck near a frozen daiquiri shop and sipped the frozen concoctions. I looked out over the flowing St. Johns River, and I said quietly, "Mike, this feels too normal. We are going to be living here."

I looked at him. "How did the interview go?"

"It went well," he said. He laughed as he recalled part of the exchange. "He asked me what my goals were. I told him to get through the job and retire."

"Did you really?" I looked up at his face. I was thinking, what kind of goal is that? "Didn't he want to hear your goals for making a contribution to the company or your goals for growing professionally?"

He shrugged. "That's my goal."

I was not sure if he was being honest with me. Mike had been very successful as a developing manager, and he surely had goals related to his role. I was not worried.

Two weeks after we returned home, Mike received a telephone call offering him the consulting job. He accepted readily and called me immediately at my work. I was excited and happy for him. I was also happy for myself. We had lived in Pine Bluff for eleven years, and I was ready for a change. I was still working the two part-time jobs, which in total time amounted to more than a full-time position, and I was ready to quit. He would start his new job in September. His plan was to go on alone, and I would stay behind with the girls until the house sold.

What was I thinking? Now, I had even more than my full-time work with three children to care for and manage. And I was playing bridge plus playing on a tennis team that was headed possibly toward a USTA 3.5 state championship. I also had to keep the house clean for prospective buyers. My schedule became unbearable at times. Aly started acting out because her daddy was missing—she was very close to him— and because of my stress. Jamie had the usual third-grade activities, including Girl Scouts (I was the troop leader), church choir, and lots of homework. Lindsey was not quite a year old, and she seemed unaffected by any of it. I was glad she was a happy baby.

Mike was gone nearly seven weeks before he flew back home for a visit. Our relationship had changed over the years, but when he walked through the gate at the airport, I remembered what had attracted me to him. He was so darn good looking, and he aroused a stirring inside of me. I felt our chemistry and the renewal of the attraction that had been lost over the past few years. It was in the middle of the day. Jamie was at school, and the younger ones were at day care. We went straight to our home and straight to our bed.

When Mike and I picked the children up later, Aly would not look at or speak to her father. She had turned three the end of September, and I knew this was a vulnerable stage in her development, particularly as it related to her relationship with her father. He would get upset with her because of her unresponsiveness and her opposition to him, but I would remind him she was upset and probably angry that he had left her.

"She doesn't understand, Mike. Be gentle with her and keep trying. You are the adult."

He continued to be playful and to show her affection, and she finally relented and was her happy, big-blue-eyed self with him. But then we had to take him back to the airport.

"Daddy's going back on the airplane. He does not want to, but he has to go back to work in Florida," I told the children gently. As soon as we drove out of our driveway, however, Aly clammed up and would not look at her daddy. It broke my heart to see her so upset. He could not prod her attention away from the window she was sitting beside. He was in the seat beside her (Jamie was in the passenger seat next to me), and he tried to put his arm around her, but she resisted and turned away from him. She still did not look at him when he gave her his goodbye hug.

We all cried during the hour-long ride back home. I thought it might be good that Aly saw our sadness, so she would not think this action by her father was directed solely at her. She remained sullen during the drive, however, and she would not cry. I said as much as I could to let her know this was not her father's desire. He wanted to be with us, but he had lost his job, and he was having to work in Florida.

We managed to get through the first seven months. The girls and I visited their father during the Easter holiday. They loved the Florida beach, and I think it helped them to see their father's place of residence. I knew they could imagine him getting on a plane, but I did not think their imagination could carry him beyond that picture of sitting on an airplane. He traveled a lot as a consultant, and he sent them beautiful postcards from Alaska and Hawaii. He called often and spoke to Jamie and Aly when he did. It helped.

We had planned to wait for the house to sell and then move, but it was still on the real estate market eight months after Mike left for Florida. Rather than continue to wait for a house sale, we decided to move the household after the end of the school year. The children and I would drive to Florida after the moving company emptied our house. I expected Mike would fly home, help with the packing of the household items, and drive us all to our new home—but he did not. I had an eighteen-month-old, a very active three-year-old, and a very helpful nine-year-old. Thank goodness Jamie was old enough to help.

My father-in-law was upset with his son for not coming home and taking care of his family. My neighbor Elizabeth was also upset, and she decided to accompany us to Florida then fly back home. I was relieved. This was going to be a fourteen-hour drive in total. I planned to spend the night somewhere along the way, but I could not imagine the bathroom stops en route. I was usually the one needing to stop, and I would have had to take all three children inside with me. Elizabeth's presence made such a difference. I was able to run in to a bathroom and leave her with the girls. I must admit I was a little miffed at my husband as well.

Life's Fear

I am running. I am not running forward, but slowly I feel myself continuously being drawn back. Back to what? This is what I do not fully comprehend, nor do I reason out why I am being pulled this way.

I can remember a time when I did have big ambitions and had something to look forward to. Life was full of promise and hope. I had something to strive for, and I was working toward that goal. But now it's all lost on me. I have lost it all, and I find myself drawing further and further back.

Yet, I feel there is hope. Somewhere, somehow, someday I will find what I have been looking for. It will all come back to me, and I will again feel the peace and security I once felt in this embittered world.

Life is full of hardships and problems. This is what I must remember, and this is what I must not be afraid to face. I must remember that I am not alone in my miseries and my problems are not alone. They, as other people's, are yet to be solved. Until they are, I shall feel the weight of them upon my shoulders.

Why do I run? To what am I running? What is making me run? I must find these answers in myself. I must see myself as I am and reason out why I am how I am.

I am running because I am afraid. I am afraid of going forward because of what I might find. Fear is the force pushing me backward, not letting me go forward and finding what's there for me. This fear is what I must overcome, and I must not be afraid to face my life openly and see it as it is. I shall overcome this hindrance, and when I do, I shall once again live with all the meaning life holds.

I shall reach my goal, and all the ambitions I hold shall come to be conquered.

I am a changing person. I have noted this, and in realizing this fact, I see that I may have more problems than I otherwise would have. I find that what I once may have loved, interests me no more, and what I have despised, I may now love. I see that my moods are ever-changing. I may be happy and free one minute, and the next so forlorn.

What makes me this way? How can I ease this retreating and start advancing toward my goal? But what is my goal? I must find my answers in time and only hope that what I do find is what will make me and all concerned happy. It is with happiness that each of us dotes upon, and it is happiness that keeps this world going. This is what I must have to live, and this is what I must live for.

But, is life worth living? How can life be worth living when all some get is pain for their suffering? Some people may feel this depressing thought, but it isn't so. There is good and bad alike, and I must face the good and denounce the bad. I must live up to my beliefs and head for my eternal goal. In working toward that goal, I am sure to find my real reason for living and the goal I am pursuing now on earth. Until that time, I can only hope and wait—wait for the time when I shall be free and ready for my world.

You have options. You now have a bridge to cross. Today can be the first day of the rest of your life. You can wallow in your sorrow and let this life event suck you under into the yawning waters of despair, or you can rise above it and stagger onto the path of self-preservation and pursue continued meaningful life. Cross the bridge. It is up to you. It takes courage to face the changes that now present themselves to you. It takes guts and daring to face the unknown, to take risks, and to take a step forward over the dark abyss. You do not know what is ahead of you. You have no idea. But you must take the step.

It takes courage to overcome the anger, the sadness, and the fear. Fear can be debilitating. Fear of the unknown can cause you to tremble and hang on to what you know. But why fear the unknown? You know nothing about it. It may be far better than you can possibly imagine at this dark season of your life. You can replace that fear with hope. You must be hopeful that you can adapt to the changes and the new life that awaits you. You can find new meaning and purpose. You can make sense of your world once again. Of course, it will be different. It is not what you planned, but does that make it bad? So it is different from what you predicted. So what?

If you expect gloom and doom, you get gloom and doom. If you expect new opportunities and new dreams, you get wonderful, new experiences. You will have to seek out those sources of satisfaction, pleasure, and beauty that are in your world. Relish in them and consider the endless possibilities. Run! The world is at your feet, and you are just standing there. Dance! Dance at every chance—music is so very soothing. It awakens and lifts the spirit. Celebrate new life!

Life is unpredictable—there are no guarantees. This is a new beginning, certainly not one you had planned. It is, nevertheless, a new beginning. And it is time to reorder your life and reinvent who you are. This is probably the most difficult time in your life, but it is a part of your life. You cannot escape it. It is what it is. He had said that to you. He had taken your life from you. You had allowed it. Now it is time to leave all of that behind and redefine and recreate you.

It takes courage to find your strengths and to forge ahead, swiping at the obstructions in your way, not letting any obstacle thwart you. It also takes holding on to your faith and allowing hope to brighten the path. It takes courage to find your new self, your new identity. You do it, so you can be whole again, without pain, without fear, without regret. It takes courage to let him go and to let your past life go.

Your life as you know it has ended, and you now start an entirely new chapter. How does your story end? You are the author. It is your choice.

CHAPTER 12

THE MOVE TO FLORIDA

Florida is where the changes took place. After the girls and I moved there, life was good. I felt I was on continual vacation. Incidentally, I did have to travel back to Arkansas to play in the USTA tennis regional finals after my team won the state championship. We made it to the finals at regional, but we were stopped there.

As a consultant with CPI, Mike traveled a lot, more than I liked, but we got along better than we ever had. He was not around for me to nag when I needed help. I missed him when he was gone; I took all the household responsibilities as my own and wanted to enjoy him when he came home on the weekends. I sometimes felt as though I was having an affair with my own husband. He was not around enough to take on the husbandly duties. I took on the duties of a part-time single mother.

We became active in the Methodist church that was not far from the area where we relocated in Mandarin. The girls and I settled in to our temporary home, and our house in Pine Bluff had been rented out. It finally sold three years later. We made plans to buy a house in Jacksonville or closer to the Beaches area. The girls and I had been driving out to the beach regularly and had spent many lazy afternoons enjoying the Florida sunshine and swimming in the waves of the Atlantic Ocean as they lapped up against the coastline.

After our house in Arkansas sold, we bought a lot, built a house, and moved to Ponte Vedra Beach in September 1991. Jamie entered the seventh grade, and Aly entered the first grade. Lindsey was in her last year of preschool. These were the best years. Mike joined a country club and played golf. I played tennis, and I found my bridge club. We met people, went to parties, and enjoyed our new life. We attended a Presbyterian church, where we were active in a Sunday school class and socialized with several of the members. Mike continued to drink, but he was not home that much, and I let it go—or I was conditioned to it.

I must have been conditioned to it, as I was surprised when a letter came from Deenie. It was addressed to Mike, but I always opened his mail since he was gone most work weeks. By now, Jamie was in the ninth grade, Aly was in the third grade, and Lindsey was in the first grade. Jamie had the lead role of Christine in *Phantom of the Opera* in her high school production, and Mike had a conference in Chicago. I wanted to go with him, and we needed his parents to stay with our children and to transport Jamie to her play practices after school. They had done that. The letter arrived two weeks after they returned to their home. I was surprised when I read the following:

> "I want to thank you and Marti again for letting us keep the girls. You are so blessed to have three girls that are so good, smart, pretty, and are so proud of their parents. Mike, again, I want to impress upon you how important it is that you spend as much time with them as you can work into your schedule. The time you have them at home passes in such a hurry and then they are on their own (you hope!). It is beginning for Jamie to be so busy that she hasn't time to stay home and it won't be long before Alyson and Lindsey will do the same. You wouldn't want it any other way but I don't want you to lose out. We couldn't have had more fun with them if you had planned every minute. I just wish we could see them more often."

I was stunned when I read further:

> "The previous two times we had been to Florida, each girl had asked me to please talk to you because you didn't love them. I told each one that, of course, you loved them and would do anything for them. They knew you didn't because when you came home all you ever did was yell at them and didn't ever do anything with them. I was just sick because I knew this wasn't true. I told Cecil what they had said, and he wouldn't let me say anything to you about it. He said you were forty-four years old and you should know how to get along with your family. When

I got back home and was trying to decide what I should do, I realized what was wrong. Most of the time you saw them was late afternoon and early evening and you'd had too many drinks. Alcohol does a lot of things to your personality and body and not any of it is good. I really wanted to lay into you, but I am sure you knew already what was happening and you are the only one that can do anything about it. I don't ever want you to lose the respect and love of your daughters so I felt I ought to tell you, and it is up to you to take care of it."

I folded the letter carefully and returned it to its envelope. Should I give this to Mike? He would be devastated. I knew he had continued to drink, and I knew he did not engage in any individual activities with the girls, but I stopped my thoughts. Have I become that accustomed to his drinking? He did not help with any transportation to their sports events. He did not take them places on his own. They begged to go play putt-putt golf with him. He always told them he would do that a day in the future. That day never came. Did they not think he loved them though?

Mike read the letter when he came home that weekend. At first, he reacted angrily, not at his children, but at his mother. "Marti, I don't drink that much." He had said that many times before, and I had always disagreed with him.

"Mike," I implored him, "think about it—that is the only time they see you. They only see you after work hours or on the weekend, and that is when you drink. Of course, you don't drink when you are at work, which is the greater part of the day, but you do drink as soon as you get home and most of the weekend. That is when they see you!" I emphasized the last statement.

"Please, just do more with them," I said. "They only want your attention."

He vowed to do better and in fact was focused on being a better family man as part of an inspirational, team-building training program he was involved in at work that included a section on personal goals. This seemed to help for a while, but his drinking did not slow down.

Jamie finished high school four years later. It was a sad day when we dropped her off at Florida State University in Tallahassee. I cried most of the way home. I knew this was the beginning of inevitable changes in our family constellation, and the changes would continue as each girl went off in their pursuit of higher education.

Mike's behavior changed significantly; he became more withdrawn, he often sat despondently and stared off, and he increased the amount of beer he was consuming. He worried incessantly. He felt he was getting old, and he acted old. I worried, I fretted, I thought about his drinking and worried anew about the self-destructive path I felt he was choosing. I had no idea it was no longer his choice.

When Mike turned fifty, which was in December of the second year Jamie was in college, I threw him a birthday party with a hundred invited guests. He had been so despondent over the past few years, and I wanted to cheer him up. I felt him slipping away from me, and I wanted to get him back. The drinking was an age-old problem, but he was showing extreme signs of depression. His brother came in from Arkansas and joined the festivities. Mike seemed rather melancholy during the celebration, and John noticed it as well.

"What's up with Mike?" his brother asked me after the party ended.

"I don't know, John. He has been this way for a while. He asked me the other day if I was happy, and I told him I was, but he told me he was not happy. He did not feel happy. I am worried about him." I continued, "I have tried to get him to go to a psychiatrist, as it could be a chemical imbalance, but he won't go. I even made an appointment, but he told me to cancel it."

Mike and John's father had been diagnosed with Lewy body dementia several years back, and Mike's emotional state seemed to decline at the outset of this news. His mother had lupus, and I knew Mike was worried about the two of them. I also knew Mike's mother had attempted suicide when Mike was in Vietnam, and Mike had asked me when we were in our thirties if I had ever thought of suicide. I said no. He said he had. I was now worried about his mental state.

Mike quit drinking beer the day after his fiftieth birthday party. He became even more despondent and often came in from work and walked over to me and hugged me. One day he said, "I don't deserve you."

"Mike, what are you talking about? What are you saying?"

"I don't know. I just think you are better than I am. I don't deserve you. I don't know what's wrong with me. I can't concentrate at work. People talk to me and it sounds like that Charlie Brown character, 'waah, waah, waah.' I have no idea what they are saying." I worried about clinical depression.

"Mike, you quit drinking. You were self-medicating. Maybe that was hiding something else—you seem depressed. Let's go to that psychiatrist now. If it's a chemical thing," my mind raced for the right words to convince him, "wouldn't you rather feel better?"

"Let's just wait it out" was his reply. He had just learned he had a hearing loss, and he hoped that accounted for his inability to concentrate. He was prescribed hearing aids.

Mike was pitiful the next few weeks; he was so sweet to me and seemed to be struggling with something inside of him. He was so down on himself. I wondered what he had done that made him appear that remorseful. I had no idea that Jamie's upcoming age of twenty years was a reminder to him and sparked memories of where he had been when he was twenty. He was in Vietnam at that age, and he had stuffed those memories down where they could not reach him for thirty years. He could no longer do that.

Mike picked up a bottle of red wine one day on his way home from work. Only three months had passed since he had quit drinking beer. He came into the house and opened the bottle of Merlot. He looked at me. "I read that red wine is good for you."

That was the beginning of the end. Mike slowly increased his drinking that year and by the summer of 2000, he had exhausted my patience. He was not being the family man I wanted him to be, and his drinking had become intolerable.

I retrieved a letter I had written to him that expressed my thoughts and my wants. I had written the letter the summer before his fiftieth birthday in 1998. At that time, I was tired of his lack of involvement with the family. In addition, his beer drinking had gotten out of hand that summer. I had held on to the letter but felt the need to bring it back out. I gave it to him one day in July 2000, and then I flew to Arkansas. I wanted him to think about his role in the family, and I wanted him to consider my time away as a separation. I did not know it then, but he spent that night with another woman.

When I returned from Arkansas, he slowed down his drinking. He did not reach the inebriation stage as often, but his willpower did not last long. He eventually began to have a glass of Merlot every night, and then two glasses, and then three to four.

He became belligerent with the girls. The girls fussed about him to me or complained to him directly. I fussed at him constantly. His drinking continued to increase, and my patience wore thin. His hearing worsened, and he quit wearing the hearing aids. He became more frustrating to talk to, as he would answer a question he thought you asked, and it was never close. His cognitive ability declined as well. Jamie noticed it in a telephone conversation when she was later in the work force. She asked him a business question, and his answer made no sense.

"Mom, Dad's not very smart," she said to me.

I knew he had been an intelligent man, and I worried. He was drinking more. His drinking had progressed to the point he was consuming four to six glasses of Merlot a night. Fortunately, he went to bed early. Unfortunately, he was becoming more withdrawn from us.

His teeth and gums became stained by the red merlot, and over time I lost respect for him. His sexual functioning declined, and he depended on Viagra. He lost his appeal. He gained weight, and I chastised him constantly.

As each girl turned nineteen and then twenty years old, his depression seemed to worsen. As he turned a year older, his emotional state seemed to decline even further. He sat despondently at the dinner table on his birthday from one year to the next. He sat despondently often. The wine seemed to make it worse, as he had a "stupid" look on his face when he drank. I hated that look, and I started to hate him. I am sure my actions and reactions to him showed it. I felt he could control what he was doing. I felt if he loved us enough, he would stop drinking.

His drinking increased to the point he was consuming great amounts of Merlot—a full one and a half-liter bottle in one night. I felt I was on a roller coaster that I could not get off. I felt consumed by him, and I lost myself somewhere along the way. No one knew what we were going through; it just kept getting worse, and I became even more resentful and angry and reacted to him in a way that I can only describe as condescending and disrespectful.

We were losing him to the Merlot, and I could not bear the sight of him. At the same time, he was becoming more withdrawn and more closed off. *Isn't there anyone that can help us?* This question played over and over in my mind. When the youngest daughter went off to college, I tried to pizzazz it up and renew the passion. It worked for a short time, but I had lost so much respect for him. I would react to his drunken states, and I would resort to my angry outbursts. I finally reached the point where I despised him.

I left him emotionally and started taking care of myself. He thought I was having an affair. I was not, but he was and had been for the previous five years. He had stopped listening to my appeals to "Please stop drinking." He started saying he could do whatever he wanted. He also started using the F-word more than he ever had. I felt my control of him slipping away.

My husband was part of a person. He was not whole. I had known that, but over the years this knowledge had faded. He had felt abandonment in his early years, and he was now abandoning himself. I would not do that to him. By the time I realized what he was doing, it was too late. He had already gone. He had left me long before he left our home. He had left himself long before that.

Mike walked out of our lives the summer before the youngest daughter turned twenty.

Love Hurts

First love never dies
The memories remain …

Memories of yesterday
Times forever told
Happy times passed away
As the days grow old.

I think you play a game
Of hurting people,
And I must be
Your main card.

I feel the beginning of the healing. I know I must heal, and I know I must pull my fragmented self together and go on with my life. I can no longer detach myself from the events, or from the feelings associated with those events, that have brought me to this moment.

The moment has come for me—that moment in which I must stop disassociating. It is time to begin to reconnect the disjointed pieces of myself and to take ownership and start to accept and embrace all that has happened. This happened to *me*. Sometimes, it is the most difficult thing: to believe that a seemingly insurmountable event has happened.

To become whole again, I must make a conscious decision to do whatever it takes to get better. I will have to be willing to take risks, and I will need to get to the point where I want to face a new future. I know I am no longer that person I was likely going to be in the future. I will no longer be married to the man who is married to Merlot. This is my chance to have an even happier future. The possibilities are endless!

When my husband walked out, I felt powerless. His leaving initially felt destructive to my sense of who I am, my sense of self. I did not know who I was anymore.

For me to heal, I am going to have to reinvent a new self, one that is different from the self I was in the past and different from any previous thought of a future self. I must establish a new identity—one without him. Right now, this is a frightful thought. I will be examining my beliefs, my values, and my thoughts about fairness, trust, and respect, as well as my thoughts about intimacy. Everyone wants to feel wanted and loved. I feel I have lost that, but I must tell myself I will have that again. Is being married to the man who was married to Merlot really such a loss? I must think now about the opportunities life is going to offer me for my continued growth.

Two months have passed since he left, and I feel I have come a long way. I am beginning to accept this change in my life, but I know I have a long way to go. The agony and the pain have been unbearable at times, but I keep putting one foot in front of the other. I go through the motions at work; I cannot concentrate on tasks that need to be completed. It is truly unbearable.

I have cried heart-wrenching tears. I have pleasured myself to ease the pain and then have cried uncontrollably afterward. I have obsessed and have thought ad nauseam about his leaving me. I have pictured him with the other woman. I have not been able to get him out of my mind. The thought of him has been a constant distraction, and I have not been able to concentrate on anything.

I have done fun activities with others and have been able to forget for a few minutes, but the thought of him leaving always returns to haunt me. Now at least I can go for longer periods of time. I can wake up in the morning, and it may not always be the first thing I think about.

It has not been easy. Memories of that last week with him invade my thought processes. The night he told me he was leaving was excruciatingly difficult. I reflect on that day's events. I had been with my friends Joan and Barb for one of our annual summer birthday lunch outings. It was late July. Joan was driving and had taken Barb home. We were pulling up to Joan's and my neighborhood when I saw Mike's car. His car pulled into the street ahead of us, and I wondered what he was doing coming home so early. It was four o'clock. He did not get off until five o'clock, and his job was forty minutes away. As we caught up to where he turned off, I saw that he had pulled in front of The Pelican Bar and Grille. I pointed his car out to Joan.

"What is he doing? Oh my gosh. He's going into The Pelican."

"I wish we had not seen this" was Joan's only comment.

I fretted. Is that what he had been doing—stopping at the bar at The Pelican and drinking several glasses of wine before he came home, then downing a few more, acting like he only had the few he drank at home?

Joan dropped me off at my house, and Mike came in two and a half hours later. He walked into one of the back bedrooms where I was on the computer.

"Did you just get home?" I asked casually.

"Yeah," he replied.

"Mike," I turned and looked into his eyes, "you just drove home." It was a statement, not a question.

"Yeah." He looked at me without changing expression. "Why?"

"Mike, I just saw your car two hours ago at The Pelican."

He gave me a "so what" expression. "Yeah," he said, "I stopped and had a couple of glasses of wine." He turned and walked out.

I shut down the computer program and walked to the master bedroom. He was at the sink in our bathroom.

"Mike," I asked him. "What's going on? What are you doing?" I had asked him this so many times in the recent weeks. He had been having anxiety attacks, which he had started having in May. Today was the twenty-sixth of July. I had also noticed his hands trembling. "What is going on?" I asked again.

He walked out of the bathroom and into our bedroom and sat at the foot of the bed. He put his head down and held his head in his hands with his elbows on his thighs. "You are going to be so upset."

A weakening feeling of anxiety arose within me. I leaned against the bathroom door jamb. "Mike, tell me—you need to get this out." I had been trying to get him to talk during the past month. I thought issues were surfacing with which he had not ever dealt. His depression and anxiety had worsened, and his physician had put him on an antidepressant.

"Mike," I repeated, "tell me."

"I can't tell you. You are going to be so upset."

I pulled myself up, standing tall. "No, I'm not. You need to tell me." I stood across the room from him and watched as he agonized.

"You're going to be so upset," he repeated, as he continued to hold his head in his hands. He started to shake his head slowly back and forth.

"Mike, I am not going to be upset." I said firmly. "You have to tell me. What is it?"

I waited and started feeling extremely anxious. What was he about to tell me?

"You are going to be so upset," he said despondently, continuing to shake his head.

"Tell me," I insisted. "I am not going to be upset. Get it out *now*."

"Marti," he said in an accusatory tone as he released his head and looked up at me. "Five years ago you were going to Arkansas, and you told me I was fat and repulsive to you."

I broke in, "Mike, I told you I was going to Arkansas and I wanted us to consider it a separation. Your drinking was too much for me. I may have said hurtful things. I was mad at you." I didn't remind him that was six years ago.

He looked down and held his head again in his hands. He continued in a mournful tone, "People fall out of love." He looked up at me sadly. "I met someone five years ago, and three months ago I realized I was in love with her." He repeated, "People fall out of love. I love her. I feel great when I'm with her." His words were a little slurred. I could tell he had downed more than just a few glasses while he had been at The Pelican.

My anxiety heightened, and I walked over to him. "Mike, that's great," I said calmly. I sat down beside him and looked at him. He lifted his head and looked at me. I continued, "Some people never find that." My tone was quiet, unruffled. I wondered how I could appear so calm on the outside yet feel so utterly undone inside. I felt as though someone else had taken over for me. I asked, "Does she love you?"

"She says she does."

I could barely breathe. I was trembling on the inside. I felt like my nerves were racing at breakneck speed, yet I continued to react calmly. He wanted to tell me more. "Five years ago, after you said that, I went to the club and this woman started talking to me. We went to her apartment. I banged her."

He banged her? He says he loves her? What a disrespectful verb to use with someone you supposedly love.

"You had sex with her?" I cried out. "How could you!" I meant that literally. "You are impotent."

He did not deny his impotence. "We didn't go to her place much," he said. "We may have gone five times over the years. I see her now at The Pelican. She's a food and service manager there."

Bartender, I thought. How convenient.

"She comes by," he continued, "and she pats me on the back. We talk. She makes me feel good. She adores me. She worships me. She puts pep in my step."

I could not imagine. I was also amazed I had not broken down. As upset as I was on the inside, I was bound and determined not to show it. After all, I had said I would not get upset. And I had said it three times.

"Tell me about her," I said gently.

What was wrong with me? The questions were pouring out. Why wasn't I screaming and crying and beating on him? A thought came into my head: This is the only way this could happen.

"Marti, you'd be shocked. I've gone from a grade A to a grade C."

And that was supposed to make me feel better?

He continued, "She's so sweet ... she's wonderful ... you would like her."

"Yeah," I said, attempting to sound serious, stifling the sarcasm, "I'd like to meet her."

"Yeah," he said, "I could do that. We could ..."

"Mike!" My calmness had left me. I raised my voice an octave, "What is wrong with you? Do you really think I want to meet her? You *are* insane!"

"Tell me about her!" Why the hell did I want to hear about her? Maybe I was the one who was insane.

"She has reddish hair." He looked at me. "She's fifteen pounds overweight." I start to picture a sweet looking, matronly, dumpy appearing person.

"How old is she?" I asked.

"She's forty-five, but she looks older than you."

"Is she pretty?" I didn't have to ask if she was smart. I already knew the answer to that.

"No, that's what I mean. You'd be surprised if you saw her. I am telling you I've gone from a grade A to a grade C."

"Then why are you doing this?" I was feeling knots beginning to form in my stomach.

"Marti, I want to be happy. You were always putting me down. You are not nice to me."

"Mike, the drinking is the issue."

"I don't think so."

I knew he was in denial, and I left that alone. Still, I was stunned.

"Mike, I can't believe you are doing this."

"I will move out on Saturday," he said.

This is not happening. My anxiety had risen to another height, and I felt twisted in knots inside. My marriage was breaking up, and I was stunned ... blindsided ... devastated.

"I feel better," he announced.

"Great," I answered. I felt horrible. "You've given it all to me." I asked, "Mike, why are you doing this to us?"

"Marti, you will be okay. You are strong. Cecil always said you were a rock. You will be fine. You are beautiful. You're smart. Now you can get that doctorate you always wanted. I think I have held you back. You have vision—you have goals. I don't have any goals."

I looked at him. I had known he had no goals, but I had not known that my having them was a problem for him. He had been so supportive and so proud of me last month when I presented at the Readers' First conference in Orlando. I had been invited by my elementary school's principal, and I had accompanied the principal and two other teachers. We all spoke within two one-hour presentations to two different groups of administrators from schools all over Florida. He had been so encouraging. I looked at my husband. Was he simply trying to make me feel better, or was he trying to make himself feel better?

"Marti, you've given me the best thirty-three years of my life. I appreciate what you have done for me. I could not be where I am today if it had not been for you. I'd be a druggie on the side of the road."

A few minutes later he was talking about her again, and he said, "When we get married ..."

I cut him off. "You're going to marry her?" I asked incredulously.

"Marti, she's so sweet."

"Mike," I said. "Sweet people don't do this to families."

"I am dying," he continued. "I think I have what Cecil had. I probably won't live more than three more years. I want to be happy those last years."

He added, "I am not going to get to the point Cecil did. I won't let it take me that far."

I knew he was talking about suicide. "Don't do anything and hurt your children further. Don't leave them with that."

"I can have a wreck," he said quietly.

"Mike, don't do anything like that."

He then told me he was thinking about ending his life earlier in June when I was at the conference in Orlando. "I could not get out of bed. I was so dizzy. I called her, and she came and helped me pee."

"She was in the house?" I exclaimed. He did not remember how she got into the house. He was dizzy. How did she get in? That was a scary thought. She had been in my home. I looked around our bedroom. She had seen my things—my picture, my children's pictures.

"She talked me out of it," he went on. "I just couldn't go on. I didn't want to feel like this anymore."

He was referring to his anxiety and his heightened emotion. He had displayed a spiraling of emotions since May when the panic attacks started, and he had experienced several bouts of extremely high blood pressure. He had appeared more depressed and despondent, as he withdrew further from us. His physician had put him on a strong, Serotonin-inhibitor (SNRI) antidepressant, and he did not like how it made him feel. We had gone on walks together, and he had told me it made him feel like he was someone else. "This isn't me in here. I don't like the way this feels." His medication was changed to a different antidepressant (SSRI) at my advice after talking to a friend who had indicated she had a good response to that type medication. But after getting off the first one so abruptly, his emotional state worsened. He eventually found himself in bed with dizziness, and he had not been able to get out of bed for those three days in June.

"She talked to me a long time when she came over," he said. "I really was going to do something. She talked me out of it."

That is why he had never answered my calls when I was in Orlando. I had called him several times, but he apparently had not been able to get out of the bed. I recalled coming home, and he had looked ragged. That was a Wednesday. He was going to try to get up and go to work the following day, but I convinced him to wait another day. He got up late that Thursday morning, and his appearance scared me. His hair was disheveled and lay in clumps all over his head. His eyes were demonic. I thought I was losing him to insanity. Looking back, I now wondered if he had truly had a nervous breakdown.

I had tried to help him in May after he told me about the panic attacks. He finally agreed to try an antidepressant, but this was the way he had eventually responded—unable to get out of bed for three days. He was really scaring me.

Mike had somehow pushed through that "dizzy" episode and had returned to work and was functioning better by the end of June. I had gone to Arkansas then (my annual summer visit to family), and Jamie had accompanied me. She and I spent time with his mother. I questioned Deenie about her parents and about their death. She could not remember much, but she told us Henry, her father, had taught Mike how to walk. How I was impacted by that casual comment! I flashed back to my sister Carol and her husband, Norman, and how they responded to and cherished their time with their new, first grandson, Luke. They were crazy about him.

Mike's grandparents must have been crazy about Mike. They must have played with him, loved him, and cherished him as well. The grandfather especially doted on him. Deenie described her father as loving and very kind. She described her mother as "more strict." I interpreted that as meaning not as warm. Mike lost those grandparents when he was two years old, and at the same time, he lost his mother who became depressed and unavailable to him.

Mike reacted to the change in his life, he missed the positive attention he had been receiving, and he started acting out his sadness and his loss. He fought for attention and ended up receiving negative attention, which was better than no attention. His paternal grandparent, Mimi, must have seen his need, and she took him away from the grief in his home.

Mike and I had talked about those early years sitting in the back glassed-in porch of our home one late afternoon following my trip to Arkansas. As we talked I could see the palm trees and vegetation swaying in the gentle breeze outside. This room was my solace, my connection with nature. I wanted him to feel the peace surrounding us. We talked for over an hour—I thought it was very important that he talk about it. I told him he had probably bottled up a lot of emotion and needed to get it out. However, he knew the real reason he was having anxiety.

Now he was telling me he was leaving me. When I brought up that porch discussion, he said, "I almost told you about her that day."

"Marti, I remember being happy and never being happy again." I could picture the happy little boy who suddenly found himself lost and confused, looking around, wondering, *Where did everybody go*?

I recalled a short trip we had taken to a coworker's wedding and what Mike had said to me while we were driving back home. "I know very few people who are really happy."

"I'm happy," I had blurted out.

"I'm not," he had said.

"Really, Mike? Why aren't you happy?"

"I don't know. I don't feel happy."

Now he says he just wants to be happy the last few years of his life. He tells me he has been wanting to tell me, but he was afraid. "I didn't know what you would do. I thought you would just tear into me. I didn't know what you would do." For some inexplicable reason, I remained calm in front of him and asked lots of questions.

There was nothing more to ask at that moment, as I was seeing my life taking a whole different turn, a detour off the beaten path. Mike went to bed, and I left our bedroom. I returned a few minutes later to get a bottle of lotion out of the bathroom, and I heard his voice even before I opened the bedroom door.

"She knows everything. It's all on the table. She knows about us." He was on his cell phone. I walked to his bedside and calmly sat down beside him. He continued to talk to her, but he was trying to get off the phone. I could hear her raspy voice through the phone's speaker. She kept asking questions. He was trying to terminate the call. "Yeah. She knows everything. We'll talk later … yeah … we'll talk later …" He finally hung up.

My heart sank as I sat there. This encounter made it more real. At one point I had thought he was bluffing. Now, I knew he wasn't. I was angered.

"Mike, are you crazy? You talk to her with me here? You are insane!"

I left the room and when I returned five minutes later, I caught him on the phone again. He immediately put his cell phone down under the covers when he saw me enter. I could hear her voice. I walked over and picked the phone up. He had just turned it off. She was gone.

That was the most hurtful thing he could have done. How easily he had dismissed me. Now, she was his confidant, the one he turned to. He showed no feeling for how this affected me. He had made up his mind, and he was going somewhere else.

CHAPTER 13

THE BEGINNING OF THE END

My husband of thirty-three years told me he was leaving me for another woman on Wednesday, July 26, 2006. He told me he would move out on Saturday, July 29. This was so foreign to anything I knew. My parents had been married for over sixty years. His parents had been married for close to fifty years. All my nine siblings were in their one and only marriage with the exception of one brother. None of my bridge group members or my tennis friends had ever divorced. Divorce was not a word I had ever wanted to apply to myself.

A disruption had occurred in my life as I knew it, but I was not ready to deal with it. I was numb, and I ran errands the next day. The day after the night my husband pulled the rug out from under me and sent me sprawling, grasping at anything I could wrap my fingers around— anything that made sense—I ran errands. When I returned home, I stopped by a store across from The Pelican, and I'll be damned if I did not see his car there. It was five o'clock. How was he getting off work so early for the second day in a row? I called him.

"You had better get out of there. If you don't want me coming in and making a scene, you had better be home in ten minutes." I was angry, hurt, sad, and bewildered.

I went home. He was there within the allotted ten minutes.

"I am your wife," I cried to him. "What you are doing is immoral, illegal, and sinful!" I was shaking and feeling out of control.

He was sheepish but unwavering. He wanted her, but he had to take care of me.

I fixed dinner. We sat at the kitchen counter and talked.

We talked each night before he left. I asked more questions. I needed to know everything. Our marriage was dying, and I needed closure.

He tried to console me, to make me feel better. "Marti, you can have the house, I'll buy you a car. You'll have guys lined up at the door." Who says this to his wife?

He also said, "You know how you always say things are meant to be? This just happened. I didn't mean for it to happen. I think it's meant to be. It is what it is. You'll be happier."

He added, "You all took a left—I took a right."

"How many other affairs have you had?" I asked him.

"You know all the ones I've had," he replied steadily. I only knew the two earlier transgressions, but I left it alone.

"I want us to be friends," he later said. "I want to call you, professionally." He wanted to seek my opinion; he and I had engaged in long talks about his emotional state, and I guess he felt the need to continue. Maybe it was helping.

"I don't think so." I said glumly.

I lay beside him each morning. He held me. He told me he wanted me to be mad at him. I was sad, but I knew I should be mad at him. I was not showing a normal reaction. I also knew this was the only way this could happen. I had been unhappy with him for such a long time. I told him I could have had affairs if I had wanted to. He told me he thought I was having one. I told him I had morals, and I could never have done that to him. I also never could have left him and hurt him like this.

I had wanted to leave him lots of times, but I knew I could not have done that to him. I could not have hurt him. I also knew his friends would hate me. I had often wished some woman would sweep him off his feet and take him away from me. I remembered having a conversation several years ago with a woman whose husband had left her for another woman. She was heartsick. I wondered why that had to happen to her. She was in love with her husband. Why could that not have happened to me instead? I thought I would have welcomed it. He was my cross to bear, the only problem I had in my life. I had thought many times, *I love everything about my life except for my husband—he is the only problem I have. I am happy everywhere else but not with him.*

Now I was devastated he was leaving me … unheard of … never considered it as a possibility. So, I lay beside him each morning, and he held me. We talked for hours each night of those last few days together.

"This is what I wanted," he told me one night as we sat beside each other, leaning back against the headboard of the bed. "To talk—to hold." He had tried to hold me when he was drunk. I had resisted. He had told me he liked holding her. Sometimes I cried when we talked. Sometimes I didn't.

"How are you doing this to me?" I repeatedly asked. "I would never do this to you."

"I'm sorry," he would say.

He had been drinking even more heavily the past few months. He was always holding a glass of red Merlot when he was at home, and, apparently, he was stopping by and drinking at The Pelican even before he arrived home after work. Aly was home from college for the summer break, and she had questioned that a few times after he had arrived home on a week day.

"Has Dad been drinking?"

"No, Aly. He just got home from work. That's his first one." I agreed he had the demeanor he adopted when he was drinking, but I did not think it was possible. He had not been home long enough, and he was on his first glass of wine, or so I thought.

He had become very sneaky, and he had become a very good liar.

When Mike left our home on Saturday, he had a meager pile of his personal belongings. He wanted nothing else except "maybe the table my Mimi had."

"I don't want all of this," he said as he waved his hand in a circle and looked around the room. We hugged. We cried in each other's arms before he walked out. He held me tight, then he pulled away and looked down at me and said, "I love you. I have always loved you. I will always love you." I knew he did, and I knew he had to go. His drinking had been destroying all of us. Was he trying to save us? Did he know what he was really doing? He turned to leave, and I pulled him back to hold, to hang on to him for just another few moments. He had been such a big part of my life—good or bad—he had been there with me for nearly thirty-three years. I couldn't imagine my life without him.

"Mike," I said, "I will let you go, just give me a moment." He held me. We held each other. We both cried again. Then he left.

Aly had spent the previous night out with friends—she knew he was leaving, and she did not want to be there. She hated him for what he was doing, and she did not understand how I was able to sit with him each night and talk to him civilly. She was wrestling with her own feelings, but I was not available to her. That is a regret I have. I was so torn up and distraught, and I could not be of help to her. I knew she was hurt—wasn't she the one who had tried to provide the sports for him to spectate, since he did not have a son to do that? Wasn't she the one that had accompanied him to his club putting championships, and when he won, he deemed her his "lucky charm?" She wanted to provide for him what he may have enjoyed had he fathered a son. She wanted his approval, and she wanted to bring joy to his life, and she had. He was so proud of her athletic ability and her performance on her soccer and volleyball teams. He was thrilled when her soccer team ended up winning the state championship and even more thrilled because she had been the awesome goalie.

Aly came into the house the afternoon after he left, and she threw out the old comforter on my bed—his and my bed. She took a white, down comforter (I think she had bought it in college), placed it on the bed and added several decorative pillows of different colors. It gave the room a feminine touch. It did not feel like the same bedroom.

"This is your bed now. Your bedroom," she announced. I was amazed at the transformation. Aly knew I was hurt, and she crawled into my bed that night to offer me comfort. She needed the comfort as well. I rubbed her back, and she rubbed mine. Neither one of us knew what to say to each other. We were both hurting.

Aly and I both went through the motions the next day. I called Frances, my college roommate. She was there for me to call anytime. I could not tell anyone else. My youngest, Lindsey, was about to take her summer college class final, and I did not want to disrupt her life until she had taken her test.

Aly wanted to tell her older sister. I procrastinated all afternoon but finally agreed, although I did not want it to get back to their youngest sister. Aly called Jamie and handed me the cell phone.

"What's up, Mom?" Jamie said happily.

I did not waste any time. "Jamie, I have some bad news. Your father and I are getting a divorce."

What I heard surprised me. "Well, it's about time, Mom," she said soberly. "You should have left him a long time ago."

"No, I'm not doing it. He's leaving me …" I was interrupted before I could finish.

"What!? What the fuck! What!? He's leaving *you!!* What the hell is going on!" I had never heard Jamie talk like this.

"He's found another woman …"

"What!? Oh my God! Who? What the hell!"

I told her about the woman at the bar. I knew she was as stunned as I had been, and I knew she needed time to process this.

"Mom, you okay?" Jamie asked gently.

"Yes, I … no, not really … but I will be okay." I fought back the tears which had become my constant companion since I was first hit with this disturbing news from my husband.

"I know this is the only way this could happen. I could have never left him, Jamie. He is doing it for me."

"I love you, Momma." Jamie and I hung up.

I did not want to think about her reaction. I knew all my daughters would be furious with their dad. Aly already was. Why wasn't I angry? All I could feel was sadness. I felt this was the beginning of something horrible in our lives, and I was still on the roller coaster, moving forward but careening around curves and bumping through the dips instead of gliding through them smoothly. The roller coaster was completely out of control. There was nothing I could do to stop it or to slow it down. It had a mind of its own, and I had no idea where it was taking me.

Lindsey took her summer course final exam, and Aly and I made plans to go to Tallahassee and move Lindsey's apartment furnishings to our home. Lindsey had lived in an apartment her first year of college but had decided to live in her sorority's house her sophomore year.

Aly was such a wonderful companion the week we waited. She helped with the decision making, as I was not thinking very clearly. With her help, I rented a Penske truck out of Tallahassee. We drove to Tallahassee on a Saturday and picked up the rental truck, then headed to Lindsey's apartment.

We entered Lindsey's apartment, and I sat her down with me on the well-worn, faded sofa in the living room. "Lindsey, I have something to tell you."

After I told her, she looked at me and said, "Shut up! Why are you saying this to me? It's not April. It's not April Fool's Day!" Her voice escalated as she spoke. She did not want this to be so. She saw my face and knew it was true. She cried briefly and erased his number from her cell phone.

Lindsey did not want to talk about her dad, and I retreated to a back bedroom. I thought she and Aly might want to talk without me in the room. I was on my cell phone for a while then decided it was time for the move. The three of us loaded Lindsey's bed, bureau, dresser, and miscellaneous tables into the Penske truck. Lindsey would not need these furniture items next year. "Look at us," I said. "We don't need men. We can do this ourselves. We are strong women!"

The following day we returned to Tallahassee with Aly's belongings and moved her things and the rest of Lindsey's possessions to their sorority house. They were members of the same sorority. I thought it fitting that their bedrooms were on opposite ends of the hall. They had grown up together and had spent plenty of time with each other. College was a time to make new friends. I hugged each one goodbye and returned to my very empty nest.

I went to work on Monday, tried to concentrate, and went home. I cried as soon as I walked through the door into my vacated house. At one time there were five of us living here. Now, I was the only one. I had never lived alone. I did not know how to do this. I was sad, but I knew his leaving was for the best. I knew that intellectually; I was not yet there emotionally.

I called Joan and Barb, my good friends, and made plans to meet them on Tuesday night. I had not yet told any of my friends for fear Lindsey would find out before she took her exam. When I did meet with Barb and Joan, they were sympathetic and supportive. I had called my sister Carol on the Saturday after I told Lindsey. I had telephoned my mother the following day. After I told Barb and Joan, I called friends at work and met with them the next day and told them. I told my neighbors, Samm and Charlie. I was able to talk about it intellectually, but I was still in shock.

When the knowledge finally sunk in, it hit hard. I cried all night. Thank goodness it was a Friday night. I felt sad when I woke up Saturday morning to my very quiet home. It had been two weeks since he had walked out. I had called Mike often those two weeks to tell him about a bill or a household matter. I felt heightened anxiety and nervousness each time just before I talked to him, and I was always sad at the end of the phone conversation.

I saw an attorney on the Monday following that bleak weekend. I had been told by friends I needed to protect myself. I was able to get through work that day and drove immediately to my late afternoon appointment. When the attorney told me he had an affair himself, I knew I could not use him—two adulterers in the same room? No. After that meeting I drove home and met with Mike. I had previously asked him to come over and discuss money.

I showed Mike how much I needed and how much the girls needed. I asked him how much he needed. He looked at my expense figures. He seemed okay. He looked okay. He looked at the figures, but he didn't say anything. He finally said he needed to poop. He then went to the bathroom. Really? Did he just say and do that?

I could not maintain my calm outer exterior and started crying when he returned from the bathroom. I lost all control and cried to him about what he had done to me, to his family. He teared up, looked sad, and then left. After he walked out, I shut the front door and told myself, "That's enough" and made myself stop crying.

It had only been two weeks since he had moved out. I was still in shock. I wanted him to see how much he hurt me.

My college roommate came in the following Friday. My sadness had been extreme, and Frances was a refreshing bright light for me. I had called her often during the last three weeks, and we had talked endlessly. She let me talk, and she was wonderful.

I do not know what got into us. I picked her up from the airport and drove straight to The Pelican. It was six thirty in the evening. I thought it would be a perfect time for her to catch Mike. After all, they were friends too. Didn't she want to say hello? After I parked, I became nervous and was not sure if we should go in. What if it backfired? He and I were being civil, but this could stir up negativity. He was mowing my yard every Saturday; I was giving him bottled water and his mail on those days. As we hashed it over, I noticed his minivan in the parking lot. It had a large round dent in the back of it.

"That's my excuse!" I exclaimed. "I can ask him what happened to the car."

We walked through the front door and entered the bar area. I saw him immediately. He was sitting at the bar with an empty stool beside him. I knew my entry would shake him, as his old world was now going to converge with his new world. Up to this point he was able to keep them separated.

I walked up to him. "What happened to the car?"

Frances said, "Hi, Mike," and she gave him a hug. What is wrong with us?

He told me he was backing out one morning and hit a palm tree. He stared off after he gave me a brief look.

The bartender, a young girl, asked, "Would you ladies like a drink?" She apparently had been looking from me to Frances to Mike and was trying to figure out who we were. Frances had been watching her.

I now looked at Frances. "Sure," she said without hesitation. "I will have a Pinot Grigio."

"Make that two," I said, "and put it on his bill." I pointed to Mike. The bartender walked away.

Mike turned and looked at me. "Oh," I said, "I have cash if you can't do that."

He said, "It's two for one. I guess I can buy one drink."

The bartender returned with the wine glasses and asked, "Do you want to start a tab?"

"No," I looked at her thinking she must be dense. Had she not heard me? "He'll take care of it." She glanced at him and as he did not say anything, she turned to another customer.

Frances, Mike, and I made brief chitchat. He chugged his glass of red wine, paid his bill, and told us we could have his seat and the one beside it. "Tell Gilbert I told you that you could have his seat."

We sat down after he left, and the bartender did not waste any time getting back to us. She looked at me. "Hi, I'm Cassandra," she said.

I said, "Hi," and I looked away.

She prodded, "What's your name?"

Now, why would she need to know my name? Furthermore, what bartender, especially a female one, asks a female customer such a question?

"Jane," I quickly replied. She looked at Frances who stated her real name.

The bartender persisted and tried to make small talk. We answered her questions with a yes or no, but we did not volunteer any information about ourselves. I knew she must be wondering if I could be Mike's wife.

Gilbert walked up behind us as we faced the bartender. "Hi, Marti!" I heard. I groaned inside and turned to him with my back to the bartender.

I greeted him and whispered, "Gilbert, you weren't supposed to say my name out loud. I did not want them to know who I was." I knew Mike's paramour was somewhere nearby, and I was not quite ready to meet her. While Gilbert and I talked, Frances watched Cassandra leave and return with a woman who was dressed like a waitress. Frances stared openly at her, but the woman had a hard time seeing me, as my back was to the bar and to her. Frances, however, had a good look before the waitress turned and walked away.

Gilbert told me the guys who played golf with Mike were losing respect for Mike, and they all respected me. That was nice to hear. He told me he thought Mike was crazy. I asked him what the woman looked like and he said, "She's not as pretty as you. Nothing special. She's pretty worn looking." I introduced him to Frances and told her he was an old golfing buddy of Mike's. The three of us chatted. Frances and I finished our wine and made preparation to leave.

"You need to see her," Frances said as we got up from our seats.

"I'm not sure," I replied.

"Yes, you do," she said firmly.

She led me out a side door and took me through the restaurant. I saw lots of people dining and having quiet conversations, and I laughed at what we were doing.

"There she is!" she exclaimed, as I noticed someone crossing a short hall just ten feet in front of me. She saw Frances and apparently recognized her from the bar and quickly slipped behind a partition. We lost sight of her. I picked up my pace and rounded a corner just in time to see her come out the other side of the partition. She was facing me, and her eyes widened. She turned quickly and walked in a different direction. I could almost hear her gasp, although she didn't. She had damaged, straw-like red hair, and large facial features. With her big eyes, nose, and mouth, she wasn't ugly as I had hoped, but she wasn't pretty either. I could not see the details of her face very well, so I wasn't sure about the worn look Gilbert had mentioned.

Frances and I laughed all the way into the bathroom. We both felt the night had been a successful one. We made Mike leave, and we scared her into running from us.

After that relaxing weekend with Frances, I had several invitations to dinner with girlfriends. I spent time with my good friend, Gloria, and relaxed often at her pool. Another friend and therapist, Cindy, had me over for some of her special Italian dinners.

Gloria and I spent Labor Day weekend in Atlanta. It was good to get away, and Gloria was good for getting me to laugh. Jamie and Lindsey came home the weekend after Labor Day, and we tried to make the best of everything. Lindsey would not talk about her father. Jamie still thought I should have left him long ago. We all missed Aly, who had stayed for an event at school.

In the meantime, I was calling Mike often when he was at work. I used the ruse of telling him or asking him about financial matters. I wanted to hear his voice. I did not want him to sound okay. He always sounded fine, and that made me sad.

I realized Mike was moving on, and I saw my second attorney, this time a woman, for consultation in St. Augustine. I thought she would be sympathetic, but I did not feel right with her. I saw my third attorney. I was told he was the best attorney in Jacksonville. He had a plush office, and he seemed knowledgeable. I just did not feel the connection I needed to feel. That attorney asked me if I felt this marriage needed to be dissolved. I could not say yes. I called Mike on the way home to see if he could say yes to that question.

"Mike, I do think we bring out the worst in each other, but I am not sure I am ready to dissolve our marriage. Are you?"

"Yes, Marti," he sounded resigned to hearing from me more than he probably wanted. "Yes," he said.

Something lifted from me when I heard those words. The finality must have hit me. There was no turning back. I called him the next day and left a voicemail message.

"Mike, I am going forward with divorce proceedings. Let me know by tomorrow if you want to settle this between us with legal counsel, or if we need to go the whole gamut with an attorney. We can save a lot of money if we just settle it."

He did not call. I called him three days later regarding some financial pieces that needed his attention. We had a good talk. I felt better. For the first time, I thought I might actually be able to move on.

I was so confused by the time I saw my fourth attorney, however. He had been the divorce attorney for a friend of mine, and I had admired what I perceived as his compassion. Betty had gone through a divorce while her twenty-year-old daughter was dying of a brain tumor. Her daughter died, and her husband of twenty-plus years left her. Her attorney had eased up on his costs when she told him she could not pay him up front. She thought he seemed to care about what had happened to her, and she convinced me to see him.

I expected to retain Barry the day I met him, but I was so confused during my meeting with him. He suggested that I go to counseling for a few sessions, then somehow get Mike in for counseling with me.

"Thirty years is too much to just give up on. Your husband is going through a midlife crazy. He is going to wake up one day and realize what all he has lost." Barry looked directly at me and continued, "At least for the children's sake you both should try this." Barry then told me a story about a man who left his wife for another woman and six months later noticed his mistress sounded just like his wife of twenty-five years.

"What happened?" I asked.

"He went back to his wife."

Can I really do this? I had been working on receiving God's grace and forgiving my husband for his betrayal of the last five years. I knew I needed his forgiveness also for how mean I was to him the last few years. Can this marriage be saved? I had always thought that was a rhetorical question.

I did not like this confusion. I had gone to Barry intending to retain him. I left him with a feeling of uncertainty. Now I planned to convey to my husband Barry's suggestion:

"I care about you, and I am getting a therapist. If you'd like to meet with someone, you could meet with mine, or you can find a different one. We could both go to the therapist together when it is time. I have an obligation to our children and to our thirty-three years together. I am inviting you to do this. If we are ending this, how much of an investment would this counseling be? We have invested thirty-three years. This would be a small investment compared to that. I will seek information from my therapist to find out something about myself and how I have been unfair to you. If we go ahead and end this after going to counseling, we will then have a well thought-out and well-reasoned decision. I cannot rush into this without trying to save my marriage first. I need to do this for the children. They are hurt."

That is what I planned to say. I would see a therapist first and go from there. Barry had told me he thought Mike was having a midlife struggle, and he would want to come back. I wasn't so sure. The alcohol addiction seemed major.

After I left Barry's office I went to dinner with some of the ladies from work. "Get rid of him" was their hasty reply when I told of my encounter with the attorney. They did not think I should even consider it. One of my buddies, Laurel, agreed with the attorney, however, and said, "If you don't try this, you will never know if it could be saved." She put into words what I was already feeling. I at least had to give it a try.

CHAPTER 14

SECOND THOUGHTS

I went to a church service by myself on a Sunday in October. The minister talked about the power of prayer. He also talked about community, and he spoke to me. I received the message that everyone has a mission, and my mission was perhaps to bring God to someone else, someone who needed God in his life. I might be that person's only friend, and, therefore, the only one who could bring God into his life.

After I left the church service, I called my good friend Cindy. I visited with her in her home for two hours. I told her I wanted Mike to get treatment. She said she had seen people return from the intensive thirty-day treatment, and they are changed forever. How I wanted that for Mike. I loved him, and I wanted him whole and happy. It would take a miracle.

I left Cindy, and I called my mother and asked for her prayers. She said she would request a Catholic Mass for him and put prayer requests at both St. Gerard's shrine and Padro Pia's shrine in Italy. She was leaving for Italy the following Saturday, and her tour group would be at St. Gerard's by Tuesday. She would also get everyone she knew to pray. I had heard that message earlier about the power of prayer and was happy it was spreading.

I emailed my brother Bob and called my sister Carol. I also spoke to my brother, Chris, who had called me. I asked them all to pray and to get their Sunday school classes or churches to pray.

We were praying for a miracle, I knew, as that is what it would take. Mike was so embedded in his drinking and in his new relationship. I only prayed it was beginning to sour. I prayed she was sounding like I used to sound—the old me.

I thought of the conversation I had with Mike the previous Monday. It was a pleasant conversation. After that phone call I had decided I would continue to show my sweet nature, and I would eventually implore him to try to get our marriage back on track. We owed it to the girls. I knew Barry was right—we had to see a counselor *together,* but first we had to start with individual sessions.

In my first counseling session with my therapist, Alice, we explored my family background. At the end of the session, I reviewed what I had learned. My mother was a model for my behavior—she had lived with an alcoholic for over fifty years. I have had lots of practice doing what I do. Mike abandoned himself years ago. He has now abandoned his children and me, just like his mother abandoned him, albeit unintentionally. Why did I settle for this life?

My therapist told me Mike left me because he wanted me to leave him alone. He drinks and wants to be left alone. She told me to tell him that I cared about the person inside and miss him and want him to come back, but he must stop drinking. He must agree to get help. Her message to me, however, indicated two opposing suppositions. If he wants me to leave him alone, why would he want to come back?

Alice talked about me making *me* happy and whole again. My husband was depressed. My mother was probably depressed handling my father's alcoholism. I guess I should be depressed as well. Why would I settle for such an existence? I thought I was trying to save my children by staying in the marriage. I did not say it to Alice, but I guess I needed to tell her that family is important to me, and I was only trying to hold the family together. I thought back to the days before Mike left me. He and I had held hands snorkeling just five days before he told me he was leaving me for another woman. I knew he was leaving me for the freedom to drink.

I called Mike two days later while he was at work. I asked him about money the girls needed for sorority dues. I knew what I wanted to say:

"I am in a different place. I am not so sure I want this marriage dissolved. Thirty years is a long time, and we both have a great investment here. We have a long history. We were best friends. We were partners, lovers … any dissolution would impact not only our well-being but that of our children, your family, my family, our friends, and on and on.

"We do have a long history, and I do still love you. I care about you. I think about CeeCee and Mimi a lot, and I feel I may be the only one who really cares about you the way Mimi did. Mimi wanted the best for you. So do I.

"I am going to therapy right now. I have been seeing my friend Cindy a lot—she is a mental health therapist, as you know—but I just started going to someone officially. I want to change the behavior I brought into our relationship. I don't want to bring that into any future relationship, whether it's a new one or whether it's possible with you again. At the very least I want us to be good friends. I want you to be able to forgive me for my behavior of the past five years, as I am trying to accept, understand, and forgive yours. I am getting there, and I need to for my spiritual growth. I love you, and I care what happens to you.

"I know who I am. I am basically happy and optimistic. The person I was when I was with you, I am not proud of that person. I am not that person, and I am already undergoing changes.

"I think this separation has been good for me to see what is important in my life. I am not ready to give up what was ninety-five percent good and that is how you described our marriage. It was not a bad marriage—it was ninety-five percent good. I don't think many people can say that about their own. I care about you. I know you may think what you are doing is what you want, and so be it. However, if there is any doubt, I want you to consider that there are other options. I am here, and I will always be here for you. I got off on the wrong track as did you, but I am wanting to find that path back to you. I know we each were reacting to hurt—we were both hurting, and I am forgiving you as I hope you forgive me."

That is what I wanted to say. However, when I called him, I lost sight of my plan and said instead, "I am in a different place. I have made a 360 degree turn and am in a different place. What about you?"

"Yeah, I guess so," he replied.

"Are you sure? Is this the place you want to be in?" I asked him.

He stumbled through his response. "I don't think … I don't know … will I ever be sure?"

"Mike," I said, "when you left, you said things happen for a reason. I think they do too. I have been alone for two months, and I have learned a lot about myself. I love you. I care about you. Mimi and CeeCee are not just rolling over in their graves right now, they are thrashing about. I care about you. I am probably the only person in the world who really cares about you like Mimi did. I am not ready to let thirty-three years of marriage go. I am going to therapy, and I am changing. You know I am a good person. I know you are a good person." I added, "You know how spiritual I am."

I continued, "I just don't think we should rush into this. Mike, I have seen attorneys, but I am getting all these messages that I shouldn't be doing this right now. I don't want to rush into anything and regret it the rest of my life. What do you think?"

"I think you need to go ahead," he said. He did not sound sure, however, and I had already heard him say he wasn't sure he was in the right place. "I can't talk right now. I'm busy."

"But, Mike, I'm just asking you to open your eyes to what's around you … open your ears … and open your heart. I am here, and I am waiting."

"I have to go."

"Mike, I …" I wanted to add the "ninety-five percent good" line. I heard a click. Too late.

Although it did not sound encouraging, I felt it was. He did not want to hear what I was saying. It was upsetting to him, and it may have been confusing him. I knew he loved me too. This would be a long process.

The next time I would have to work in the ninety-five percent comment.

As desperate as I was, I was not going to give up on him. I also knew I was on a different journey, a sad one, and I wanted healing. I had looked for resources to aid my healing and had read several books. I persuaded a friend Trudy into going to a Saturday evening "healing service" at a church in a town approximately thirty miles from Jacksonville. I did not know what to expect, but I was willing to try anything. I wanted to feel better.

During the healing service I prayed for help for Mike and me, and I put Mike, the children, and some of my friends on the prayer list. The service was powerful. The minister gave each of us a personal blessing that ended up being a bit humorous. Trudy needed to be back at her house by eight, as she had a sitter. It was after seven, and we still were not in line for the blessing. Our pew was finally directed to move to the line and after ten minutes of standing, I touched Trudy's back to get her attention. She was standing in front of me.

"We have to go on up there or you will be late," I whispered. The minister was blessing each person individually at the communion rail. We were standing in a line in the aisle, waiting our turn. I noticed the corner on the far right was empty—no one was standing at the rail. They had been, so I knew it was available. I gave Trudy a small push.

"Let's go to that corner," I whispered as I pointed to the right.

Trudy knew she was running late, so she walked toward the corner without any hesitation. We turned from the aisle and walked in front of the first row of pews and saw why no one was standing there awaiting the blessing. A rather large woman was lying supine on the floor—she had fallen back when she was blessed. We had seen several people fall back when the minister blessed them. Two gentlemen were always there to catch them and lay them down gently. Here lay another victim. We had momentum and could not turn back. We walked alongside her body and felt kind of bad when we stepped over her, but we had to get healed before we left. We had come so far, and we now had to leave. We stood at the communion rail, waiting for the "bestower" of blessings. He was at the far end of the rail but was headed back our way. It would only be a matter of minutes.

I prayed, "Please get up ... please get up," as I noticed the woman's left foot was just to the right of my right foot. I was afraid I would step on her or fall on her if I, too, fell back when I was blessed. Trudy was to the right of the woman's other foot and stepped up onto a step at the rail and moved over to her right, giving me room. I stepped up beside her and was instantly relieved that I was no longer touching the woman's foot. A moment later someone tapped me on the shoulder and told me to step back down so I would not fall. I did as I was told and moved as far left as I could. Trudy had to step back down and straddle one of the woman's feet. I worried. How is anyone going to catch Trudy? They would have to step over the inert woman, which, by now, I was assuming was a corpse!

The minister finally arrived and saved the day. He placed his hand on Trudy's head and said a brief prayer. Nothing happened. She was still standing when he turned to me. I was expecting a long litany of prayers from him—I was asking for so much—but his blessing was brief for me as well. He walked away. Wait, I wanted to cry out. That wasn't enough. I need so much more. I was afraid it didn't take. Neither of us fell. We stood for several seconds, and we finally turned around. Unfortunately, Trudy had to step over the lady who had not moved. Needless to say, we made a hasty exit.

Trudy and I laughed all the way back to Jacksonville. We weren't being sacrilegious—we were just seeing the humor in what had happened. She was going through a divorce as well, and neither of us was finding much humor in our lives. I left her where I had picked her up and went home.

When I arrived home, there was a message from Deenie on my voice mail, but all she said was, "Mike." I called him on his cell phone and left him a message to call her. I called Deenie the next morning before I went to church. She told me Mike had not called her, but Jamie had. Jamie had asked her to put Mike on her prayer request. She said she did not know why and did not want to know why. She surmised, "It must be his drinking."

"I love him and worry about him," she said.

"I love him, too, and only ask that you pray for him."

She replied, "When I leave this world, I want all of my family to be Christians and to be together."

"You should tell him that, Deenie."

"I wrote him a letter." She added, "Don't stay with him if he won't stop drinking. You're young, and you could find someone—you have a lot of years ahead of you. I wouldn't blame you, Marti. I had to tell Cecil I would leave him if he kept drinking the way he was, and he stopped. You don't have to keep taking this."

"Please pray for us, and let's leave it in God's hands," I said.

I finished getting ready for church and once again marveled at the sermon and its message for me. I realized it was true that we put more energy into beginning a relationship than in maintaining it, and I received that message loud and clear. We are selfless when we do something for others, and we don't expect anything in return. When we devote time to others, we engage in selfless acts.

I never thought Mike devoted time to me. I never considered him a selfish man, but now I reconsidered. Did he ever show selflessness? I am sure he had, but I could not think of one instance of it in that moment sitting in the pew of that church. How does one become selfish? I thought if a child at two or three years of age experienced disturbances in the home or trauma during those years of egocentrism, he or she could become stuck in the emotional growth process. It made sense to me that that child could continue to be egocentric and eventually selfish. I could imagine that other problems would emerge as well.

The minister made it clear that when we are frustrated or angered, we need to talk to the other person and let the feelings go. We don't need to keep those negative feelings inside of us. We should forgive those who hurt us, and when we do, we let the angst go. We free ourselves.

We should ask ourselves certain questions: With whom do we need to be more unselfish? Are we critical of anyone? Are we able to admit we are wrong? Are we able to say we are sorry … to say forgive me? Who do we need to forgive?

I left the church service with much to ponder.

I called Deenie again that evening before a dinner engagement, and she still had not heard from Mike. How distant he had become. He had not called me either. I thought I had opened the door with my call to him on Saturday night when I left a message that his mother had called. I asked him to call me so I could tell him about her phone message, but he never called.

I was very sad the next day at work. I never liked Mondays anyway, but I had started to think it might be hopeless—or it just took too much out of me. I was trying to heal, but I had been so down in the dumps. I was leaving the door open for him, I was not pursuing the divorce, and I was receiving counseling. He was enjoying drinking, and he was with someone else. He was not doing any of this mental work. I still could not believe he made this choice.

I called Deenie after I arrived home from work. She told me Mike had not called her. I called his cell phone and left a message that I had mail for him. I also wanted to tell him about something I had heard over the weekend—something good for him to know.

Mike called me two hours later. I could not believe it. Oh, why does my heart beat so fast when I hear from him?

"Hey," he said, "what kind of mail do I have?"

"Just State Farm something, New York Life, Merrill Lynch, Fidelity annual reports, and some other pieces," I replied.

I could not hear his response, so I jumped into what I wanted to tell him. "Mike," I said rather excitedly, "I was talking to someone over the weekend, and she was describing symptoms similar to what you said you felt. She was put on an antidepressant, and she felt worse. She was put on a second one, and she could only live 'a day at a time.' I realized that is what you always said. She said she was up and down, having panic attacks, and just not feeling like everyone else. She didn't care about anything. She couldn't get anything done. You have said the same things."

I continued before he could stop me, "She went to a psychiatrist who asked her about her symptoms, found out she had attention deficit disorder as a kid—I think you may have had attention deficit hyperactivity disorder—and the psychiatrist put her on Adderall. She said it was life changing. She felt blissful, calm, happy. She felt like other people said they felt."

I paused briefly and then said, "Mike, what if?"

He asked, "What was the name of the medicine?"

"Adderall," I repeated. "You should look under your insurance and find a psychiatrist though. If you have a chemical imbalance, the psychiatrist would know what to try based on your symptoms. He'd know the right medication."

I then said, "Mike, we are all praying for you. I hope that's okay."

"That's okay," he said softly.

"I know you don't want me to say anything, but I know what part I brought into this." I was talking fast. I did not want him to hang up on me before I got it all out. "I was on a different path—we were both on a different path—and I'm working on it. I want to be that sweet person. I do care about you. I can't throw away thirty-three years of marriage that quickly. I hope that's okay for now."

"That's okay." His tone was gentle.

"I don't know what's going to happen," I said. "I just don't want to do anything right now."

"Okay."

I hesitated. I was stunned to be hearing "That's okay" and "Okay" to all I was saying.

There was silence between us. He finally said, "I'll call you tomorrow. I'll come pick up my mail."

"Okay," I said, and then, before I could stop myself from saying it out of habit, I ended the call with "Bye, sweetie."

But he never called. I wondered if this man would ever stop disappointing me. I had been so hopeful after our phone conversation, even blissful. I went to play bridge with my bridge group afterward, and I was happy. I felt good for a change. I thought he might wake up after all.

What a roller coaster this was, but I still put my faith and hope in God to deliver me from it.

He did not call the next day either. At five thirty p.m. I went out to get my mail, but my mailbox was empty. I saw my neighbor pull several articles of mail out of his mailbox, and I thought that strange. Where's my mail? Did Mike swing by and get *my* mail? Good excuse to call him.

I called him and asked him if he came by and took mail out of the mailbox. He said, "No."

"Are you going to pick up your mail?" I asked him.

He answered, "What is it again?"

I told him what the various pieces were, and he said, "Just put it in the mailbox."

"Mike, why can't you come up to the door and get it?"

"Just put it in the mailbox."

"Can you not look at me? Can you not face me?"

"Marti, it just always goes south."

"Mike, I have been going to church, to Bible study, and I am changing. You know I think sometimes *big* things happen so people can realize what's really important. I know what's important. I know the part I played in it, and I am changing. I cannot throw away a thirty-three-year marriage just like that. Can you just keep it open?"

"I'll keep my mind open."

We both said goodbye.

I called him right back. I had not said anything about the medication, and I had a question. "Mike, I was talking to that girl about the medication thing. Do you ever feel like you're not in your right skin?"

He hesitated as he spoke, "I don't think so."

"Well," I said slowly, "that's what the girl described."

I changed the subject. "Well, I have that name for you—the psychiatrist's name."

"Just email it to me."

"I will put it with your mail."

He said, "I'll come get it sometime," and then, "Bye."

I hung up the phone.

CHAPTER 15

HOPE SPRINGS ETERNAL

I called Mike early the next morning at work to see if he had put money into my account for the girls' sorority dues. He told me it should come in the mail. I said, "Thanks," and we both hung up.

I saw Alice, my therapist, after work. She asked if I had used the script with Mike. I told her he had sent a mass email out to the girls and to me. I was feeling hopeful. Although the email was just a list of company phone numbers and a website for searching for numbers, it was his first email communication with any of us. I wondered if he was trying to make a reconnection. I am sure she did not think so.

I had talked to Jamie about it, as she had asked about the email. "What has happened? Why is Dad sending us all an email?" She went on before I could answer, "I forwarded it to Eric, and he asked me if Dad had broken up with his girlfriend. He told me he was trying to reach out to us all." Eric was Jamie's boyfriend. Had we all lost it?

I told Jamie what happened. I told her about my conversation with Mike and how he had said he would keep his mind open. I didn't tell her he said it always went south. She thought it was "pretty amazing." I told her to keep praying, and I said I was glad Deenie was praying for him. "I think a mother's prayers are very strong. I think a child's prayers are strong too. Keep praying."

I told Alice about the email and about Monday's conversation when he said "Okay" about me not doing anything right now. I was so hopeful we could work this out. I did not get to tell her about the other conversation when he kept telling me to put his mail in the mailbox, as he did not want to see me.

Alice moved over to the sofa where I was sitting, sat beside me, and placed a large flip chart across our laps. She started drawing on the spread-out sheet. She drew family members as I named them. She started recapturing family patterns, and I quickly became very interested. I told her about my mother telling my father she was not a virgin. She told him shortly after they married. She did not tell him an older man, her employer, had taken advantage of her. My father was devastated; that was important to him. He thought she was a virgin; he would not have married her if he had known she was not. It put a major strain on their marriage.

I described how my father turned mean and verbally abusive when he was approximately sixty years old, how he called my mother a whore and other disrespectful names. He would drink and then curse her.

Alice listened quietly, as I told her my father had wanted to marry a different woman before he met my mother, but the woman's parents did not want their daughter marrying a poor farmer. I recalled talking to my father when I was in college and telling him not to go see that woman. He had located her in Little Rock and had made plans to see her. He eventually bought a new car and drove to Little Rock to meet her. I knew he wanted to show that he had become a success, and he apparently thought his shiny, new Impala was evidence of that. He anticipated meeting the young woman he had fallen in love with, but he met an older woman he did not recognize. He was not attracted to her. I remembered my mother's reaction when she found out he had gone to see her. She was hurt and saddened.

I told Alice that my mother wrote me a letter when I was in my early thirties, asking for help. I visited my parents shortly after and tried to talk to my father on that visit and on many subsequent visits. I did not visit them often enough in their hometown of Morrilton, but when I did, I felt my dad and I had great sessions. (So now I am counseling my parent?) He would complain about my mother, he would cry, but he could not forgive her. I tried many times to tell him she had made a mistake (I had only his story at the time and did not know that it was my mother's employer), and he had to find it in himself to forgive her. He could not do that. He just kept drinking.

It pained me when I revealed to Alice that my father lost his mother when he was nine years old and was mute the following year. His mother had gall bladder complications that required surgery. The traveling physician attempted an emergency surgery on the family's kitchen table, and my father heard the agonizing cries of his mother as she lay dying on her own kitchen table. He did not speak for a solid year. He attended a Catholic school, and the nuns were worried about him. I wondered why no one reached out to him.

My father's mother had lost three children to spinal meningitis before my father was born. My poor grandfather! He lost three young children, and then he lost his wife. How emotionally available was he to my father and his siblings? My father's depression was evident, and the precipitating events were clearly laid out in my mind. This was nothing new to me; I had hashed and rehashed my father's past many times over the years.

Alice and I went over all the interactions between my siblings and parents. She asked me about my parents' relationship. Nothing came to mind. I could not describe their relationship. Vacant? Nonexistent? My father had worked on his farm and in his winery. My mother had worked in the house and in their wine and beer package store. We children worked wherever and whenever we were told. I told Alice that when I was growing up, our home always had tension and stress. My home with my husband also had tension and stress when we lived together.

Alice drew parallels. Of course, I had always reflected on relationships in my parents' home and had seen the similarities in my home with my husband. It did not hurt to revisit the parallels, however. My parents did not have a loving relationship—at least not visibly to us children. Mike and I did not have a loving relationship. I pointed out that when at home, my maternal grandfather sat in a chair in the corner, my father sat in a chair in front of the television, and my husband sat in a chair in front of the television. All three isolated themselves and were withdrawn from the rest of their respective family members as well as from the family events.

Alice said we should look for the ideal when we consider having a relationship. We may not find the perfect relationship, but if we find ourselves nagging, we should stop, turn, and walk away from it. When we find ourselves nagging and trying to change someone, we are apparently seeing characteristics that are counter to our ideal.

In a better relationship we learn to tell the other person what we need from them instead of just telling them what to do.

Unfortunately, some of us just happen to fall in love with the wrong guy—or with an alcoholic.

I had worried about the path my husband was going down during my entire life with him. I continued to worry that he would spiral downward even further into his alcoholism, and it would kill him. I had prayed for him, I had others pray for him, and I prayed to God to take it from me. I wanted to leave it in God's hands. I didn't think I could do anything more.

Yet, I kept looking for his car every time I drove by The Pelican. It was sad to me that my husband of thirty-three years was sitting at that bar almost every night since he had left me nearly three months ago. That was not what my daughters' father should be doing. How did I know he was there? I had to travel down the street that goes by The Pelican Bar and Grille almost daily—it was my route to work. He selected this bar that was just outside of my neighborhood. I know he selected it because his paramour worked there, but it was at the entrance to my neighborhood—our neighborhood.

Although it was usually there, I had not seen his car at The Pelican for several nights. I had been surprised each time I looked and had not seen it parked in its usual spot in front of the restaurant. When I did finally see it, I had toyed with the idea of making a visit and was still considering it.

I had been reading the week's lesson from my Beth Moore Bible study, The Patriarchs, and God seemed to be speaking to me. Some of the words seemed to literally jump off the page at me. I took the words and formed my own prayers, asking God to please not pass me by. I wrote Mike's name in the blank on one of the pages, thinking he had been overlooked. He may have been desperate for an identity change, while I was destined for one.

I gleaned from the pages that Mike's difficulties and the path he was taking were somehow tied to a God-led track for me. His and my relationship and his uncaring, however, were blocking me and holding me back. What I saw as an obstacle may have been the opening to a new passageway. I realized God could change anyone—him, me, any of us.

I finished the lesson and felt peaceful. Beth's words and the accompanying words from the Bible always left me with a feeling of peace. I wanted to go see my husband while I was feeling it.

I dressed to look my best, and I drove to the restaurant where I knew he would be. Of course, my heart started beating fast when I pulled up and parked. As I stepped out of the car, I felt the nervousness to which I was accustomed start to seep into my body. This always happened just before I saw him. Still, I had to see him. I was afraid he was starting to forget about us.

He was inside, sitting at the bar. I walked straight to him and ignored the looks the other guys in the room were giving me. Hey, I knew I looked good. I touched his back and squeezed myself in between Mike and the guy sitting to his right.

"Mike, hi," I said.

He turned his head toward me. I moved further toward the bar, so I could make eye contact.

"Did you get my message?" I asked, expressing concern.

"No, what message?" he asked.

"Deenie called last weekend and said, 'Mike.' I was afraid something was wrong. I called you. Did you get my message?" I asked again.

"Yeah," he said, "I did."

I said, "Is she okay? Is anything wrong?"

He picked up the mail I had laid on top of the bar.

"No," he said, "let's go outside."

We walked through the bar and as we walked out the door, I repeated my question, "Is she okay?"

"No. Someone told her I moved out."

"No, they didn't. Who?"

"Either you or one of the kids."

"No, Mike, no one told her that. She doesn't know you moved out."

"John told me she knows."

"Have you talked to her?"

"Yes."

"Did she say that?"

"No."

"Then she doesn't know."

We walked toward his van. He opened the door and put his mail on his seat and turned back toward me.

I looked up at him. I asked him if I could do something and leaned toward him, saying, "I'm not going to kiss you. I just want to pass a blessing on to you."

I felt foolish and impulsive, but I was thinking about the personal blessing I had received with Trudy. I put my forehead to his forehead. I told him, "I was blessed and want to pass it on to you."

I stepped back and again looked into his blue eyes. He *was* in there somewhere.

I felt helpless and searched for words. "Mike," I started, not knowing what I was about to say. "Can I have a hug?"

He hugged me and then stepped back. "You look good," he said with admiration, as he looked down at my slender body. I was thinner than I had been when he left, and I was wearing a close-fitting shirt and tight jeans. I knew I had firm lines where I needed them and curves where I wanted them. My brown hair had grown longer as well. I wanted him to think about what he was letting go.

"Thank you, so do you," I said, and I meant it. His eyes were bluer than I remembered, and he looked good to me in that moment. He was sober as well.

"Mike," I tried again, "I've been doing this Bible study, and it is really speaking to me. It talks about you and me. Let's just keep an open mind, okay?"

He agreed, and he waited.

"You know I said something big happens, and it shows us what's important in our lives. You are so important to me. I am going to send you an email and tell you some things." I turned away.

"Okay. Bye, honey," he said.

"Bye," I said.

I walked to my car and turned and watched the back of him as he strolled back into the bar.

I wondered, as I drove away, how Mike would react when he read his mother's letter. Deenie's letter was in the pile of mail I had left with him. I had unsealed it and carefully sealed it back before I took it to him. The first paragraph of the letter included general information about her physical state. I had been saddened when I read the following words:

> "Mike, Jamie called me tonight to put you on my prayer list. You and John and families have been on it some time and I hope God has helped both of you with any problem that you haven't been able to solve. She didn't say what you needed to hear from God, but you are on my mind and in my prayers. I knew it must be important for her to call me. I am sorry I am not able to come and see for myself what kind of help you need and I would try to do it.

> "I hope you know that you and John and families are my life and I love all of you dearly. I know He will try to help you if you just give Him the chance."

Deenie went on in her letter to talk about her ailments, John's schedule, the weather, and closing the Mount Nebo cabin for the winter. She continued with her concern for Mike.

> "Mike, all of us have had good lives and we need to thank God every day. I miss Cecil more each day and hope he

is happy wherever he is. I didn't ask Jamie what your problems are, but I will ask God to be by your side and give you all the help you need. It makes me feel guilty that so much I have called on God to help me and some time I haven't given much time to Him. I have asked His forgiveness and thank goodness He has said, ye shall ask and I will give!

"Honey, this letter will be hard to read and I can't help it, but I will speak with God tonight and tell him you need His help, and I am sure He will be there.

"There are times when your mother wishes she had been closer to God. I am sure all of us feel that way when it is time to die, but we do the best we can. I know you are a grown man, and you don't need your mother preaching, but I love you and can't be by you to help.

"Please tell Marti, Jamie, Aly, and Lindsey that I miss all of you and do take care."

My mother-in-law had no idea that my husband had walked out on us. She did not know that Aly had not spoken to him since the day he left, nor did she know that Lindsey had deleted his number from her cell phone and thus from her life. She had heard from Jamie, who had been there during the better years with her father, who had not seen the heavy drinking of the past eight years, who had not seen the change in her father as her two sisters had witnessed.

Jamie had heard from me in years past and knew it was bad at her former home, but she was not there. Jamie remembered the good days with her dad. She had not seen him stumble through the house with that "stupid" look on his face when he drank. She had not witnessed him turning from the driver's seat in the car and breathing out forcefully on her sisters who were in the back seat after they complained they could smell his breath—the stench of the alcoholic's breath. She had not witnessed his trembling hands when he tried to pick up a Scrabble tile when his daughters and his wife guilted him into playing "just one game." She had not seen his distant gaze, his look of appearing to be someplace else, his inability to concentrate.

She had not seen the transmutation the Merlot had done to her dear father.

They had not seen his alcoholism first hand, and I was glad Jamie and his mother were praying for Mike. I kept up with my own praying and talking to God, and I continued to attend Sunday services at a local church. The sermons never failed to amaze me. The last sermon focused on growing spiritually. I thought of Mike when I was reminded that we can pray for other people's spiritual growth. I considered him when I acknowledged that when we accept other people's differences and value them, we affirm their worth. We show we accept them when we stop insisting they become like us.

I also thought of Mike when I heard the greatest gift of love is our attention, our time. We can help others grow when we show them affection and appreciation. It was Mike I thought of when I received the messages to pray for those who need God's love and pray they do what is right, to admit our mistakes, and confess to one another so we can be healed emotionally.

I knew the importance of making a commitment to Christ and striving toward godliness. It helps to have a partner. Rather than deal with commitments, however, we tend to run, escape, or change spouses. We need to invite Christ into our lives.

I was not going to give up on Mike yet.

I called a friend, Stacey, and I told her about the sermon. She, too, was going through a divorce and was having a hard time letting go of her husband of fifteen years. She said, "You are going back with Mike." I felt hopeful, and I replied, "I am not going back with Mike—I am going forward with him."

I wanted to say so many things in my email to Mike, but later that day I sat down at my computer with notes I'd made, composed myself and typed the following email:

> "Mike, I just wanted to say that the last two and one-half months have taught me a lot about myself and what I have done to our relationship. I have been hurt, but I know I have hurt you even more. I am sorry for all that I have done, and I only hope you can forgive me, as I have forgiven you. Yes, I have forgiven what you have done, as I know and understand why you left me.
>
> "I have been seeing a therapist, I have been going to a wonderful Bible study, and I have gone to church services. I am changing. I have a long way to go, but I do know I am not that person you knew the past seven years. I don't like that person, and that is not the real me. You know who I am.

"There is a lot more to this relationship than the past few years show. You even said that when you described our marriage as ninety-five percent good. Not many people who are married can say that. We really did have something good, and I played a terrible part in destroying that. I humbly ask for your forgiveness. My hope is that we can both keep our hearts and minds open until we are sure what it is we need to do. This life is too important!

"I told you I would let you know more about the medication I mentioned to you. A friend was telling me she was feeling agitated, panicky, just "not right," and had never felt right. She was put on an antidepressant, and she got worse. Her family doctor put her on another one, and she was no better. She even tried a third and was living one day at a time. She could not look ahead and was living day to day.

"She finally went to a psychiatrist, and he tried her on a medication for attention deficit disorder (she had ADD as a child), and she felt happy and blissful after two weeks. She said she had never felt happy like most people say they feel, and it was life-changing for her. She learned that some people do react poorly to antidepressants, and she was told that is because it's the wrong medication for them.

"Only a psychiatrist knows the neurology and brain chemistry symptoms and knows what medications are best for what symptoms. She told me people come from far away to see this psychiatrist because he is so thorough, he is so good at matching the symptoms to the right medication, and he won't stop until the patient feels right. Just wanted to let you know.

"I am glad I got to see you Saturday. It had been a long time, and it was really good seeing you.

"Lindsey is coming in this weekend. I would love for you and her to see each other. She was not here when you left, and I think she is having trouble with all of this. You two got along the best as of recent years, and I think it would be good for her to see you and just enjoy you (like you two used to do when you'd watch TV together).

"Take care, Mike."

I pushed "send."

CHAPTER 16

SURRENDER

I sent Mike the email late Sunday night. I am sure he read it on Monday—probably first thing in the morning.

I had loved seeing him on Saturday. My heart was beating hard the whole time I was with him. I felt hopeful. He had seemed so sweet. I saw him at four in the afternoon, but his car was gone when I drove by at seven thirty. That was unusual for a Saturday night. He may have returned later, but I never drove back to see if he had. I assumed he had read Deenie's letter that night. It could have upset him.

After I sent the email, I had not planned to talk to him for at least a week or two, but a corporate American Express bill came in the mail. I left Mike a message at his office to ask him what to do with it, but he did not call me back. He had me so up and down—up on Saturday and then down on Monday. I was only expecting a response to my bill inquiry, not to my heartfelt email. It seemed every time I opened the door, he shut it.

The Bible study had inspired me to hold that door open. It spoke to me about us and reinforced the idea that I could not pursue a divorce right away. It confirmed the possibility of the impossible and that miracles happen when we are ready to throw in the towel.

I continued to pray for that miracle—that Mike would see a psychiatrist and get on the right medication. He seemed more like himself when I saw him on Saturday. I had not seen him like that in months. He told me he was on his third antidepressant, but I knew he was seeing his family practitioner. Dear God, I prayed, please let him see it won't hurt to try a psychiatrist, one who knows what these medications do.

As I prayed for him, I knew I needed prayers for me as well. I had been feeling a lot of emotional upheaval, and I had one night of heart-wrenching cries when I saw with clarity what I had done to this man. I had fussed at him for eating while standing in the kitchen, for God's sake. I could not leave him alone. I stared at his fat stomach when he walked into the room, and he visibly would suck it in. He would ask, "What's for dinner?" I would get annoyed and say, "Food," but I would not have anything planned. He did most of the cooking the last year—I had been having a year that was "all about me." My youngest had moved off to college, and I had been liberated from child-rearing. It was my time to be egocentric. I had given all of myself to my children for twenty-seven years.

It *was* all about me. I dressed differently, as I was making a conscious effort to make myself look more attractive. Jerry had told me things the previous spring that made me feel desirable, and I liked that feeling. Jerry was a businessman who had delivered some items to me one day while I was at school, and when he was in my small office area, he seemed flustered. I had no idea why he was acting so nervous, but he later called me and said he did not know what it was, but he could not get me out of his mind. I did not believe him, but I was very flattered, as he was nice looking. Mike did not dole out compliments, at least not to me, and how I wanted them.

I had examined myself during that emotional onslaught and found a false sense of security. I was not as self-assured, secure, or confident as I may have appeared to others. It was all a front or a facade to the scared, insecure, inadequate feeling person within.

My spirit is strong, but my human weaknesses are plenty.

So, I had those heart-wrenching cries, and I begged God to forgive me for what I had done to one of His creatures. I tore Mike down, and I tore him down until he had no recourse. I understood why he left me. I always wondered why he stayed. I know how mean I had become to him. He often said to me, "Why are you so mean to me?" I just thought I had lost respect for him because of his drinking, and I no longer liked who he had become. Now, I wondered if my fear of his becoming like my father made me treat him in a way that made me perceive him as being like my dad. Mike was not my dad, but my fear that he would be an alcoholic like my dad made me treat him so negatively. "You are going to be just like my dad, and I will not take care of you like my mother took care of him." My fear made me suggest to him that he would turn out like my father—a self-fulfilling prophecy. What was wrong with me? I knew how damaging those messages were. I was always so angry!

Was I angry at my father?

Perhaps I became my father. He verbally abused my mom after a certain point in his alcoholic demise. I had verbally abused my husband and had beaten him down as my father had beaten down my mother.

Which was my greater fear—that I would turn out like my father or that my husband would?

This revelation bore into my being. Again, I found myself emitting uncontrollable sobs, begging God to forgive me. I wanted to understand why. I knew it was not mine to understand, but it was mine to change. With awareness can come change.

The part I played in my destroyed relationship was a lot larger than people realized. Mike never heard me say one good thing to him in the past few years. I thought about all that negative energy directed at him and what that alone must have done. I thought I hated him, but I essentially hated myself and all I represented.

I knew why Aly was so conflicted—Aly and I had faced many challenges in our interactions with each other. I was sweet in public and would greet everyone I saw. I was not so sweet at home. I barked orders, I yelled, I was enraged at times. Why though? I needed to know. Was I so very unhappy with Mike? I really didn't think so. We had many great years—the years we attended church together and were both closer to God. During those years we each said "you are awesome" to the other daily and even several times a day. I was and had been very stressed. My perfectionistic tendencies got in the way. I wanted everything to be just right and to be my way. I wanted control.

I had never given anyone else a chance. I recalled what Aly said to me when she was just eight years old, "Mom, I am who I am. You can't make me into who you want me to be. I am who I am." I heard her profound statements and marveled at her wisdom at such a young age. Did my eight-year-old just say that? Maybe God does speak through us. She said something I needed to hear.

I applied Aly's words to her, and our relationship improved. I should have applied those words to my husband. I would not let him be who he wanted to be. I nagged him about everything. He never did anything right—my idea of right. I didn't consider it nagging. I was trying to edify him. Maybe some people just can't take edifying.

The separation, even with his infidelity, may have been the best thing that ever happened to us. I needed to wake up! I was in such a negative holding pattern. I had eventually stopped fussing at Mike about everything he did, and I started ignoring him and doing my own thing.

He said he had wanted to hold on to us, but I had already gone. He had tried to pull me in—he had reached for me, but I had resisted. My libido was gone—I was not attracted to him. I didn't think anyone else could be. I never gave that a thought, didn't even conceive the idea, although I had in the past wished someone would sweep him off his feet so he could leave me. I was not happy with him, but I was happy everywhere else. People loved me, or so I thought. I was friendly, sweet, and positive. Why wasn't I this way to my husband?

So, who was I really? That is what this self-discovery would need to divulge.

I did have my libido after all—it returned as soon as my husband left. Maybe out of anger at him for leaving me and having sex with someone else or just out of a need to feel comfort. Or maybe it was out of a fear I would not be able to get aroused with a man in my future due to lack of use. I learned the benefits of masturbation.

Having grown up in a strict, Catholic family where the word "sex" was shunned and masturbation was considered a sin, and having been raised in a generation where women did not speak in sexual terms or even say aloud the names of private body parts, I can say this was not easy for me. However, I think it is important for women to acknowledge their sexual needs and to feel comfortable talking about a normal biological function without feeling shame or guilt.

I went to The Pelican Bar and Grille on a Saturday to give Mike his mail. I wanted to give him that American Express bill I had called him about, but he had never called back. He had not taken care of canceling a small life insurance policy on me either. I had asked him to cancel it, as I did not want to continue to pay the premium. It was of no benefit to me and not enough to help my daughters out in the event of my death. I had planned to tease him and say, "So, you just want me to come here to see you? You don't come get your mail or call me back—I can only assume you want me to come up here." That is not how it happened.

Mike's van was in the parking lot, but he was not seated in his usual place at the bar. I followed a couple to the back of the bar, and I saw a redhead that could have been his paramour sitting at an outside table. I could see her through a window, and a wall blocked the person she was talking to. She was all smiles. I glimpsed a masculine arm that moved from behind the wall toward the window, and with a sunken feeling, I knew it was probably Mike sitting there.

I continued to follow the couple out the door to the outside, and the girl approached Mike and the redhead. I don't know what happened to the guy. It was no longer a couple I was following. Mike's paramour did not see me, but he did. I motioned for him to "come here," as I did not want her to see me. He got up from his seat, but he said something to her, and she flashed him a wide-eyed look. She did not look my way, but I am sure he told her I was there.

When he approached me, I asked him, "Is that her?"

He nodded, "Yes."

Without thinking, I said, "Introduce us." What the heck was wrong with me?

He studied my face. "Are you sure?"

"Yeah," I said.

We walked back to the table, and I looked down at her. She had big, heavily made-up eyes and broad features framed with straw hair. She looked cheap and fake in my eyes. *Mike, what are you thinking?* He introduced us.

She looked up at me and smiled, "Nice to meet you."

I looked back at her. "You too," I said. She looked down my body to my legs. I was wearing a skirt. I knew I looked good, so I didn't mind. I turned away from her, and Mike and I walked to the car.

"She doesn't look as bad as you said," I commented casually.

He said, "What do you mean? I never said she looked bad."

"Yeah, you had horrible descriptions of her when you were leaving." I dropped it.

We walked on to my car, and I pulled the mail out from the front seat and handed it to him. He had a hard time taking the various pieces from me, and I had a hard time giving them to him. I think we were both shaking. He wouldn't look at me. I took off my sunglasses and looked at him. He still wouldn't look at me, so I said, "Look at me." He did. I was surprised I did not feel anything other than perturbed. I had walked in on them, and it was a rude awakening.

"How's work?" I finally asked.

"It's okay," he said.

I pointed to the mail and explained some of the pieces and what he may have to do. I also asked him to take care of a dental insurance issue that occurred at his company. I then looked at him again.

"Are you happy?" I asked.

"Yeah, I'm pretty happy," he mumbled. He had not been able to say that before.

"Mike, you know you'll have to do it—I don't want to divorce you."

He turned away. I asked him, "Are you going to church?"

"No, I'm not going to church," he muttered.

"Mike, you're a good person. You're in a bad place right now. You're a better person than this." I was referring to the bar and to the cheap woman.

"I've got to go back in. I have friends in there. We're getting ready to do something."

"Wait," I said, "can I have a hug?"

He hugged me and I said, "I mean we were married for thirty years." I felt a hug was appropriate.

He walked away.

I got into my car.

I found out later he and his friends, and of course his paramour, were going to a concert he and I had talked about last spring. I had started looking for tickets at that time, and he told me he would get them. I had completely forgotten about the concert. I guess he had found tickets after all.

Oh, the ups and downs! That night I went to see *Joseph and the Amazing Technicolor Dream Coat* with my good friend Barb, and we had a fun time. We had a glass of wine afterward at Aroma's, a cigar bar, and watched salsa dancing. After we left each other, I gave in to despair and cried in the privacy of my home.

I sought comfort and watched a Bible study video in the midnight hour. I wrote some of Beth's statements onto the pages of my Bible study workbook, and her words provided the relief I needed. I felt the peace return, and I knew my faith would pull me through. I also knew God was up to something big, and I had to wait it out.

After the video, I read my insertions in the workbook, and I thought how my reactions to Mike had been selfish and mean. I prayed for the Holy Spirit to renew me so I could be more godly in my behavior. What a difference that would make for my marriage. I knew I had to trust Him, and I had to trust that it would work out according to His plan. I felt there was something bigger happening, and I knew I would have to be patient.

I felt spent the next day and talked to my friend Stacey that evening. "It is probably time to surrender it to God," Stacey told me. And Stacey's not even religious.

I was feeling melancholy, and I knew she was right. I would surrender it all and prove my faith in God.

I did just that, and Mike filed for divorce the next day, unbeknownst to me. He filed on October 23 and requested that it be officially filed on

October 27, our thirty-third anniversary date. I had no knowledge of that while I was packing that same evening of October 23 in preparation for the next day's travel to an annual state conference in Orlando. I had no idea what was in store for me on that trip either.

I rode to the conference with my co-workers Toni and Laurel. I sat in the back seat and was heavy-hearted. I had agonized over the past three months about the end of my marriage and the end of my life as I knew it, and I could not find comfort. I told Toni and Laurel how I just wanted to get help for Mike. The man he had become was not the man I married. I told them how I had left the door open in case he had a change of heart. I was miserable, and as sad as I was, I was still trying to make the best of it. After all, I had surrendered it.

We freshened up after our arrival, and the three of us went to the conference registration booth to pick up our packets. We then headed out to dinner. The first person I saw in the hallway was Dale, a guy I had met four years earlier. We had become friends and always greeted each other and had conversations intermittently during the conferences.

"Hi, Marti!" he said loudly as he walked by. He was wearing workout clothes and was walking briskly toward his destination.

"Hi, Dale!" I replied. "You've been working out!"

He nodded. He was some distance from me even as he passed, and neither of us slowed down or stopped walking. I gave him the thumbs up, and we both kept walking away from each other. Toni, Laurel, and I continued to the hotel restaurant, had dinner, and listened to music at the piano bar before we called it an early night.

I woke up early the next morning and walked to the weight room. Dale was in the lobby, and we greeted each other. I hurried past him, as I was not wearing any makeup under my glasses. After my workout, I showered, dressed, and headed down to the conference. My roommates, Toni and Laurel, had already gone down to their first session.

I walked through the long hall of the conference and opened the door to the room where my first session was occurring. A man was at the door and would not let me enter. He said it was full and at capacity, and no one else was allowed. I walked back down the hall, looked down at my schedule, and wondered where else I could go. That was the only session I had marked off as an interest. The door to my left swung open rather abruptly as I was passing it, and I looked away from the schedule and turned to face Dale.

"Hi!" we both said rather eagerly. We started small talk. He stared at me.

"You look different," he said.

I hoped that was a positive statement. We talked more. He had told me in the past he was in a separation with his wife, and he was still separated.

I said, "You must have rubbed off on me. My husband left us last summer."

"Oh, Marti," he said with sympathy in his voice. "I'm so sorry." My spirits were starting to lift, and I said, "It's okay. I think it needed to happen."

I told Dale that Mike was with a cheap-looking redhead.

"What's wrong with redheads?" he asked. He then told me he had been with a redhead when he was first separated from his wife. I told him his redhead was probably a professional. My husband's was a bartender/ waitress type. (She could have been an attorney; I would have still found fault with her profession.)

We talked for two, maybe three, hours. Various people stopped by to say hello to him—all women. He seemed quite popular, at least with the ladies. I looked at him. He had sandy blond, graying hair, blue eyes, and a great smile. He was nice looking, and he was gregarious. He made no move to get away from me, so we talked between the interruptions. He eventually had another commitment, so we separated.

That was the beginning of my ability to release my fears. I had expressed fears to Alice, my therapist, that I did not think I would find a man I clicked with—one who would have conversations with me, who would interest me—or one that I would interest. I had not yet realized I needed to find myself first.

Dale and I saw each other that night at a party given by one of the conference attendees. We talked forever. He told me his wife was having trouble conceding to a divorce, and he was unhappy. We later kissed, and my worries were erased. Somehow, right or wrong, I felt God had placed Dale in those halls for me. He was the first person I saw after my arrival, the first person I saw in the morning on my way to the workout room, and God finally pushed him out a door practically on top of me. He was a diversion, an opening in the dark skies that had surrounded me. Every moment with him was more special than the one before. I felt desire I had not felt in years. I knew this was probably just a break in my mourning, but it felt good to feel good. We kissed long and hungrily.

We went out to lunch the next day and drove around in his midlife-crisis car, a silver Porsche convertible. We danced that night at the conference party, and afterward we kissed some more. Dale was always a gentleman, and I was having trouble holding back. When he told me, "I love your heart and your soul," I melted. When he said, "I am so into you," my knees got weak. We joked about my weak knees. We laughed about a lot of things. We enjoyed each other's company, and we did not want it to end. But it did, and it was an awkward goodbye.

"It feels like summer camp," he said as I turned and walked away.

I was a different person on the drive home. God had answered a prayer and had shown me there are good, fun, nice men out there, and I would be okay. I was not so unattractive—I had also received attention from one of the better looking male vendors, and Dale had said he was jealous.

I had surrendered my burden—all of it—to God, and although I felt I would be healed and whole again, I knew deep inside it was not over. I felt a sense of dread, but I did not know for what. Dale was my escape, and I was on cloud nine. Dale and I had something special, and we both knew it. Would it last? That was the big question. Even if it did not, I knew that he was helping me through a rough period of my life.

I arrived home, and I rested before I made my way over to The Pelican Bar and Grille. It was five thirty p.m., and I thought Mike would probably just be getting there after a long week of work. It was Friday, October 27, and it was our thirty-third anniversary.

When I drove into the restaurant's parking lot, I saw Mike's van leaving. I hailed him down and marveled that I got there in the nick of time—I would have missed him if I had arrived seconds later. He pulled over into a parking space. I parked in the row across from him. I had his mail and collected it from the seat beside me. I leaped out of my car and walked over to his van. He had been drinking, and he appeared drunk. It was only five thirty.

"Mike," I said. I did not give him time to greet me before I continued. "I just wanted to tell you, it's okay now. I'm okay. You made your choice, and I'm ready to let you go. I won't hold you back. I'm in a different place now, and I am happy."

"Did you find someone?" he asked.

"No, but I've had a taste of it."

"I'm a happy person," I said. "You're not a happy person."

"No, I'm not a happy person."

"But I want you to be happy, Mike. Go to that psychiatrist and get on the right medication."

"Yeah," he said, "the medication is not helping." He added, "I'm seeing a neurologist."

"Good," I said. I had told him to go to a neurologist the previous summer. "Have they found anything?"

"No, not yet." He held out his hand. It was shaking.

I then told him about Marchiafava-Bignami disease, an alcohol-related neurological disorder, that results from great quantities of red wine consumed over an extended period of time.

"How much is great quantities?"

"Two to three glasses a night over six to seven years." I had recently attended a presentation by a neurologist who had given that information. Two drinks every night over a period of six to seven years could result in harmful neurological conditions, she had said. She went on to tell her audience that cardiac specialists will tell you the benefits of red wine for the heart, but they will not tell you how it affects the neurological system.

He didn't reply. He held his hand out to me, and I placed mine in his. "I hope you have a good life," he said.

"Mike, this is not the end for us. We have the girls, and I hope you'll be able to meet me sometime to talk about them."

He looked at me. "I filed the petition today."

On our anniversary. I looked at him and saw what he had become. He was no one I wanted to be associated with. Heartless. Soulless.

"Happy Anniversary," I said, and I turned away from him and walked back to my car.

CHAPTER 17

ROLLERCOASTING

The months passed, and with the passage of time I recognized that I was truly moving toward a better place. I had let go of my past, and I was embracing my new identity, my new self. I was in the process of shedding each layer: the sadness of the loss of my marriage, the anger at my husband's betrayal and infidelity, my lost self, and the need to be in control and thinking I knew what was best for my loved ones. I had not completely discarded all the layers, but I was moving in the right direction.

The path was less daunting, but the nagging feeling that it was not over continued to hound me. I tried to shake the feeling of dread each time it surged up within me, but I continually found myself bracing for something unforeseen.

I managed to get through the divorce proceedings with Dale at my side, or at least in my ear. It was a long-distance friendship, and he and I were usually on the cell phone after I left my attorney's office, when I was having a low moment, or after the mediation settlement. He took my mind away from my dismal existence with financial disclosures, alimony agreements, splitting of our financial assets, and the endless list needing to be completed before the divorce decree was signed and the marriage was dissolved. He gave me hope for a better future; I had released my fears, and I knew I could be attractive to someone, and I knew I could at some point have a relationship with someone else. I knew Dale was not that one, but I also knew he was in my life to help me get through the worst period I would ever experience.

I was wrong. It was not the worst period. I had known it was not over, and the dread was with me when I signed my name to the divorce decree. I felt the roller coaster continuing, and while I knew I could not stop it, I did not want to get to the end of the ride. I did not know how the ride would end. I was scared. I was scared for my now ex-husband. I was scared the roller coaster would crash.

My dread increased during the three months that followed the signing of the divorce decree. I will never forget the date: May 19, 2007.

I had just sent the bridge ladies off. They had all stayed at my house the previous night after we had gone to see *Mamma Mia!* in Jacksonville. We played bridge until three a.m., and we woke up at nine a.m. We had "omelets in a bag," which they raved over, and then they were all gone— both the bridge ladies and the omelets. Mike had just recently given me the recipe for the omelets.

I called Mike to see if he could come over to sign the refund check we had received from the IRS. I also needed his half of Aly's expenses for her London trip. She, along with the Sport Management department at Florida State University, were spending six weeks in London. They were leaving in June. He readily agreed and was at my house within the hour.

Both Aly and Lindsey were still in college and both were home that weekend. Lindsey was home for the entire summer. Aly would soon be traveling to London. Lindsey was home when he arrived, but Aly had spent the night at a friend's where she was house and dog sitting. I prepared an egg omelet for Lindsey and for Mike. They sat at the kitchen counter and ate together. Mike was quiet; his demeanor was sad.

After Lindsey left the room, I told him about my sister-in-law's parents and how they spent time together even though they were divorced. Brenda was married to my brother Bob, and she told me her parents had coffee together every morning. (Her father was a recovering alcoholic, and they had divorced years ago.) I told Mike we could see each other, have dinner sometimes, even go dancing. He and I danced well together, and I loved to dance. I had been doing a lot of that since our divorce, which was signed by the judge and final on February 19.

Mike appeared forlorn; he seemed friendless. I wanted to reach out to him. After all, he was my children's father. He did not respond to my suggestion that we could see each other. Mike never said much, so I did not expect him to talk to me.

We talked about Aly's trip to London and the costs. He wrote a check for four thousand dollars, and I asked him, "What about the hundred?" His half was forty-one hundred.

"I'm only giving you a check for four thousand," he said.

"Fine," I said, knowing I would have to make up the difference.

He signed the IRS refund check and handed it to me. "Where's Aly?"

I said, "She should be here any minute."

Aly called a few minutes later and was upset. She had locked herself out of her friend's house and was frustrated with herself. Her car keys were in the house. I relayed that to Mike, and he said he would pick her up. He asked me to go with him.

I picked up a second set of car keys for Aly's car, and I left with Mike. She rode back to the house with him, and I drove her car back. She later told me she and her dad did not get to talk, as she was on the cell phone with the homeowner and was trying to figure out how she could get back into the house.

After we arrived home, Aly went to take a shower with the idea she would be seeing her dad when she finished. However, he did not stay that long.

I did not know Aly and her dad had not conversed; I assumed they had, and I thought he was just ready to go. His interactions with us tended to be brief, so it was not surprising that he was ready to leave after a short visit. I was glad Aly was able to see him. She had last seen him the end of July, and I recalled her last words to him, "Look at me. You will never see this face again."

How hurt my daughters were when their father left me. They felt he had left them too. I think they also saw how his alcoholism had progressed. I cried when I thought about how his leaving affected them.

Mike said he needed to go, and I walked outside with him. He hugged me, a long hug, in the kitchen before he walked out. He seemed so woebegone. As he pulled himself up into the van into the driver's seat, he said, "Marti, I'm sorry I wrecked your life. I'm sorry I wrecked the girls' lives." He closed the door and rolled the window down.

I said, "Mike, we are doing what we can—we are trying to get through it. Right now, I think the life you wrecked is your own."

He nodded in agreement and sat in the driver's seat. He appeared forlorn, and I walked closer to the van.

I said, "Mike, we can get help for you; we can get you treatment. I will go to therapy with you." I hesitated. "We can try to see if this is salvageable."

"Marti," he said, "it's so much more than this." He waved his hand in a circle outside the window.

"Like what?" I asked. "What do you mean?"

"There's so much more stuff."

"What stuff?"

"There's just so much more stuff," he answered.

I walked up to the driver's window, and he reached out with his left hand and put two fingers on my right cheek.

He looked at me and said, "Remember this. I love you. I have always loved you, and I will always love you."

When Mike said those words to me, I looked at him sharply. His words and tone sounded final. "Mike, I don't like the sound of that. Promise me you will not do anything." He did not answer. "Promise me!"

He said quietly, "I will try not to."

"No," I said. "Mike, you can't do anything. You can't leave that legacy to your girls. You think you have wrecked them now. You will have really wrecked them. Promise me you will not do anything."

I thought for a second, trying to give him a reason not to do anything rash. "You won't be able to anyway. Deenie wasn't able to carry it out. Do you think Cecil and Mimi would allow that to happen? No, and you can't either. They won't let you."

I knew I was talking crazy, but I was grasping at whatever might make sense to him. Cecil and Mimi were dead, but I imagined their spirits could be guarding their loved ones who remained here on earth.

Mike looked right at me and flashed that boyish grin I had not seen in years. With it came a flood of memories of a younger, happier Mike combined with wistful images of earlier days filled with love and hope. His smile assured me there were better years, and those were the ones I needed to grab onto and keep in my memory bank.

Now he was turning on the key; he was starting to back out of the driveway.

"Wait," I said, "Mike …"

He kept backing out, and I knew I had lost him. He did not want to wait. He did not want to say any more. I knew in that instant that he could not and would not overcome what had beset him. I knew he had gotten to a place in his life from which he could not climb out. He would never get over what he had done to us, to himself, to his life. Mike was never going to be or feel any better than he did in that moment in time. He could not pull himself out of it. I realized all of this, as he backed out of my driveway.

With the realization that my ex-husband would never rise from the abyss into which he had fallen also came the thought that if I attempted to Baker Act him, he would laugh at the police officer who stopped him, and he would tell that officer that I was crazy and that I made accusatory statements like that all the time—ever since he divorced me. I also wondered why he would bicker over one hundred dollars if he was planning to do something to himself. What difference would it have made? He had refused to give me the one hundred dollars needed to complete his half of Aly's London expenses. He was apparently wanting to hang onto and use that hundred. He would not do anything.

With that last thought, I let him drive off.

CHAPTER 18

A PLEASANT ENCOUNTER

As I watched my ex-husband drive away, I had a very gloomy view of what his life had become. I thought back to the Saturday two weeks before. Mike and I had met that day as we needed to pick up flight tickets at the airport. Lindsey and I were flying to Arkansas in June for my niece's wedding, and we were using a Delta fly-one-companion-flies-free certificate. The ticket had to be purchased from an airline ticket agent with the original Delta American Express card that was in Mike's possession. He and I had agreed to meet at his empty office building early that Saturday morning. I picked him up, and he rode with me to the airport.

It was awkward at first. Our conversation was stilted. After we had completed our task at the airport, we went back to his office and picked up his car. At his invitation to have coffee together, I followed him to a nearby Starbucks, and we both parked on the street. We walked in together, and he mentioned he had never been in a Starbucks. We took our coffee cups and sat at a table inside the coffee shop.

Our visit was pleasant. We talked. I told him I had never thought I would be divorced, and he said he never had thought he would be either. I saw Mike for the first time in nine months—my Mike, the old Mike. His eyes were clear again, and I could see *him* and not that sordid, soulless human being I had been interacting with during the past nine months—the one that had left me the end of July. This Mike was not unlike the guy I had married. How many times over the past eight years did I ask myself, Where did that guy go?

I looked into his eyes that day as he sat across from me at the Starbucks table, and I said in a matter-of-fact tone, "I love you, you know."

He replied, using the same tone, "I know, and I love you."

I changed the subject. We made small talk. He greeted a customer that walked by our table, and I asked him if she worked at his office.

"No. She's a waitress at a nearby restaurant."

"Oh," I teased, "so, you're still trying to pick up waitresses?"

He laughed and said, "No, not at all."

I asked him what had happened to him and his paramour. I still could not call her his girlfriend. I knew he had moved out of her apartment the end of March.

He replied, "Too much drama."

"What do you mean? Her drama or her kids' drama?"

"All of them. There was just always drama. It was too much." He would not elaborate.

"At least you were happy for a little while—when you were with her." He denied that he was.

I asked to see his apartment. He had moved into this apartment when he moved out of his paramour's place.

He said, "It's not far from here. We can walk."

We walked to his apartment, feeling the congeniality between us. His apartment was a depressing place. He had no furniture other than a bed, a shabby chest of drawers, and a television set, which were all contained in the single bedroom. What his life had become hit me like a sledge hammer. This was what his life was reduced to: a single bedroom of furniture. I was left with our home, our three daughters, and all the responsibility associated with that. Mike had forsaken all responsibility, but at such a cost.

Mike did not belong in that apartment. He belonged at home with his family. How did it get to this point?

I mused about my ex-husband and our current state as I backed out of my parking spot. Mike and I had hugged before I left. A few minutes after I drove away, my cell phone rang.

"Marti," Mike said on the other end of it.

"Yeah?"

"I just wanted to tell you I enjoyed those last few hours just now with you."

"I did too, Mike."

"I really enjoyed that," he repeated.

"Well," I hesitated. "Maybe we can do it again. I could meet you for dinner sometime, Dutch treat. We can talk. We can be friends.

I've already told you I'd like to go dancing sometime." My friend and his friend, Gloria, and I had reached out to him after Easter and had suggested going dancing. Dancing and music had lifted my spirits many times during the past three months after the divorce was final.

"Okay," he said. We hung up.

Mike had appeared remorseful—he *was* remorseful. I later told the girls what I had witnessed. Aly called him the next day. She had not spoken to him since July 28, the night before he moved out. She later told me he cried when he heard her voice.

"Aly," he said, "you have no idea how much this means to me. I love you so much."

He cried out loud and without shame. Tears came to Aly's eyes when she heard her father, and she told him she loved him before they hung up. They made plans for lunch, but he could not set a date and time.

Aly called her father four times to set the lunch date over the next two weeks, but he made an excuse each time. They never got together. The only time she saw her father was on that date, May 19, when he came to our home, and she had gotten locked out of the house where she was housesitting.

CHAPTER 19

A SCARE

I was worried about Mike the week before he came over to the house. He had called me that Monday when I was on my way to Quinn-Shalz funeral home for the visitation service of my next-door neighbor's father.

I saw his number on the screen when I reached for my cell phone. "Hi, Mike," I said.

"Hey," he replied. We made small talk, as I drove to the funeral home. I was in the process of parking my car when I heard him say, "You'll be okay if something happens to me."

"No, I won't, Mike," I answered quickly, stepping on the brake half way into the parking space and stopping there. "I won't be okay."

I let my foot off the brake and eased into the parking spot. What was my ex-husband saying?

"Yes, you will," he said. "I left you on all my life insurance, so you will be okay."

"Mike," I repeated emphatically, "I will not be okay." He sounded down; I did not want to get off the phone with him sounding like this, but I had to run in and see my neighbors and then I had to pick up a friend for bridge night.

"Mike, I need to run into the funeral home," I explained why I was in a rush. "I will call you back in a minute."

I had an eerie feeling as I stepped out of my car and realized Mike had said final sounding words while I was sitting in front of Quinn-Shalz—a funeral home, of all places. As I walked to the door, I wondered. Is he saying what I think he is saying? Does he have a medical condition he's not telling me about?

I called him back ten minutes later, and he talked to me as I drove to pick up my friend Joan who was riding with me to the bridge hostess's home. He sounded dismal. I tried to offer him encouragement. I told him Aly had tried several times to make a lunch date, and he said he would call her. I told him Jamie was coming home for Memorial Day, and it might be nice if he could grill steaks for the girls. I could leave if he did not want me there. He said, "Maybe."

"How's your face?" I asked.

"It's better. Hartley did a pretty good job on it."

Mike had told me previously that he had gotten hit by a golf ball that had ricocheted off a tree about two months earlier. He had broken several bones in his cheek, and he had an indentation where the ball hit. He had been treated by a maxillofacial surgeon, who had been a former neighbor and was still a good friend.

"Mike," I said, "about what you said earlier. I repeat, I will not be okay if something happens to you." I hesitated. "Do you have something I don't know about?"

"No," he answered. "I'm just saying you'll be okay."

We talked about Aly's upcoming trip to London. I told him she would be going with the Sport Management department from Florida State. "Will you pay for half of it?"

"I guess," he said. A few weeks earlier he had said he would not help with her costs unless she started talking to him again.

I told him I'd call him later in the week, and we hung up just as I arrived at Joan's house.

Although I was concerned about Mike's telephone call, I dismissed it from my mind. I enjoyed Monday bridge night with the girls, and this night was no exception. The eight of us were making plans to see *Mamma Mia!* on Friday, and we discussed our plans while we played.

Shortly before ten p.m. my cell phone rang. I looked at it and saw it was Mike's number. I answered, but no one was there. I had trepidation in my heart, as he never stayed up that late. Now he was not answering when I called back. I had a mental picture of him doing something to himself and calling me as he was doing it or calling me to keep him from doing it. My anxiety heightened as I made a second attempt to call him back. He still was not answering. I called back three more times before I returned to the bridge table. Luckily, I was the dummy, and bridge ended after the next hand was dealt and played.

I told Joan about the phone call, his not answering my call backs, and my fears as we drove to her house. She knew I was worried, and she gave me a hug when she left my car.

When I arrived home, I called Mike's cell phone again. Still no answer. I asked Aly to call his house phone while I kept trying to call his cell phone. We were discussing our next move while we dialed. Should we drive out to his apartment? We were at a loss, and we were both worried.

Finally, after about the twentieth attempt, Mike answered his cell phone.

"Mike!" I exclaimed in relief. "Where have you been?"

"What," he said in a muffled tone. "I don't know," he mumbled.

"Mike, you called my cell phone forty-five minutes ago, but you didn't answer when I called back."

"I didn't call you," he said.

"Yes, you did," I said with emphasis. "Your number showed up on my caller I.D. What are you doing?"

"I don't know," he sounded confused. "I think I was asleep."

"Have you been in bed?"

"Yeah," he answered, but he didn't sound so sure.

"Are you okay?"

"Yeah, why?"

"Well, it was strange." I waited a few seconds. "You're never up past nine, and you called around ten, then you didn't say anything when I answered, then you didn't pick up when we kept trying to call you."

"I've been asleep," he said again, this time more clearly.

Maybe we had caught him in a dead sleep. "Okay, go back to bed."

I hung up the phone.

I called Mike after I arrived home from work the next day.

"Are you okay?" I asked him gently.

"Yeah," he said.

"You scared me last night. I didn't know what was going on. Are you sure you're okay?" I did not like the depressed sound in his voice.

"Am I okay? I'm probably not okay," he said, then continued, "Marti, I don't belong in this world. I don't have a place here. I don't fit in. I have never fit in."

"Mike, of course you have." I did not want him to think that. "You're just going through a mess right now."

He sounded like he had been drinking, and I had learned well that you could not talk to a drunk. Luckily he said it first, "I'll talk to you later." I was not the one who had to end the call this time.

The following Friday was when the bridge group saw *Mamma Mia!* Mike had come over that next morning after everyone left to sign the IRS refund check and give me his half of Aly's London trip expenses.

I was sad for Mike that Saturday after he left me. I was also worried.

Aly, Lindsey, and I went out to dinner that Saturday night, and I told them I was worried about their father. Afterward, Lindsey and I went over to my friend Dawn's house, and I felt a sharp pain in my stomach around eight thirty p.m. Jamie later told me her stomach was hurting her at that same time.

The next morning, Aly, Lindsey, and I met my friend Gloria for coffee at a local café. I told her how Mike had seemed, and we called him to see if he wanted to meet us for coffee. He did not answer the phone. Gloria tried him on her phone. We thought maybe he was avoiding me. He did not answer. We each took a turn. No answer.

I tried again later. Still no answer. Aly tried. I tried again. Lindsey and I went shopping, not knowing our lives were about to be drastically changed. One of us called off and on all afternoon. By the time I went to bed, I was extremely worried, and I had to keep calming myself down. You are being dramatic, I told myself. He is okay. I will call him tomorrow and set up a dinner date.

I didn't know that Aly was also worried and was also having trouble falling asleep.

CHAPTER 20

PLEASE BE OKAY

I woke up Monday morning feeling despondent. I couldn't shake the ominous feeling I had. I tried to reassure myself that Mike was okay. Why would he bicker over one hundred dollars if he had planned to do anything to himself? He knew Jamie was coming in Memorial Day weekend, which was just the next weekend. He had the girls to consider. I told myself he wouldn't do that to them. I told myself I had too active an imagination. He was okay.

I called his office at seven a.m. He always went to work early. He had always said he was able to get more done in that one hour, from seven to eight a.m., than he could the entire rest of the day because he had no interruptions. He did not answer. His voice on the answering machine said, "Today is Friday, May 18 …" I started to panic, then I remembered the apartment he moved into was only blocks away from his office. He didn't have to leave early and avoid the traffic on Butler Boulevard anymore. I told myself again that he was okay, but I still had a sinking feeling.

Aly woke up when I did. She dressed and left to go to a babysitting job but asked me before she left if I had reached Dad that morning. "Not yet." I was trying to sound chipper while hiding my anxiety. She told me she would be sitting all morning and would be back at the house by one p.m. She kissed me goodbye, and I fretted.

Mike, please be okay. I knew I had to plan the dinner with him soon, and we would talk. I went to get dressed, and just after I pulled a skirt from the upper rod in my walk-in closet, a doll rolled off the shelf below it. I had placed several of the children's favorite toys on that shelf years before. That doll had never, ever rolled off that shelf before now. I put the doll back on the shelf, and it would not stay. It rolled off again. I thought of Mike for some reason and mentally asked, *Are you here? Are you doing this?* I finally shoved the doll hard, and it stayed in place.

"Oh, Mike, please be okay," I whispered aloud as I stood in the middle of my closet. That doll had been on that shelf for years, and I had not been near that part of the shelf when it fell off. It felt eerie. I felt Mike's presence or spirit or something not quite definitive in the closet with me, but then shrugged it off and again prayed he was okay.

I arrived at my school where I worked as a school psychologist, and I called his office again. The recording still said the wrong date, and my heart sank. Mike faithfully changed his outgoing message. He never forgot. Maybe he was on vacation, I hoped. I called my friend Gloria who was on her way to work.

"Gloria, Mike's still not answering the telephone. I'm worried."

"What do you want me to do?" She was ready to help in any way she could. "You want me to drive over there?" She was referring to his apartment building.

"Do you mind?" I hesitated. "Will you call me if his car is there?"

"Yes," she said. "I'll go now."

"I'm coming if you tell me his car is there."

I sat with fear in my heart but also with hope. If he tried anything, he could still be alive. He could be saved—his stomach could be pumped. He would be okay. I still hoped he was on vacation.

I couldn't just sit there. I called Gloria back.

"Gloria, would Victoria know someone in Mike's department? I want to try to call and see if they have heard from him." Victoria was a mutual friend of ours who worked at his office.

"I'll call her and see," she said.

She called me back with a name. I dialed the building's main number on my office telephone and asked for the person. I was getting very nervous, and I could feel my anxiety level rising.

"Hi," I said to the voice that picked up on the other end. I gave Mike's name and asked if he was expected in today, or was he on leave?

The female voice told me she would check, and she put me on hold. The seconds felt like minutes. Finally, she was back on the phone.

"No, he's not on leave."

"Then that means he's supposed to be there?"

"Yes," she answered. "Can I help you with something?"

"No." I was certainly not going to tell her my worst fear. I hung up.

My cell phone rang seconds later. "Marti," Gloria's voice said, "Victoria is going in to see Tom, and she will call you in a minute." Tom was Mike's boss.

I hadn't wanted to alert Mike's boss. I didn't want to give him any idea that one of his employees could be capable of ... of doing what I considered to be my worst fear.

I couldn't wait. I dialed the building's main line again and asked for Tom myself. He answered the phone after just one ring.

"Tom, this is Marti, Mike's wife." I had met Tom and his wife on numerous social occasions. He knew who I was.

"Yeah, Marti, Victoria was just in here, and I have already checked. Mike should be here."

It was nine a.m.

"Tom, I'm worried. He's never late, and his outgoing voice mail message says it's Friday."

"Marti," Tom said, "I'm worried too. Mike's been acting just real bizarre the last two months. I've been really concerned about him."

"I'm scared. Something's wrong," and this time I knew it, but I still held on to hope.

"Do you want me to go to his apartment?" Tom asked.

"Would you ... could you?" I hated to ask this of him. "Gloria's on her way now."

"I'm on my way," he said. I quickly asked for his cell phone number before we hung up.

I didn't know who would get there first. Gloria was driving from the beach. Tom was only blocks away. I wasn't sure how soon he could get out of his office building.

I called Gloria and let her know Tom was on his way.

"I'm going to pick up Victoria," she said. "Tom will probably beat us there."

"Gloria, call me as soon as you get there."

"I will," she promised.

I was so anxious. I sat and stared at the phone. I prayed. Please be okay ... please be okay ... please be okay. I waited.

"Call me, Tom," I said aloud. My phone was still. I stared at it a moment longer, and then I called Tom's cell phone.

He answered, "I'm on my way."

"Will you call me as soon as you get there?"

"Yes," he promised.

I waited. Time seemed to stand still. I was overwrought. Hurry, I prayed. Call me. Let me know he's okay. I worried. No one was calling me. Ten minutes had passed. The office was probably five minutes away from Mike's apartment. Why wasn't Tom calling me?

I called Tom. No answer. Maybe he was tied up talking to the apartment management people. But still, he said he would call me. At this point I just needed to know if Mike's car was gone, if it was parked in front of his apartment, if ... I didn't want to go there.

I wanted to call Gloria but resisted. Tom had not answered *his* phone. I sat helpless with worry and felt my anxiety mounting.

I think by now Gloria was worried too. She and I had talked about Mike's mental condition numerous times over the past few months. We both knew he had made a bad decision nine months ago—heck, five years ago. We both knew he was spiraling downward, and we both feared he would hit rock bottom. Mike was Gloria's friend, and she supported my concern about him, even if he had left me and had committed adultery. We had talked about him, his alcoholism, his depression, his declining mental state, and his seeming inability to rise above it all.

Gloria had been with me a few days before Easter when I had called Mike and had invited him to a passion play. She and I were going. He declined but said he would do something with us another time.

"Are you sure, Mike? This would be so good for you. I've already been to it once and am going back with Gloria. It's beautiful."

"That's okay," he said. "You two enjoy it." He did not sound good.

"Are you okay?"

"Not really," he said. "I'll be okay. I think you are happier though."

"Mike," I wanted to assure him that I had to make that choice or be dragged under by it. I wanted him to make the same choice. "I choose to be happy. I am not going to let myself get stuck in it. I have to keep going."

"No," he said, "I think you're happier without me."

"Mike, that's not true. I'm trying to keep going."

"Are you seeing someone?"

"No," I answered, "I'm nothing to go after."

"Marti," he said, "I think you are probably one of the most perfect people I know."

Where is this coming from, I wondered.

He continued, "I don't know anyone as wonderful as you."

Why does he do this to me? He was no longer with his paramour, so he was not needing to say this to ease his own guilt. Why? Why now?

He went on, "I was lucky to be with you all those years."

"Mike," I exclaimed, "what are you saying?"

"Just that I was lucky I was with you. I never deserved you."

Here we go again. How can the love of my life feel he never deserved me?

I thought of this conversation now as I waited by the phone.

Why isn't Tom calling me? With that thought came a loud sound above my head that I have never heard before. A rattling, banging sound that was directly overhead. "Oh, Mike." I started crying. "That's you, isn't it?" I cried, praying I was wrong.

Why isn't Gloria calling me? I was overwrought with worry and with fear. I dialed her number.

"Gloria, what's happening?"

"Marti, I don't know. They won't let us through. They're acting strange. I don't know what's happening."

"What do you mean? Who?"

"The apartment manager—she won't let us go past this point. Tom's there, but we can't go over there." Her voice lowered, and she said without much hope, "They have the area taped off."

I did not like the sound of any of it. "Should I come?"

"No, stay there," she said.

"Tom's not answering his phone." I was starting to get frantic. "I just need to know."

"I'll try his number again." I hung up.

I dialed Tom's number. No answer. It kept ringing. Tom, I prayed, answer the phone. But he didn't.

I stood up from my chair. I needed to use the restroom. I took my cell phone with me. When I exited the ladies' room, I saw a coworker, Karen, in the hall. Karen worked with me, and she knew all about Mike and me and all that I had been battling since the previous summer.

"Karen," I called to her. She was only a few feet away, and her back was turned. When she turned around I said, "I need you to come with me."

She saw my stricken face and apparently knew right away that this was not a casual request. "What's wrong, Marti?"

I motioned for her to follow me, then told her when we were in my office. I finished with, "I need someone to be with me."

"Oh, Marti," she said. We were there only a few minutes, then my cell phone rang.

"Marti," I heard Gloria's voice. "Marti …" she hesitated. "Mike's …"

What, I was crying inside. *What!?*

"Mike's … dead."

"How." It was not a question. Did I really want to know?

"He shot himself." She waited before she said, "He shot himself in the head."

I said nothing.

"Victoria and I are on our way to you. Are you at your office?" She knew the school where my office was housed.

"Yes." There was nothing else to say.

I hung up the phone. It hit me.

"*No!*" I screamed. I screamed again wordlessly. I remembered that students were in classes nearby, and I did not want them to hear me. I had to muffle my cries and my desire to scream.

Karen held me. I cried. I couldn't believe it. *Mike dead?*

No, no, no, no … this isn't happening.

CHAPTER 21

THE SHOCK

I needed to do something. I knew I had to make phone calls, I had to make arrangements … I had so much to do. I felt my thoughts racing, and I tried to hold onto them. They kept racing around in my head though. I felt helpless.

Since then, I have learned that people who face the death of a loved one take on an urgent need to be doing something. It is likely a coping mechanism—something that keeps the harsh reality from permeating our sanity. If we let the reality of a tragedy hit us all at once, we might snap.

"I have to call the kids," I now said to Karen. "I have to call John, Mike's brother. I don't know who to call first."

I tried John's number. No answer.

Now what? My mind continued to race. I pictured my dear children hearing this devastating news. I have to call Jamie. She is in Chicago, and she has to get here. I needed her to get here, but I couldn't talk to her yet. I dreaded telling her. I dreaded telling Aly and Lindsey. Aly was babysitting and would not be home until one p.m. Lindsey was at home. I needed to try John again.

John still did not answer. I dialed my niece's number. I was afraid if I called my sister-in-law, I would have to tell her, and I wanted to tell John first.

"Katie," I said when she answered.

"Hi, Marti," she said.

I interrupted her. "Where's John?"

"He should be at work," she answered.

"He's not answering his phone. I have to talk to him." I was starting to panic. I needed Mike's brother to help me with this. I was not comprehending it, and I did not want Katie to be the first one I told. I did not want to lay that on her. I would let John do that.

"What's wrong, Marti?"

"I just need to talk to John," I said more urgently. My voice weakened, "Would you get him for me?"

"Sure," she said. She must have heard it in my voice. She asked no more questions. I hung up.

How was I going to tell Jamie? How was I going to tell Aly and Lindsey?

Karen stayed with me. I started muttering about getting my psychological evaluation reports typed. She tried to keep me grounded.

I called John back. No answer. I started feeling angry. Where the hell was John? I did not even consider it absurd that I expected him to be there because I needed him.

I called Katie back. I could feel my panic and near-hysteria rising.

"Katie, I really need to talk to John," I pleaded.

"He's not answering his phone, Marti," she said helpfully.

I knew that! I was exasperated.

"Marti, what's wrong?" she asked me again.

I was desperate, and I turned mean—not toward Katie but toward the tragic situation in which I now found myself. Unfortunately, Katie took the brunt of it.

"Katie," I cried out. "I need John! Mike's dead. I need to talk to John!" Even as I said the words, I regretted saying them. Katie did not need to hear about her uncle's death from the ex-wife who was now yelling this news to her in anguish. What was wrong with me?

I grabbed onto any bit of sanity I had left. "I'm sorry, Katie. I am just so upset, and I need your father."

"Marti, I'll try him again." She sounded calm. I was not.

I dialed John's number again but still no answer. I knew Katie would not get to him either, but now I knew she would try his office number, and I did not have that number. I had been calling his cell phone.

I tried his number again. I was surprised when he answered.

"John," I said with some relief. "Have you talked to Katie?"

"No," he said. "I just got out of a meeting. What's up?"

"Are you sitting?"

"What?"

"Are you sitting down? Where are you?"

"I just walked into my office."

"Okay, sit down …"

"What's going on?"

"John, your brother's dead. I just found out. Mike's dead."

"How?" he asked.

"He shot himself." I was beside myself. "I don't know what to do."

I know I stunned John, but I was still in shock. "I don't know," he said. "Should we have the funeral here?"

What was he saying? Funeral? There? What was he talking about? I just told John that his brother had committed suicide. He wasn't reacting normally. I guess I thought I was. I looked at Karen, who was still with me. I pointed to the phone and made a face. What's with this guy?

I shook my head. I cleared my thoughts. "No, we have to have the funeral here. Jamie will fly here. We have friends here. He works here."

"Let us know when," John said. "We'll want to be there."

What, I thought, is wrong with Mike's brother? No emotion—nothing. Just tell him the date and time of the funeral. They will be there. This was making no sense.

"Okay," I said meekly. I guess I was not getting any help from John. "Bye."

"Bye," he said, and I thought I heard a sob before the phone disconnected.

I knew we were both in the shock stage, but even so, it hurt. I felt pain for my husband, pain for my children, pain for his brother, and pain for myself. The shock stage evidently carries hurt with it, yet John and I were both numb, and we were able to go through the motions. How can you feel pain and numbness at the same time?

I found out years later that Katie had called her mother, Becky, who in turn called her husband before I reached him. Becky told me she had asked John to leave his meeting, but he did not. She asked him to leave again and ultimately screamed at him to "walk out of the meeting now!" She told him as soon as he walked out of the door of the meeting. Becky had a corner office in a bull pen, and she said all her coworkers were staring at her when she hung up the phone. I must have caught him as he was walking back to his office. He apparently was already in shock before I spoke to him—he gave no indication he had already heard the tragic news.

I was no longer alone. There were now four of us sharing the pain and trying to cope with what I considered the worst of the worst. There would soon be more.

CHAPTER 22

GOD LOVE ERIC

I knew I had to call Jamie. She was the farthest away, and she would have to get a flight to Jacksonville as soon as possible.

"I am going to call my daughter," I said to Karen.

"Do you want me to stay with you?"

"No, I need to be alone."

After Karen stepped out, I called Jamie. No answer, of course. Where is everyone when there is an emergency? Unavailable! What had I expected?

I had her boyfriend's cell phone number on my cell phone, and I called Eric.

"Eric, where's Jamie?"

"Hi, Marti." At least one of us was polite. His next words made my heart sink. "She's in Philadelphia."

"Philadelphia? Oh!" I said, not sure what to do or what to say to Eric. I had hoped Eric could be with Jamie when I called her. They worked at the same company.

"What's up?" he asked.

"Eric, I need to talk to her, but I wanted you to be with her when I tell her." I was thinking quickly, and my thoughts were racing. I did not want to tell Jamie if she was alone, and especially if she was far from her home. She would have to fly back to Chicago, unpack and pack again, get a flight, all while contemplating what I was about to tell her. It was too much for her to endure alone.

"How far is Philadelphia from you?"

"About a two-hour flight …"

"Oh," I interrupted him, "could you go to her?"

"Well, sure, if I need to. What's going on?"

"Eric, I need to talk to Jamie, but I don't want her to be by herself."

"Marti, what's wrong?" he asked gently.

Do I tell Eric before I tell Jamie? Why did I think there was an order to such things? Again, my thoughts were racing. Maybe I need to tell Eric, so he'll see how important it is that he go to her and be with her when she receives this devastating news. Okay, that is what I must do.

"Eric, Mike's dead."

"Oh my God." Eric's voice was subdued.

"I just found out … maybe I should wait and tell Jamie when she returns."

"No," he said, "you know Jamie. She'll be upset if you don't tell her right away. What do you need me to do? I'll do whatever you need me to do."

God love him.

"Can you go to her?"

"Yes, I can get on a flight right now."

Wow, I thought. He would do that. But, what was I thinking?

"No, that's crazy," I said. "I need to call her right now."

"She's probably not there yet. Her plane should land in about fifteen minutes. What do you want me to do?"

My head cleared. It was a momentary opening in this dark cloud that had formed all around me and had enveloped me. "Eric," I took charge. "Can you pack Jamie's bag and meet her at the airport and get her to Jacksonville? I will tell her to fly back to Chicago from Philadelphia when I talk to her."

"I'll get the tickets and get her stuff," he said.

"I want you to get here tonight." I needed my three daughters, and I knew they would need me. I wouldn't want any visitors this first night. Only us—and Eric.

"I'll take care of it," Eric said.

"Bye, Eric."

"Bye," he said, "and I'm so sorry."

I called my mother. I knew I couldn't tell Jamie for another fifteen minutes, and I couldn't tell Aly and Lindsey until Aly returned home from babysitting. I would be there waiting for her and would tell both her and Lindsey at the same time.

"Hi, Mom," I greeted my mother when she answered. "What are you doing?"

"I'm just sitting here, watching TV," she replied. My mother had broken her hip a month earlier, so she couldn't do much else but sit.

Good, she was seated. Of course, she would be.

"Mom, I have some bad news." I gave her a few seconds to prepare for it, before I said, "Mike's dead."

"Oh my gosh!" she exclaimed.

I continued, "He killed himself, Mom." How could I be saying this without screaming it out of me?

"Oh," she said, "you were worried about that ... oh my." She did not know what else to say. I knew she was shaken, and I hated doing this to her.

"Mom." I waited. I needed to talk to someone. I felt so alone. "Mom," I tried again. "He shot himself in the head!" I wanted her to know—I was so horrified. I had to say the words out loud and get them out of me. "He shot himself in the head, Mom." I repeated the words in disbelief. Maybe my saying it would help me to believe it.

"That is horrible ... the girls ... I'm so sorry." She sounded stricken. I was sorry I had to tell her this horrible, new event in my life. She had already heard enough about the divorce. Could she take this? Could I take this?

"Mom, I'm scared for him. I've always been scared for him. Where does the soul go when there's a suicide?" I knew my wise mother could tell me the answer.

"No, it's not what they used to say about that," my precious mother was saying to me. I held onto her words, "God is merciful, and if Mike believed in Him, he's okay."

"Will you let me know where it says that?" I felt some relief, but I needed proof. I needed to know Mike was not condemned to hell for taking his life.

My mother needed to process this. I needed to process this. "I'll call you later." I pushed "end" on my cell phone.

Karen returned to my office with the school principal. Karen had apparently informed the principal that my ex-husband had died.

The principal hugged me. "Marti, I am so sorry. Please tell us what we can do for you." I told her I was making calls and to just pray for me and my daughters. She offered her cell phone number, and I asked Karen to put the number into my cell phone.

I picked up my office phone and called my district supervisor and told her I'd be off the rest of the week, including today. It was Monday, and Wednesday was the last day of my ten-month contract with the district.

I would have to make up these three days, as I had reports to complete before the summer break. "Don't worry about the job," she said. "Go do what you need to do."

CHAPTER 23

JAMIE BABY, BREATHE

The school principal and Karen stayed with me during my conversation with my supervisor. My supervisor gave me her cell phone number, and I could not get it into my cell phone. I handed my phone to Karen to input the number. She had already recorded the principal's number.

Jamie called. I asked the principal and Karen to give me privacy. I was about to tell my eldest that her father had died.

"Hey, Mom," she said.

"Are you just calling me?"

"What?"

"Are you just calling me for no reason?"

"Eric told me to call you. I just talked to him." She sounded pleasant, without a care in the world. I really hated doing this to her. I really hated shaking up her perfect world.

"Oh." So, he did not let on, and she did not know anything was up. "Are you sitting down?"

"No, Mom," she sounded slightly irritated now. "I am walking through the airport." She sounded hurried.

"Jamie, I need you to sit down."

"Why?" Maybe her anxiety was rising, hearing my voice and intuitively knowing something must be seriously wrong for me to call her in the middle of a workday morning. "I need to get to my appointment!"

"Jamie," I said firmly, "sit down for a minute. I have bad news."

"What, Mom, what is it?" Now she sounded concerned, but she had no idea what was coming.

"Are you sitting?"

I could feel her struggling with the idea of walking and making it to her destination without delay or doing what I was asking her to do.

"Jamie," I repeated, "are you sitting?"

"Okay, I'm sitting," she replied, sounding just a little bit frustrated.

"Jamie." I was not prepared for this message delivery. I had not planned what I would say. How was I going to tell my beautiful twenty-seven-year-old daughter that her father killed himself?

"Mom, what is it?"

"Jamie," I said as I started crying. I knew I was blowing it, but I was hit again by the news, and I could not control what was coming out of my mouth. I blurted out, "Your dad shot himself in the head." I had not meant to say it like that. I did not know how I was going to tell her, but certainly not like that. I couldn't take it back. The damage was done.

I couldn't hear her. I could hear sobs, but I couldn't hear her breathing. She was crying quietly, but she wasn't saying anything.

"Jamie, can you hear me?"

There was no answer. "Jamie baby, breathe," I implored. "Breathe ... take a deep breath." I was afraid she'd hyperventilate. I could hear her attempting to take sharp breaths, but she made no sounds. "Breathe, Jamie ... talk to me."

I pictured her collapsing in the chair and crying out but without sound and without breathing.

"Jamie!" I said loudly.

I heard a loud gasp and could hear her taking deep breaths. "Mom," she cried.

"Jamie," I said quickly, "I need you to listen to me. I'm so sorry you're in an airport, but I need you to turn around and go to a counter and get a flight back to Chicago. Eric is waiting there at the airport for you. He will have your flight tickets to Jacksonville. He'll also have a bag packed for you." Eric had told me Jamie had gone to Philadelphia only for the day and was returning that evening, so she did not have a bag with her.

"Can you do that?" I asked my little girl.

"Yes," she said weakly. I could sense she was fighting back her tears.

"Okay. I love you, baby. We will get through this."

Jamie later told me she walked to a counter as I had directed, and there were several people standing in the line. She stood for a few minutes, then fell in a heap on the floor and started crying. One of the ladies behind the counter walked toward her and asked her if she could do anything for her, and Jamie tearfully told her what she needed to do and why. The attendant helped her up and took care of everything for her. To this day I do not know how my daughter got through those next few hours, alone and without anyone to comfort her after hearing that her father had shot himself.

I did not know those would be my first words when I told Jamie. They were impulsive and raw, and I think that the horror of it was hitting me. I also was having a difficult time believing it. It was too terrible for words. It was tragic, and I knew no other way to say it. I hoped, however, that I would find a better way when I told my other two daughters.

Somehow life had not stopped. The minutes ticked away. It was ten a.m., and I could not tell Aly and Lindsey this devastating news until after one p.m. I dreaded telling them as much as I had dreaded telling Jamie. How can we possibly get through this? I knew we had to, and I would make sure we did. I just felt so sad for Mike and for my daughters. I couldn't get out of my mind what I perceived as the last few moments of my ex-husband's life.

I had to do something. I could not let myself think of his last hours and how sad he must have been to commit such an act. I called my sister Carol. I told her, and she immediately started crying.

"I am on my way."

God love her. She knew what to do. I told her, "Not today. I love you dearly, but I need my girls tonight. Come tomorrow."

"Okay," she said. She continued to cry.

"Carol, will you call Barbara and Chris and tell Mom to tell everyone?" I needed to get the word out to my other brothers and sisters. "Mom already knows," I added.

She could barely talk. I hated this. I was not going to call anyone else. I had to get to my girls. "I love you," I said before I hung up.

Karen returned, and I waved her into the room. I did not want to be by myself. She told me she had not told the principal the cause of death. I was grateful. I did not know how that would be handled, but I did not need the gossip just yet.

Karen was with me when Gloria and Victoria walked in. We all hugged but did not have much to say to each other. Gloria drove my car home, and Victoria drove Gloria's car. Thank God for women. They sat with me at my house, waiting with me until the next dismal hour. Lindsey had been up late and was still in bed. I dreaded telling my Aly and my Lindsey, as I had dreaded telling my Jamie. Hopefully, I would choose my words more carefully.

Detective Barker called while we were sitting in my Florida room. Tom had given him my number. The detective asked a few routine questions of me. "When did you see Mike last?" "How was his demeanor?" "Did he have a girlfriend?" "Had he been suicidal in the past?" After I answered his questions, he declared it a suicide. He told me there was a life insurance policy on the floor beside him when they found him, and his head was facing a framed picture of him and three young girls. "He has three daughters?" When I answered affirmatively, he said, "It looked like they were on a boat." He offered his condolences, and he hung up.

I flashed back to the previous summer and our last family vacation in Key West. I was there attending a state association conference, and I wanted all the family members to accompany me. Jamie and Eric flew in to Key West. Mike kept hedging, saying he did not want to go. That was Mike. I told him we were all going, and he had to be there. It was the first time the entire family had done a vacation since our Caribbean cruise in 2001.

He drank most of his waking time when we were on that cruise and in Key West. I remembered how unhappy he had seemed then in Key West. He frequently stared off, and his affect appeared sad and depressed. I knew he was fighting a mental battle. I just did not know it included an affair he had been having and a decision he had just made to leave me. I felt sorry for him (not knowing the true situation), and I held his hand when we snorkeled one evening while we were there. I took some good photos of the girls and their father on that snorkeling excursion. One of those pictures was the last vision my ex-husband had before he pulled the trigger.

How many times have I wondered about what he was thinking those last moments of his life. How was he able to buy that gun, knowing that he was planning to do with it? We now know he bought it the Tuesday before the Saturday he died. He had written across the top of the receipt, "Pick up Saturday morning." He was at our house that Saturday by twelve noon. I shudder when I think it was probably in his car then.

What could possibly have been his thoughts as he raised the gun to his head, and as he looked at the picture of his three beautiful daughters gathered around him? What were his words to them? "I'm so sorry." I was convinced that was his last thought before the darkness came to claim him.

I shook off my reverie, and I waited with Victoria and Gloria for the one o'clock hour. I still had a need to do something. I called the funeral home and asked general questions. Tom rang me as I just ended that call, and we counseled each other. He said they had brought in the crisis intervention team, and he told me, "You need to know and the girls need to know that a lot of Mike's coworkers need counseling."

Tom told me many of Mike's coworkers were struck hard by his death and were not handling it well. "He was loved by us all," Tom said before he hung up.

Mike's death affected so many people.

I called my church and talked to the pastors about the service. We tried to establish a date and a time. I then called John to let him know the service would be on Thursday, and he said they were "making arrangements to be with you all tomorrow." Thank goodness. I guess the shock had lifted somewhat for him, and he was taking action, as I was.

Then the one o'clock hour was upon me. Lindsey was still asleep. Knowing her sleep habits, she probably did not go to bed before three a.m., and she would be in bed another hour if allowed. I called Aly to see where she was. She said she was on her way home. "Good." I lied. "I finished some things at work and got caught up. I'm home." I tried to sound cheerful. I succeeded, as she responded, "Oh good. You can make me that chicken salad."

"Sure." I wished that all I had said to her was true. I wished that I could make her the chicken salad she had requested yesterday instead of delivering this devastating news to her and to her sister. "Hurry home."

Gloria and Victoria said they would leave so I could be alone with the girls. I thanked them both. We hugged, and they left. I was alone. Lindsey was still asleep. I waited.

CHAPTER 24

ALY AND LINDSEY, PROMISE ME

As I waited I felt my insides churning. I was about to change my youngest two children's existence. I was about to break into their lives in a way that was totally inconceivable to me. No one I knew had ever committed suicide. It was unheard of. It was unspeakable. But now I would have to speak of it. I wanted to deny it. I wanted it to not be true. It was too hard to accept.

I heard the garage door open, and I knew Aly was home. She was parking in the driveway and would soon be in the house.

"Lindsey," I called out. "I need you to get up." I wanted to tell them both at the same time, and I did not want to delay this any longer. I walked through the kitchen to the door that led to the garage.

"Lindsey!" I yelled louder just before I reached the door. I turned back and looked toward her bedroom, which was on the far side of the house from where I was standing. "I need you to get up right now!" I really wanted to tell them at the same time. I could only go through this one more time.

"Lindsey," I screamed even louder, "come out here now!"

So much for staying in control and saying the right words and breaking this to them gently. I was a complete mess, but I wanted Lindsey with me when Aly walked in.

"What, Mom!" She came to the door of the family room, across from me. She appeared groggy and slightly annoyed.

I looked at her. "I need to talk to you."

Aly walked in just then and saw me. She brushed by me and said in a matter-of-fact tone, "He's dead, isn't he?"

Lindsey did not hear what Aly said. She had left the doorway and had gone back to her bedroom for a moment. She returned. She was walking toward us, and I could not hold it in any longer.

"Girls," I said, "your dad is gone. He's no longer in this world. He's passed on."

Aly's worst fear was true. She started crying, and I grabbed her and held onto her. Lindsey let out a loud, soulful cry and fell to the floor four feet away from us. I held onto Aly, and we went to Lindsey. We huddled together on the floor, holding each other, crying together. Aly asked how. I cried out to them that he had shot himself in the head. They cried out. We all cried louder. It seemed like we were in that holding, crying pattern for an eternity. Lindsey finally jumped up and ran to her room.

Aly and I sat together. She told me she already knew when she arrived at our home. She had been worried the night before, and she felt he was gone when she was driving home. She had cried on her way home, fearing the worst.

I hugged her, and through my tears I said emphatically, "Promise me. This legacy stops here. This will not be a pattern. It does not go on. It stops now. Nothing like this will happen again in your life or your children's lives. Promise me! No alcoholism! No suicide! Promise me!"

Aly cried, "I promise, Mom." We held each other and sobbed.

After she pulled away, I went to Lindsey's bedroom and repeated the same imploring message to her. We held each other. We cried. She promised.

Lindsey's friend Casey came over then. Lindsey had moved away from Aly and me so that she could call her. Casey had a cousin who had committed suicide, and Lindsey needed her. Aly went to her room and called some of her friends. I had to take phone calls from the church, the funeral home, and Mike's boss. All were helping with the funeral arrangements. I was on the phone most of the afternoon.

My two daughters later told me they resented that. They needed me, and I was talking on the phone. They apparently did not realize what all needed to be done. I was in the "keep busy" mode which tended to be my modus operandi—I had done that all my life to avoid seeing what I did not want to accept. I regretted doing that to them though. They needed me, and I was not there for them.

I wanted to spend that day with them and did not want visitors. I had proclaimed that earlier. Jamie had the same thought. "No visitors, Mom."

However, the visitors poured in. I was as much overwhelmed by the number of people who reached out to us as I was by the tragic event and the aftermath that was occurring in our lives.

Tom and I talked to each other several times that afternoon. Mike's company was going to provide additional food for the funeral service reception. "Marti," he said, "I am hearing from companies all over the country. People are coming from all over. We will supply more food."

I could not believe it. I had planned on two hundred or three hundred people. I had no idea there would be that many from Mike's work. Tom said he was expecting at least two hundred from work. They were shutting down on Thursday, the day of the funeral, so everyone could attend.

Did my ex-husband have any idea how much he was loved? He was respected by so many at work. How did he manage to be so successful at his job and be so clueless when it came to his family? Mike had lost all our respect over the past few years because of his drinking. The girls had complained to me multiple times when I had been away about how drunk he had gotten while I was gone. Apparently, the increase in his drinking habit over the past few years had to do with his living a double life. He had been seeing his paramour for five years. He was living a lie and drinking more. I had forgotten about his background, his PTSD, his depression, his anxiety, and his need to self-medicate for escape. I had forgotten that a drinker develops tolerance and must have increasing amounts of alcohol to achieve the same effect as the initial quantity. And I had forgotten that drinking often disguises underlying emotional issues.

After he left me that July, his drinking increased—he was not happy. What had he said to me that day at Starbuck's when I told him he was at least happy for a little while—when he was with her? "No, Marti, I was tormented the whole time." Hadn't I been told by neighbors and friends how drunk he was when they saw him at The Pelican? Didn't I know that he was speaking the truth with the words he said to me that day he left our home? "I may be making the biggest mistake of my life." I knew he was. He was not himself. He was not using good judgment, and what he had said to me the day he told me he was leaving was nothing a man would say to his wife of thirty-plus years. At that time, I knew my husband was going to self-destruct, and I knew I could no longer stop him. I saw it as a behavioral choice—I had erased his depression and mental suffering from my mind.

Now I had to plan his funeral. My husband had walked down that self-destructive path from which I had managed to keep him during the over-thirty years I was with him. Once he got away from me, it took him only nine and a half months to get to the end of that path. I had always known Mike was self-destructive, and I also knew I could not and would not ever abandon him. He did that to himself.

Tom was indispensable. He furnished the soloist in addition to part of the food. He agreed to speak at the service, as did Gloria. Tom loved Mike and was already missing him. He told me Mike had been having a very difficult time during the last two months at work.

"I was curious last fall when Mike finally told me you were divorcing, and he was seeing someone who was working at The Pelican Bar and Grille," Tom told me. Mike did not tell Tom until November. Tom said he went to see "the other woman" out of curiosity and told me he could not believe it. He said he sat Mike down the next morning and said to him, "You are an idiot. You are a complete idiot!"

I guess that gave Mike the validation he was seeking. He had very little self-worth at that point. His seeing someone like her only indicated to me where his self-esteem was, and it was apparently very low. As I told myself that, however, I knew my descriptions and feelings about her were wrong. It is easy to dislike and denigrate "the other woman" when your husband chooses her over you. It really is not about her. It is about him.

Tom said he was in complete disbelief that "Mike left you for someone like that." Maybe that was supposed to make me feel better. But what I think is that Tom was seeing Mike taking a path that was unhealthy and not good for him. He told me that Mike came in on some Monday mornings with alcohol reeking from his pores. He thought Mike must have been drunk the entire weekend. I had seen Mike's car parked at The Pelican, and I knew he was at the bar a lot. It still hurt me to think he would choose that life over a life with his daughters. They had class, and he knew it. How could he let himself be defined this way, and didn't he know how that life choice affected them?

Another side of me wondered if he really had a choice. Did he choose the self-destructive path, or did it choose him? Was he so embedded in his alcoholism that there was no turning back? Was he at that last stage where the disease had taken over, and he was powerless within its grip? I knew the only way he could stop drinking in that last stage was with effective treatment delivered over an extended period of time.

Tom also told me Mike had not been functioning as well at work. I, too, had seen how he had displayed a decline. "Losing cognitive ability?"

"Yes," he said emphatically. "That exactly." He went on to say Mike and several of his coworkers would return from a meeting, and Mike would tell Tom everything was taken care of, and the team had reached resolution. Tom would later consult with the rest of the team and find out nothing had been resolved.

I thought back to what Victoria had told me when she was sitting in my porch earlier. She told me Mike was handing out name tags the end of March at a user's conference in Orlando, and the girl working with him noticed he never gave out the correct name tag. The person who was registering would give his or her name, and Mike would look for the name tag while the girl sitting with him signed in the individual. Mike always handed out the wrong name tag. The girl finally started to pick up each name tag and hand it to Mike before she signed the person in. Of course, his difficulty could have been partially explained by his limited hearing. He had stopped wearing his hearing aids.

Additionally, Mike was missing important discussions and was not staying focused. Tom said he had reprimanded Mike numerous times over the past two months, as Mike was not attending to or processing what was being discussed. Was this part of "all that stuff" Mike was referring to the day he died? Was there more going on than just the hearing difficulty?

How do you make sense of all that had occurred in our lives during the course of one full school year? It was too much to comprehend, but I knew for my recovery I had to make sense of it.

For now, however, I had to plan the funeral of my husband of thirty-three years. We were divorced a mere three months. I was never again going to call myself a divorcee'.

I was a widow.

CHAPTER 25

FAMILY

Jamie and Eric arrived that evening. We hugged. We cried. Jamie's good friend Anna came over announcing, "I know you said you all wanted to be together, and you did not want visitors tonight, but I had to come over." What a friend! All our friends stopped by, and they were still calling or coming by at ten p.m. I was amazed at how quickly the word had spread. I had called no one.

Unfortunately, the girls and I did not get our quiet moments together that night. I could not turn our visitors away.

Somehow, we were able to get through that longest day of our lives. We had lots to accomplish the next day with funeral arrangements, obituary writing, and calls to make. I woke up early and made several calls to finalize the funeral arrangements. I also had to call my schools, Mike's office, and close relatives with the date and time of the funeral.

Jamie woke up early and helped me write the obituary. I don't know how we accomplished all that we did, but everything seemed to be falling into place without complications. I knew that was a blessing, and I was grateful.

The medical examiner's office called and gave a report of his findings. I was surprised to find out Mike had a malignant tumor on one of his kidneys. Had he known? The examiner also said there were signs of excessive alcohol consumption.

"What signs?" I asked.

"Fatty liver," I was told. The forensic autopsy report also showed both a mildly-to-moderately enlarged heart and prostate gland. (I found out later that Mike had just been diagnosed with Type II diabetes, and he had an MRI that had shown abnormalities.) I wondered if he knew about any of these medical findings and if they were also part of that "stuff."

John, Becky, Katie, and Callie arrived just before Dr. Carol DiGiusto, the associate pastor at Palms Presbyterian Church, showed up to plan the service with us. Carol brought several copies of a brochure about suicide that gave hope to those of us who were concerned about Mike's soul. She handed the brochures out and gave us a few minutes to read them. Then she asked what verses we would like to have quoted from the Bible. No one had an answer. Aly opened the Bible and pointed randomly to a verse and it was perfect. She read the King James Version of John 14: 1-6 to us:

"Let not your heart be troubled: ye believe in God, believe also in me. In my father's house are many mansions: if it were not so, I would have told you. I go to prepare a place for you. And if I go and prepare a place for you, I will come again, and receive you unto myself; that where I am, there ye may be also. And whither I go ye know, and the way ye know. Thomas saith unto him, Lord, we know not whither thou goest; and how can we know the way? Jesus saith unto him, I am the way, the truth, and the life: no man cometh unto the Father, but by me."

Carol suggested the next verse and read the King James Version of Romans 8: 37-39 to us:

"Nay, in all these things we are more than conquerors through him that loved us. For I am persuaded, that neither death, nor life, nor angels, nor principalities, nor powers, nor things present, nor things to come, nor height, nor depth, nor any other creature, shall be able to separate us from the love of God, which is in Christ Jesus our Lord."

My three daughters requested "Amazing Grace" be sung by the soloist. Their father had loved to hear each of them sing. All three girls had taken voice lessons, and their father was proud of their voices. They wanted the solos to be spectacular—for him. Jamie selected "Silent Night" for the end of the service and suggested that we all raise lit candles at the beginning of the third verse, a tradition of the Christmas Eve service that was her father's favorite. Their dad had always said "Silent Night" was his favorite Christmas song. The congregation would join the soloist in singing that third verse:

> *"Silent night, holy night*
> *Son of God, love's pure light*

Radiant beams from Thy holy face
With the dawn of redeeming grace
Jesus, Lord, at Thy birth
Jesus, Lord, at Thy birth"

Carol asked about some of our good memories with Mike that we could share, and we all sat still, staring down at our feet. No one said anything. I sat on the sofa and was saddened by the thought that none of us could come up with good memories. The bad memories were unfortunately at the forefront. The girls attempted to make a few stabs.

"He loved to raise the candle when we sang 'Silent Night' at the Christmas Eve services," Jamie offered, knowing this had already been discussed. She chuckled, and there was hushed laughter. She continued, as she had a memory that she wanted to relay. "One time we went to a different church, and no one stood up when he thought they were supposed to. Dad stood up and held that candle high, and the rest of us all looked at each other, not knowing what we should do. We finally stood up with him. Slowly, other people stood up until the entire congregation was standing." She grinned, remembering his bold move and the outcome.

Aly recalled being his putting championship caddy. She had gone to the putting championship several years in a row. Mike had won the championship the first time she had accompanied him, and he called her his "good luck charm."

Lindsey loved that he was at the football and basketball games when she cheered, although she knew "he was there to watch the game." She added, "But he watched me too."

All three recalled his attendance at their activities: Jamie's star roles in high school musicals, Aly's star role as soccer goalie on her high school state champion soccer team, and Lindsey's star role as captain of her high school cheerleading squad. They all recalled the look on his face as he watched them sing at their senior voice recitals. Sometimes, they each noted, they saw tears in his eyes.

Jamie remembered he had called her "no-neck" when she was a toddler. He called Aly "Aly-Oop." He described Lindsey as waking up to a new day every morning. He was always amazed that she saw each day as a brand-new day, and she was excited to see the morning.

The memories made us laugh. They made us smile. It was a good exercise, and our spirits were lifted a little.

After the minister left, Callie decided to rest—she was three months pregnant, and the flight and emotional strain were fatiguing. Becky stayed with her, and John and Katie went with my daughters and me to the funeral home.

As we walked up to the entrance, I remembered the ill-fated cell phone conversation I had with Mike in front of this very same funeral home and how eerie that had been. I shook the feeling off as we entered. We were shown a picture of Mike taken by the medical examiner's office. It wasn't so terrible. I expected to see the worst, but I was surprised. He had a white sheet encircling his head, and the right side of his forehead had a band-aid covering where I knew he had placed the gun. I wanted to cry out loud when I saw the picture, but I stifled it, and it was a muffled cry. I was in a room full of people. I preferred crying when I was alone. Everyone looked at it except Aly, who could not and chose not to look. She did not want to remember her daddy that way.

John was going to have Deenie pay for the funeral and all the costs associated with it. After all, I was not Mike's next of kin. That financial burden would fall on his children. I knew who would have paid if his mother had not, however.

How could I not be Mike's next of kin after all I had been through with this man? Three months, I thought. Three lousy months out of thirty-three years, and I was relegated to, I guessed, a mere acquaintance. I was not of kin. My daughters were, but I was not.

After we returned home, I took my cell phone with me and walked to our guest bedroom. I lay on the bed and cried until I fell asleep. I took a nap and woke up to the cell phone ringing. Stacie, my niece, was on the other line.

"Marti, I don't know what we are thinking here!" She was calling from Arkansas. "I told Mom we have to go to Marti's husband's funeral. I asked her, what are you thinking?" Stacie went on to explain that my sister had decided it would be impossible. Stacie's sister was getting married in June, and they were attending her bridal shower Wednesday night. There was no way they could get to Florida and attend Mike's funeral Thursday morning.

"I understand, Stacie. Really, I do understand. You all will be at the shower the night before—you can't miss Ashley's shower!" I knew they wouldn't miss the shower nor should they, but I did want them here with me. I loved my sister Barbara and her husband and children. I loved Stacie and her husband, Doug. I needed family here with me at this saddest time in my life.

"Well, I don't know how, but we will figure it out. I will talk to you later," Stacie said, and we hung up.

I looked at the clock. My sister Carol had managed to book a flight, which would be arriving at the airport within the hour. It took forty-five minutes to get to the airport from my house. I hastily freshened up and walked out to the rest of the house. My daughters were together on the porch, and Eric, Katie, and Callie were with them. I had not spent any time with them, and I vowed I would do that upon my return with my sister. John and Becky were sitting at the kitchen table. John was making plans to go to Mike's apartment and empty it. None of my daughters wanted to go, and Katie had told him she would go with him. John planned to go the next day. Becky and Callie would stay behind and help with the food coming into our home.

I thanked John for taking care of that and left. This was the first time I had a chance to be entirely alone. Even as I lay on the bed earlier, one daughter or another would open the bedroom door and peek in and ask me if I was okay. I was not okay, I thought, but I knew I had to get through this. I also knew my daughters needed to see me grieve. Lindsey had said something to me earlier that made me freeze in my tracks. "Mom," she had said, "I feel bad for you. You have to be strong. You have to be strong for us."

What is being strong? I wondered. Looking stoic and not shedding a tear? Acting happy and avoiding the pain I was feeling? I decided being strong meant I needed to show I was grieving, so my daughters would feel free to do the same. Being strong meant I needed to cry when I felt the tears well up in my eyes. I needed to feel the pain and let it work through me, tackling this grief monster one day at a time. I decided a familiar phrase was true—grieving was not for wimps. And I was going to embrace my grief until it was all used up. I did not want any remnants of it lying around … lurking. I was afraid if I did not work completely through my grief, it would fester and cause me more pain and harm in future years. I knew what the lack of grieving had done to my now-deceased husband.

My thoughts were on overload as I drove to the airport to pick up my sister Carol. My thoughts turned to my husband's last few hours. I felt agony for him, and I could not shake off what I could only imagine was his state of mind during that last hour of his life. I cried anew as I drove down Highway 9A, praying I would not lose it completely on the busy thoroughfare. I stopped crying before I turned off 9A onto the entrance to Interstate 95. The airport exit was just minutes away.

As I approached the Jacksonville airport arrivals section, I became confused and missed my turn-off to the airport's nearby hotel where I planned to sit and await Carol's call. I had to circle through the airport road, and I started to feel disoriented. I shook my head to free the cobwebs. What in the world am I doing driving alone? I can't do this. I think the reality of Mike's death started to sink in at that moment.

I reached the hotel and pulled into a parking place to the side of the entrance. Carol called a few minutes later, and I again became confused when I exited from the hotel. I missed the arrivals section and had to circle through the airport road again. I called her and let her know I would be there soon.

I managed to stay lucid during that drive-through and picked Carol up in short order. We hugged before I loaded her luggage. I told her I was disoriented, and she offered to drive. I told her I might as well drive, as she did not know how to get us back home. I was sad, and she was my support.

After we arrived home, I received a telephone call from each of my eight other siblings. Barbara was still trying to figure out how they could get to Florida after Ashley's shower. My brother Chris and his wife, Sue, who lived in Atlanta, would get there the day of the funeral. Geralyn and her husband could not get away. She was a teacher and had to pack up her classroom as she did at every school year's end. Annie, Bob, Ray, Philip, and Brian all offered their condolences but could not get away from their obligations.

I had friends dropping by or calling, as did my children. The food was pouring in; it should have been overwhelming, but my feelings were numb to anything but the constant deep pain I felt within my heart.

Somehow, we were able to get through the second night and the next day and night. It was all a blur. I spent a lot of time on the guest bed, wishing to be alone, crying when I felt the tears. (I had assigned the master bedroom to Jamie and Eric—that made more sense than if I had taken the master suite for just myself.) I regretted not attending to my daughters and only hoped their friends were. Carol and Becky stayed busy in the kitchen, handling the food and preparing meals for all of us. They seemed to be okay. I was not.

CHAPTER 26

THE OUTPOURING

The funeral was incredible. My sister Barbara and her husband, Steve, their daughter, Stacie, and her husband, Doug, and Ashley's twin Melanie all left Ashley's wedding shower the night before and drove all night to Jacksonville Beach. The rest of us, including my brother Chris and his wife, were gathered in the hall outside of the church when they arrived. Barbara and her family had stopped at a service station and had freshened and changed clothes. They walked in five minutes before the start of the service. The service started at eleven a.m., and it was miraculous that they made it in time. I had been thinking I should have scheduled the funeral service later in the day.

My siblings and their families, as well as Mike's boss, Tom, and my good friend Gloria accompanied us as my daughters and I, along with Eric, John, Becky, Katie, and Callie, walked the long church aisle to our designated pews at the front of the church. The service was uplifting with the soloist singing beautifully and the minister saying words I needed to hear. Tom's and Gloria's eulogies spoke to both the girls and to me. My daughters cried. They had not cried in the safety of our home as I had. I had cried buckets already and could sit and listen, marveling at the wonder of this service. My husband was well-loved, and he never knew it. Or he couldn't accept it. Something had hurt him in his past, and he did not know what to do with the love that had been offered to him.

A large crowd—an estimated five to five hundred and fifty people—gathered for Mike's service. There were employees of affiliates of Mike's company with whom Mike had made connections. I was introduced to individuals from Fidelity, Washington Mutual, Bank of America, and other corporations. There was a multitude of employees from Mike's company. I had friends from church, bridge, tennis, and work. I saw my district supervisor, teachers with whom I worked, and other school employees, as well as my school psychologist buddies. My daughters' friends and their families were in attendance as well as friends I was surprised to see but grateful they took the time and cared enough to come.

The church women had gathered and prepared food, and Mike's company held up to its promise. The abundance of food matched the copious display of flowers and plant arrangements that had arrived from the funeral home. I was astounded by the compassionate outpouring. I felt the love from those that were gathered there for us and for him. It was both inspiring and comforting.

The girls and I, along with my siblings and their families, Mike's brother and his family, Tom, Gloria, and close friends left the service and reception, awed by the event we had just witnessed. Eric had set food out for anyone that was coming by the house. We ended up with a full house. One of Mike's golfing buddies had brought a "trunkful" of beer and wine the previous day, so we had plenty of food and beverages. The eating and drinking continued into the night.

At one point in the evening a good friend and bridge buddy asked me, "Marti, how are you doing this? First the divorce, and now this. How are you doing it?"

I had to think for a moment. I had just gone through four devastating days of living with the tragedy that had beset my daughters and me— four days of grieving this man that I had married. I had already grieved him once, when he left me. I had just started to feel that weight lifting and to feel better about the possibilities in my future when I was slammed again. You keep knocking me down, and I just keep getting back up, I thought.

I looked into the eyes of my friend. "My spiritual faith," I said simply. "My faith is what is keeping me going. It is what I had before, and it is what I have now. We will get through this."

Many stayed late that night. I was exhausted. Becky and Carol tended to dishes, kept the kitchen in order, and were such a big help. Eric was wonderful. He was there to do whatever was needed, and he, too, was a great help.

After everyone left, all was quiet. My daughters and I were now faced with a new event in our lives—one more distressing and heartrending than the previous one. We had already experienced my husband's alcoholism and depression. We had experienced his betrayal and abandonment. I had experienced a divorce I had never anticipated. Now we were having to face the aftermath of the worst of the worst.

CHAPTER 27

FACING THE AFTERMATH

I had been waiting. I sensed the feeling of waiting all during the divorce. I knew it was not over. I had too many hints from my husband that he was self-destructing. I felt the very thing I had feared during our married life was happening, and I could not stop it. Now he had done the act I had feared most. How does one make sense of a suicide?

I called my family law attorney and told him what had happened.

"Barry, what I feared most happened. My husband, Mike, committed suicide." Even as I said the words, I was in disbelief.

"Marti," Barry said, "I was also afraid of that. I never told you, but when I met Mike at mediation, I saw a broken man. He looked like he had hit rock bottom. I thought at the time he knew what he had done to you, and he was full of regret. I am not surprised. I have seen this before. I am very sorry."

I hung up from our conversation and cried once again for Mike. Will I ever stop crying for him? How do you grieve a man twice? I grieved when he left me, and now I find myself crying again over his death. How does one make sense of a suicide?

My husband suffered from depression most of his life. He was fractured when he went off to the Vietnam War. That experience shattered him even more. He self-medicated with alcohol, and then he ended his life. I knew all his life events pointed toward that final act. First, the loss of his doting grandparents when he was only two years old, then the loss of his mother's accessibility, and, as he perceived, her love, when she was grieving her parents' death. She was only twenty-four years old—just over a year older than my second daughter. I could only imagine her grief. I knew what my death would do to my daughters.

What does a youngster do when his life is turned upside down? He acts out his distress. Mike's acting out only distanced him further from his parents. His father had trouble with his behavior and probably rejected him as well. His grandmother, however, was not grieving. She rescued him, and it was probably because of her that he was able to survive the loss of love that he felt in his own home. He acted out, and he was often mean to his younger brother. Children who inflict pain on others are usually in pain themselves.

The second event, the Vietnam War, only compounded and exacerbated his emotional difficulties. However, I was wrong about that. That was not the second experience that had an impact. I had forgotten Mike's mother had carried an infant to full-term and delivered him in the hospital, only to lose him eleven hours later. His poor mother experienced a second heartbreak, as her newborn struggled and succumbed. She was discharged from the hospital without her third son, and I could not imagine the depth of her sorrow. Mike was nine and John was seven when their brother Joseph was buried, and they, too, must have felt sadness.

The family home had once again been struck by tragedy, and the feeling of comfort and security in the home had shifted with it. How could Deenie possibly tend to her sons and meet their needs when she herself was in mourning? How could she be fully emotionally available to them when she was heavy-hearted and grief-stricken? Aunt Kathleen and Mimi came to the rescue and took John and Mike, respectively, as often as they could so that Deenie could wrestle with her pain and grieve without interruption.

I decided I needed to face my pain head-on, if I were going to heal from all that had happened in the past ten months. I did not want to later inflict pain on others or on myself. I would heal. I knew I would go through the stages of grief. I would go through denial. I would go through hopelessness at times, just as I did when he left me. How distraught I was during those first few months of our separation. I wanted to right my world. I desperately hung on to what I knew, and all I knew was a lifetime of marriage.

I would once again embrace my hurtful pain, and I would once again let it work through me. I had already done that once. I could do it again.

They say it takes five years to get over a suicide. "No!" I would always exclaim when I heard those words. I had spent a good six or seven years worrying about my husband and facing the knowledge he was in trouble. I had already grieved for him. He left me emotionally well before he physically left me. I realized that I had left him emotionally as well. It goes both ways. It takes two.

Then he left me for good. How do you grieve someone three times? I erroneously thought I had grieved him twice. I had forgotten about grieving the loss of the man I had married even when I was married to him.

As I looked forward to my healing, I was convinced that you must face your pain. If you do not face it, and if you do not allow yourself to feel it—I mean really feel it and let it out—you will not heal. You will compartmentalize it, and you will ignore or deny it, but it will come back to haunt you in ways that are far worse than if you had dealt with it when it was first occurring.

CHAPTER 28

MYSTICAL SIGNS

After the funeral, the girls and I prepared for the summer events. Somehow, I went back to work and finished the psychological evaluation reports I had left on my desk. I was on automatic as I worked, and I did not allow myself to think about anything other than what I was writing—staying in the moment.

I was on summer break after that, and I found myself sitting at the breakfast table with piles of papers that were related to Mike's estate. I was completely overwhelmed, and Aly came to me and asked what she could do for me. She saw how distraught I was, and I told her I did not know.

"How about I get you some file folders and we start organizing all of this? Should that be a first step?" She looked at me, waiting for my answer. I knew she was concerned, and I was thankful and grateful.

"I guess so." I felt confused and was not at all myself. There was so much to do following Mike's death. I did not want to meet with the attorney and deal with probate or handle his estate. Lindsey had been designated the administrator, but all of us knew she would not be able to take care of the responsibilities that position entailed. None of my other daughters could have handled that either. Lindsey unfortunately was the only one consistently home that summer.

Aly left the house and came back forty-five minutes later with blank files. "Come on, Mom, let's get on this." She was leaving for England soon, and she apparently felt the need to get me over the hump. She picked up each piece of paper and asked, "What is this?" When I told her, she double-checked with me before she placed it in the appropriate file. She was systematic, she was persistent, and she saved me that day.

After she organized the many pieces of the probate paperwork, Aly prepared for her departure to England. I hated that she was having to go abroad just two weeks after her father's death. She hugged me and reassured me.

"I will be okay, Mom. Dad would want me to do this."

I knew she was right, and I knew her father had been proud of her. He told everyone he knew that she worked for Florida State's athletic department. He was a big Seminole fan and had been ever since the eldest attended that university.

My girls were strong women. She would be fine. I just wanted to make sure she gave herself time to grieve.

Lindsey and I prepared to take our trip to Arkansas. Mike and I purchased the "buy one—one flies free" from Delta. The memory of his and my time together then flooded me as I packed for the flight. Lindsey and I, along with Jamie and Eric, were attending my niece's wedding. Ashley was getting married on June 24, just a little over a month since Mike's death.

As I packed, I reminisced over the events of the past month. Our small family had experienced many mystical signs that were reassuring and that had lifted each one of us as they occurred. First, we saw a hummingbird outside of our Florida room one day during the week of Mike's death. I had never seen a hummingbird outside of the glassed-in porch. One of the girls spotted it and brought it to my attention. One of the first tasks Mike and his mother had always completed when they arrived at the cabin on Mount Nebo was to fill the hummingbird feeder. They would hang the feeder on its pole near the bluff, and we would all watch the hummingbirds flit about as we sat in the old wooden rocking chairs on the back screened-in porch.

I was awed at the sight of this one. It lifted my spirit.

During the week following his death and funeral, several occasions aroused my wonder. Early in that week I went to Office Depot to pick up computer paper. A gentleman at the counter waited on me and said something that made me smile. The smile felt foreign to my face, and I realized I had not smiled much in the week that had passed. I walked out of that store and remembered that Mike and I had promised each other years ago that we would send the other a sign when we died. As I walked to my car, I considered that promise. *That's right. You are supposed to send me a sign. Okay, I am ready. I want to see that sign now.*

Without thinking, I turned around and looked back at the store front. I looked up into the sky and saw a cloud shaped like a bear. The bear cloud was standing and facing toward my right. I saw its head, the profile of its face, its right arm that was bent at the elbow and extended forward, and its legs and feet. It was in full form, and I marveled.

Of course, I thought, in awe at the miracle before me. *Of course! A bear cloud. Why not? Your nickname was Bear. Of course, it would be a bear cloud.*

I hugged the spectacle to my broken heart, and as the cloud dissipated, I walked slowly to my car. I felt as though I were walking on that cloud. It warmed my heart, and I felt hope for my girls and for my future. I also felt hope for his whereabouts.

That night I heard from Jamie. I was spending the night with Aly at a house where she was babysitting. Aly did not want me to sleep alone in my house, and I readily agreed. She and I spent the evening playing with the children, and after she tucked the children into bed, she and I sat together on the sofa. I was comforted by her concern and by her empathy. I went to bed with a serene feeling I had not previously experienced. I woke up at three a.m. and carried my cellphone to light my way to the bathroom. I saw that my cell phone had a voice message.

"Mom," I heard the voice of my eldest on the voicemail message. She sounded excited. "Oh my gosh, Mom, you will not believe what just happened." I shook away the grogginess I felt so I could comprehend her words. It was good to hear excitement in her voice. I knew how sad she had been when she left on Memorial Day and flew back to Chicago.

"Becky and I are at a bar. Eric's with me, and Becky's boyfriend is here. Becky and I just played three songs on the jukebox. I was standing by the jukebox, and the first song was playing, and Becky went to the bathroom. That song finished, and the second song came on. It was 'Bad to the Bone.'"

"We didn't play it, Mom," she exclaimed louder. "I couldn't believe it. We did not play it. I looked at the jukebox, and 'Bad to the Bone' was not even listed. Becky came running out of the bathroom and said, 'Oh my gosh, Jamie! I never believed in this kind of thing. I believe in it now. Oh my gosh! That song is not even on the jukebox.'"

Becky had flown to Jacksonville and had attended Jamie's father's funeral. She was a close friend of Jamie's, and I was sure she had heard lots of stories about Jamie's father.

Jamie had left the message two hours before I picked it up. I knew it was too late to call her, but I could not wait to talk to her. "Bad to the

Bone" was a song her dad had played on the CD player when the girls were with him in his car. I had also been in his car with him when he turned it on for them. He would open the sun roof and roll down all the windows and play it at maximum volume. They would all sing the chorus, "B-b-b-b-bad to the bone!" Ironic, that "Bad to the Bone" was their father's song. Somehow, I was able to get back to sleep that night.

I called Jamie the next day. "We could not believe it, Mom. That song just came on. It made me so happy. I felt so happy after I heard it."

I told her about the bear cloud. "Wow, Mom," she said. "That is cool."

After we hung up, I held on to our witnessing. I felt a lift in my spirits.

Two days later, I was looking for something, and I opened a drawer in a chest in the spare bedroom. I felt wetness. The clothes in the drawer were damp. I leaned down and smelled a scent that I thought was urine. I thought of the ferrets the girls had at one time in their lives (their father's idea, not mine), but I knew they had been long gone. Did an animal do this?

Aly and Lindsey were in the family room, and I walked toward them. "Why is this drawer wet?"

"What drawer?" They both asked in unison.

"The second drawer up from the bottom in the chest in the guest bedroom," I said as I walked back to the bedroom. They followed me. Aly peered closer and smelled the urine. "Ooh," she said, as she wrinkled her nose. "That is pee. Lindsey probably did it. She was naked on the couch in the middle of the night. I think she was drunk."

"I did not pee in that drawer," she exclaimed. She did admit to being drunk. She was having a particularly difficult time dealing with her father's death. She had said several harsh words to him in the previous few months. I am sure she felt bad about that. I wished I could help her, but I knew we all grieved in different ways, and she would go through her own process. I just wanted her to know that her anger was normal, and it was better for her that she expressed her feelings to her father. I had told him that once. I told him Lindsey needed to get that anger out, and that was what she was doing when she went off on him. He said he understood. I think he knew what he had done was bad—bad to the bone.

"Lindsey, have you ever done anything like this? Have you ever walked in your sleep and peed in a drawer or a jewelry box?"

"Mom, what are you talking about? A jewelry box?" Lindsey and Aly both looked at me as though I had lost my mind. I was not making sense to them.

"Your father used to do that. He would get drunk, and after he was in bed for a while, he would sleepwalk and pee where he should not have. He peed in my jewelry box once. He just lifted the lid and peed. He peed in the closet another time. He tried to pee on me once, but I woke up and caught him and yelled at him until he snapped out of it. He even almost peed on his mom one time when we stayed with them in Fort Smith. When she finally startled him awake, he cried out like that Indian chant, you know, like an Indian chief cries out when he wears his head gear of feathers and performs a rain dance." I smiled at the memory then turned serious.

"Have you ever done this before?" I looked at Lindsey.

"No, Mom, of course not."

"I think you would know." We all felt weird about it. Lindsey had taken on a behavior her father had exhibited, a behavior she had never displayed before now.

A week later, Aly left for London. I sadly let her go. I knew she would be okay, even though I wasn't. She had been such a comfort, and I hoped I had been a comfort to her. Lindsey left for Maine a week after that, just before Father's Day. It concerned me that all my girls would be alone and away from each other and away from me their first Father's Day without their father. Jamie was in Chicago.

Lindsey's trip to Maine was not strictly pleasure. She accompanied a family on their vacation trip and served the role of the children's nanny. She had babysat for the family off and on for the previous three years. They needed her help with the children while they were on their flight and during their time in Maine.

Lindsey called me from Maine on Father's Day. I was so glad to hear from her. "I was thinking about you, Lindsey. I hope this is not too tough of a day for you."

"It has been hard," she replied, "but listen to this. We were going to a scheduled sailboat tour, and while we were driving to it, the mom told one of the kids to sing a Father's Day song for me. They were all celebrating Father's Day with their dad, and I guess Jenny thought that would cheer me up.

"Mom, it was the weirdest thing. She told Toby to sing it, and he started singing 'Silent Night.' Jenny told him that was not a Father's Day song, and I wanted to cry but I didn't. I told her, 'Yes, it is actually.' I told her it was Dad's favorite Christmas song and that we sang it at his funeral. She remembered then. She was there. Even though it was strange that Toby would sing that—how would he know? I thought it was really cool." I knew Toby was only four years old. He was not at the funeral, and he would not have known.

Lindsey returned one week later, just in time for us to leave for Arkansas. She and I flew out the next day, and we arrived at the Little Rock airport in the late afternoon. We picked up the rental car and waited for Jamie and Eric. After they arrived, we headed for Mount Nebo. Our plan was to spend the night at the cabin, get up early the next morning, and drive the seventy miles to visit with Deenie, who resided in a nursing home just outside of Fort Smith. We would then go another ten miles to their Uncle John's house to shower and dress for Ashley's wedding. From there we would turn back and drive the one hundred miles to my hometown church.

We managed all that and made it to the wedding with little time to spare. Ashley was a radiant bride. Her groom had lost his father when he was a young boy, and there was a tribute that included his father's picture with flowers surrounding it. It was directly in front of us. I thought that was a nice touch, but it was a little too close to home for the girls and me. We made it through the service with the shedding of many tears and made our way to the reception.

Jamie experienced the first-time realization that she would not have a father-daughter dance at her wedding when she saw Ashley and her father take the dance floor. She was not yet engaged, but it was assumed that she and Eric would one day be married. She left the hall in the middle of the dance and walked outside, and Lindsey followed her. I followed Lindsey, hoping we were not making spectacles of ourselves. Jamie and Lindsey were both crying just outside the door, and I let them cry for a few minutes. This was the first wedding they had attended, and it would likely be the hardest. They would make it through the father-daughter dance and the father's toast in future weddings. The first is always the hardest.

I was proud of them both. They sucked up the last few tears, wiped their faces, and walked back into the hall. The dancing had continued, and the wedding party was dancing. As soon as they finished, all were welcomed to the floor, and my girls and I took Eric by the arms and led him to the dance floor. The music was fun and uplifting, and we literally danced the night away. There was lots of drinking—good ol' Catholic wedding—and we imbibed.

We were relaxing at our table after a couple of hours of dancing, and Lindsey picked up her purse and announced she was leaving. It was ten p.m., and the reception would not end until eleven.

I looked at her. "We are not ready to leave yet, Lindsey."

"I am ready to go, and I will walk home," she announced.

"You don't know where Grandma lives." I was being reasonable. "You can't walk to Grandma's. You have no idea how to get there." We had left Mount Nebo that morning with the plan to spend the night at my mother's house.

"I don't care," she said irrationally. "I am going home."

I looked at her face. She had clearly drunk too much. She reminded me in that instant of her father and of the times when he reached a point at a party that he was simply ready to go home. He would tell me the same thing. "I am going home." He would get rather mean about it if I protested, and I would have no choice but to follow him out the door.

"Lindsey!" I grabbed her arm as she moved away from me. "You can't leave. You have to wait for us." She shrugged me off and walked quickly down the long table where we were seated. I jumped up and called to Jamie and Eric to stop her. They had just left the dance floor and were walking toward us, and she was headed in their direction. Jamie saw my concern and would not let her pass. I caught up to them and sat her down in the nearest chair. She glared at me. Why did she remind me of Mike just now? The look on her face was comparable to the look he had after he had too much to drink. She was scaring me.

Jamie and Eric said they would catch another ride if we wanted to leave. I took Lindsey by the arm, and we walked out. We were silent on the way to her grandmother's house. I did not like what I was seeing, but I knew she would work through it, or it would work through her.

CHAPTER 29

LIVING IN THE MOMENT

July passed by slowly. Aly was still in London and would not return until the middle of the month. She and I communicated regularly by email, and she wrote long narratives that were full of her adventures. I was glad she was enjoying her trip.

Lindsey had another opportunity to go on vacation with that same family, but this time they were headed to Hawaii for three weeks. I was so jealous. But I had my own treat. The family offered me the chance to sit at their place of residence on the beach while they were in Hawaii. It was a spacious home, and I could sit and watch the surf through the window and write. I made notes about the events leading to and following the horrific news of my husband's death. I cried out loud and knew no one could hear me. I screamed at times, knowing I could not be heard. I purged. I poured out. I was relentless in letting out my grief.

The nights were difficult. It was a monstrously large house, and I slept in the back part of it. I knew someone could enter the front of the home, and I would never hear them. I managed to catch some sleep during those overly vigilant nights.

The days were equally difficult. Grief attacks seem to occur at full force when you are alone and when you are not occupied. Mine tore at me when I was in that house, but I knew I needed to let the attacks happen, and I knew I needed to respond and let the anguish, the hurt, the sadness, and the pain out.

I gave myself frequent breaks, and I ran. I loved the feel of the hot sand under my feet and the wind coursing around my body and through my hair as I ran down the beach. I would walk away from the crowded areas and once I reached the unoccupied, deserted strip of the beach, I would take off my over-clothes and run in my bikini. It was so liberating. I felt I was fleeing, running from it all. But I also felt I was free. I was running away from my grief-stricken circumstance, and I was running to something better—I was running toward recovery. I found my escape, and I ran, and I ran. I am not a runner, so it was miraculous that I could even run as far as I did. It was such a release. It felt wonderful. I was set free in those instances. The joy I felt was boundless. I felt light, and I recalled the saying about the walk in the sand where only one set of footprints was visible. I knew God was carrying me. I could not have run that distance without Him.

I stayed at the beach house one week and then returned home. The family's housekeepers took over for the second and third weeks.

Aly returned from London and spent a few days with me before she left for Tallahassee. She excitedly told me about the soccer tournament she and the other students had worked. She told me about the pubs in London and how friendly everyone was there. She described the students she met from the other universities. "It was fantastic," she said in an attempt at an English accent. She made me laugh, and I was happy to have her with me.

I hated to see her go, but she was still taking summer classes. We hugged tightly the morning she left. "Don't worry, Aly," I told her. "I really will be okay. I know you are and will be okay also. We are going to get through all of this."

I was in the middle of the probate process, so I had plenty to keep me busy. I found the paperwork as overwhelming as it had been when Aly first helped me organize it. There was so much more to it than those first piles. My plan was to write up and hand in whatever the probate attorney requested (and he seemed to be making requests way too often), and Lindsey would sign all documents that had to be signed by the administrator when she returned from Hawaii.

When the life insurance check came in a few days later, I cried that I did not want Mike's life insurance money; I had only wanted him to stop drinking.

Lindsey came home from Hawaii a few days before I left for Sedona, Arizona. I picked her up from the airport, and she told me she wanted both of us to go to Roy's Restaurant. She had been to a Roy's in Hawaii, and she had loved everything she tried at the restaurant. We went home and dressed for dinner. I had eaten there before and had not been that impressed with the food, but she told me you had to know what to order. I let her take charge, and she ordered for us. She proved to be right. From the appetizer to the entrée to the dessert, every bite was delectable. She and I also enjoyed the time with each other. She regaled me with stories of Hawaiian adventures, and she had me laughing throughout each course.

My girls are so good for my soul.

I left a few days later for Sedona. I met my college roommate, Frances, and my college cheerleader buddy, Paulette, at the Phoenix airport. We were all in pursuit of healing. Frances had lost her husband to lung cancer fifteen years earlier. Paulette had been diagnosed with Lou Gehrig's Disease (ALS) the previous year. The three of us were searching for hope. We were yearning for peace. We were looking for healing, and in our interactions and in our love for each other, we found it. We had quiet, spiritual moments. We felt a positive energy while we were in Sedona, and we were all determined not to let our difficulties take us down. We would arise from our dark pits, and we would forge ahead and walk our paths of recovery, wherever they might take us.

When I returned from Sedona, I felt recharged. I called Lindsey when I arrived at the airport and told her I was going to drive to the house, pick her up, and head to Mickler's Beach, a few miles from the house. I wanted to keep the peaceful, serene feeling I had attained when I was in Sedona, and I already felt some of it slipping away. It was ten p.m. by the time we walked across the boardwalk to the beach. We climbed up onto the lifeguard's chair and sat side by side. The soft slush of the waves returned that peaceful feeling to me.

We talked quietly, but we felt the serenity and stopped talking after a while. We sat and breathed it all in. It was a beautiful, iridescent, full-moon night, and I thanked God for this special moment with my youngest daughter.

I finally spoke. "It has been such a short time since your dad's death, and there is so much I will learn from this. I have already learned one thing, though, since he left me. I never lived in the moment before, and I am really trying to do that. I am doing that right now. How can you not be in the moment with this beauty in front of you?" I watched as the moon's luminescent path saluted us; the path started at the lower rim of the moon and rolled out like a golden carpet toward us, where we sat high above the sands. I felt such peace, and I was grateful.

Lindsey turned to me in surprise. "What do you mean?" she asked. "Doesn't everyone do that?"

Now it was my turn to be surprised, but I said nothing. Of course, this dear, young woman always lived in the moment. Wasn't she the one that always woke up to a brand-new day? Wasn't she always "happy-happy-joy-joy"? Of course! How could she not be? She was always living in the moment.

I had to read and search and research to discover that I needed to stop waiting, stop worrying, and start staying in the present moment. My youngest daughter had been in the moment all her life. I had never heard her complain about an event in the past. I had never heard her make judgmental statements about others or about herself. I had never heard her express worry. She had frequent, observable moments of joyfulness. She lived life fully, without resisting and without manipulating. She simply let it happen. She showed no fear, and she tended to think and act deliberately and with confidence.

She always seemed to have been in touch with another realm. Wasn't she the one who sat upright in the bed one night when I was tucking her in and surprised me with a profound statement? She had looked directly at me and said, "I didn't know *you* were going to be my mother." She was only five years old, and the look in her eyes vanished as quickly as it had appeared. I knew what she meant at the time, and I hugged her to me.

All the searching I had done, and the best example of living in the moment and having inner peace was right under my nose the whole time. I could certainly learn from her wisdom. I had always resisted during my life. I resisted what my husband was doing. I resisted what my children were doing. I resisted and complained about my workload, both at my job and at my home. I was never satisfied. I had to be in control, and I had to make sure everyone else was doing the right thing. After all, I knew what was best for them. That is what I used to think. I finally knew better, but first I needed to mourn, let go, and prepare myself for the new me. Again.

CHAPTER 30

THE LAST LAUGH

People tell you "it takes time." It doesn't just take time. I know that. It takes hard work. It takes facing your pain and feeling your pain. Time alone does not take care of your mourning. But, what you do with that time is what ultimately leads you to the place you desperately want to go—the healing place.

I learned that at the first session of my grief support group. My life had taken a pause, and I knew I needed to mourn before my life could resume. I wanted to grieve and do it right, so I signed up for the grief group. I had a lot confirmed during that first session. I knew I had to cry and express the emotion I felt, or I would not heal.

The group leader told us that people who mean well ask us, "How are you doing?" We all agreed we hear it constantly. What do they really expect us to say when they ask us that? Only if they have been in our shoes would they know what to expect. If they had, they would not even ask the question. They would know we are not doing well. The leader told us there is no way any of us could be doing well three, six, or even nine months after a loved one has died.

In that first group session, we introduced ourselves and told the members why we were there. We talked about the person we had lost, the circumstances surrounding their death, and what brought us to the grief support group. Two elderly couples had lost adult children—one from suicide. One elderly lady had lost her husband. Another fortyish woman had lost hers as well. My friend Jane had lost her husband, Mark, to cancer. Then there was me. We learned we were not alone.

I started attending the grief group in early September. It was a twelve-week commitment and would end in December. In the meantime, the girls and I had made plans to lay Mike's ashes to rest and decided to have the event in October. We knew where he wanted them to be scattered.

Mike had told me twenty years earlier that he wanted to be cremated when he died, and he told me where he wanted his ashes to lay. I later relayed his request to my daughters in case something happened to the two of us so they could carry out his request and include my ashes.

When Mike told me he wanted his ashes thrown off the bluff behind the Mount Nebo cabin, I had protested and had referred to our daughters when I said, "No way! With our luck, you'd create a big gust of wind just as we released them, and they'd blow right back into our faces." I could envision that happening as we all stood on the bluff. I never thought we would have to fulfill his wishes though ... and never this soon.

The girls and I arrived in Little Rock on October 19, a Friday. I don't think any of us realized the date—Mike had died on May 19, a mere five months earlier. We rented a car and drove to Russellville and discussed how we wanted to carry out the memorial on Mount Nebo. The girls dropped me off in Russellville and headed up to the mountain with some of their cousins. I attended the Arkansas Tech University homecoming alumni event that Friday night, along with college "Rat Pack" buddies—Frances, Paulette, and Sherri. We had a great time with all our college friends and carried our communal banter well into the night hours.

Frances and I woke up early the next morning, and she drove me to Mount Nebo. I wanted Mike's brother, his family, and my three girls to hold a private ceremony first. We walked out to the bluff behind the family cabin. Frances stayed at the cabin and deterred the early arrivals until we were ready for them. I wanted us to have our own personal time, and I was thinking we could have a practice run with the ashes.

I thought it would be morbid or sad, but I found it otherwise. John's wife, Becky, opened the bag of ashes in the black box where they had been housed since May. I was sure she was ready for this, as I knew she had retrieved the box of ashes from her bedroom. John and Becky had taken the box with the bag of ashes when they left Florida after Mike's funeral.

I brought three small, plastic, sand bucket shovels, and we had the three daughters go first. We tested the wind. We laughed. We all enjoyed being with each other. These ashes belonged to our husband (or ex-husband), father, brother, brother-in-law, and uncle. The girls reached over the bluff and sprinkled them over the side, and they fell in a downward splatter. For some reason someone was playing a guitar below us. We could not see him, but we could hear him. I was hoping he would stay and play soft guitar music during our ritual.

I did not like how the ashes just fell unceremoniously. I had planned to do a practice throw after each of my daughters released a shovelful of ashes. It was finally my turn. I dipped my shovel into the bag that was in the original box container and stood on the side of the bluff in ready position to sling them out and up. Jamie shouted, "Mom, be careful." I was close to the edge of the bluff, and she did not want me to go with them. I did a far reach-out from the bluff and swept my hand out and up and released the ashes from the shovel. The result was beautiful. I heard exclamations behind me. The ashes billowed up and flowed into a formless (almost spirit-appearing) cloud and billowed up and up into the heavens. John, Becky, and Katie went next and copied my motion, and their ashes did the same thing. Someone announced, "We'll do it this way." The girls took another turn, and we all had to run back from the bluff as the ashes blew back toward us. There was lots of laughter.

A few minutes later, a man's head appeared at the level of the bluff, and then his whole body appeared as he walked up and over the bluff. He was slapping at his head, and dust (ash, really) was flying from it. He carried a guitar and looked a little sheepish as he barely said, "Hello." I couldn't look at him. I did not know who was more embarrassed—him or us. I guess he figured out what was happening. How awful for him. We somehow thought it was funny.

My daughters walked over to the far side of the bluff, away from the ashes area, and sat on a large, flat rock that rimmed the mountain's edge. I heard them talking quietly and resisted interrupting them. After I could no longer resist, I retrieved a small shopping bag I had set on the ground before the practice with the ashes and walked toward them.

"Girls," I said. They turned and looked at me. "I wanted you to have something of your dad's, so I had these made for you."

I sat down beside them and opened the package. I pulled out three boxes. One was different from the other two, and I handed it to Jamie. I handed the other two to her sisters. They opened the boxes simultaneously and pulled out necklaces. I had taken their father's ring and had a friend who was a jeweler make diamond drops for each daughter. One diamond was bigger than the other two, and it went to the eldest. Each diamond was placed in a setting comprised of both silver and a portion of the gold that came from their dad's ring. The setting was attached to a silver chain.

"These are from your dad's ring," I told them. "There were three diamonds, so I wanted each of you to have one."

"Oh, Mom, these are beautiful," Jamie said as she separated the clasp and pulled the two ends of the chain to the back of her neck. Lindsey and Aly expressed their thanks, and they all helped each other affix the necklaces. We stood up, and we all hugged. It was time for the ceremony.

A small number of Mike's friends from Pine Bluff arrived, and some of my friends showed up. Of course, the Rat Pack was there, as were some of Mike's fraternity brothers. Both of our families were well-represented. They assembled behind the cabin and faced the bluff.

John and I stood together in front of the small crowd, and John welcomed everyone but then got choked up and could not talk. I continued where he left off.

"Thank you for coming to this memorial for Mike. Mike loved Mount Nebo, and he loved bringing me up here. When we were dating, he and I would sit on the bluff—sometimes we might have kissed a little …" I heard my daughters groan, but I continued, "We stayed up here an entire summer while he and a friend worked on the cabin. Mike loved this place—it was his haven. After the girls were born, he loved taking them up here. They loved the mountain too. Twenty years ago, Mike asked that he be cremated when he died and that his ashes be thrown off the bluff of Mount Nebo. We are honoring that request today. Before we do that, I will read to you a portion of the sermon that was delivered during Mike's funeral service by Dr. Tom Walker, our pastor at Palms Presbyterian Church in Florida. It was meaningful to us, and, hopefully, it will be meaningful to you."

I then read:

> "As we gather today, we come as those who acknowledge the darkness but hold onto the light. We come as those for whom the shadows have lengthened and are more imposing, but as those who have seen and claim light that continues to shine. We come in the face of death, to claim life and to claim that even though death and despair seek to darken our lives, the light continues to shine.

> "As we come, I think it is important to share stories, to share stories and laugh, to share stories and smile, even to share stories and cry. Today, we have gathered to give thanks to God for the life of Mike."

I got choked, as I read the words, "the life of Mike," but I continued.

"We have come to remember Mike and to seek comfort for ourselves with the promises of God in the face of death. Each of us comes to this day with memories, moments, and stories to share and tell about Mike: stories of teddy bear hugs and laughter, stories of pride about his daughters, stories of Lake Tahoe and golf.

"These are stories that I hope you will share with each other in the days ahead for these stories provide comfort and hope, they shine light into the darkness. They celebrate the gift that God has given each of us in the person of Mike and the impact he had on our lives."

I paused and said, "And now I invite any of you to share a story with us."

Tony told the story about me calling Mike a creep one night, and since John was his brother, he, too, was a creep. Cecil was his father, so he was a creep also. Tony had asked, "What about me?" I had replied, "And you're a creep by association!" I looked at Tony then during the service and said, "And should I tell everyone what Mike had done? No, I won't embarrass him and do that." I did not tell, but I remembered exactly when that had happened and how mad I had been with Mike. We had been to a fraternity party and Mike had been very flirtatious with the other girls and had been looking up one girl's dress all night long. He picked up the hem of her dress and lifted it up high—lots of times! She had screamed and laughed and pushed him away. I was always so jealous of the attention he gave to other women, because he never gave it to me.

Other people told stories. Some of his Cavalier friends told stories. My sweet mother told a story and ended with, "We loved Mike," as she sat down. Her voice cracked a little. My brother-in-law Norman walked up and stood by John and me and addressed the small gathering. He talked about Mike's big heart and how he and Mike had the commonality of being married to sisters. He told how they'd tell stories on us and laugh about us. When he finished, he teared up and hugged John, then me. Both John and Mike had worked for Norman in his men's clothing store when they were in college. I always thought Norman probably felt like an older brother to the two of them.

After the story telling, I read a few last lines from Dr. Walker's funeral sermon:

"Telling stories is important. Telling these stories does not deny our pain, does not negate our sorrow, but telling stories reminds us of the truth that we so need to hear in the face of death. Telling stories reminds us that Mike was a gift of God to his family and friends, a gift death cannot finally take away. Telling stories reminds us that God is the ultimate storyteller and will tell the final story of grace and promise for our lives. In the face of darkness and death, telling stories is a most precious gift that we can give each other, as they can shine the light of God's promises into the darkness."

John turned to me when I finished and said, "Cleve has a Bible passage he wants to read." Cleve was Mike's cousin. He read a passage about forgiveness. I was surprised but assumed he thought that was necessary. My girls and my family knew it was not.

I looked at my daughters when he finished and said, "Girls." They followed me over to the bluff where the box of ashes sat. We picked up the box and carried it closer to the bluff's edge. Aly said something and laughed. They were all three being giddy, and I looked back at the solemn crowd behind us. "Girls," I admonished, "don't get too silly. People are watching us."

Jamie took one of the small shovels, filled it with ashes, and slung it as she had previously practiced. Mike's ashes billowed up toward the heavens. Aly filled the shovel and repeated Jamie's movement. Her ashes joined Jamie's. Lindsey did the same, and the billowing seemed to expand. The formless cloud rose up toward the heavens, and some of it came back toward them, and they ran back to me, laughing. What the heck, I thought, Mike would want laughter.

It was my turn. I did the same thing, and the cloud seemed celestial, as it made its way upward. Again, it appeared soft, hazy, almost spirit-appearing. I watched in amazement as it went upward. I could hear the admiring "aww" from some of the crowd behind me. I then looked down and saw the butterfly. It was black- and yellow-spattered, and it flew lazily back and forth where the ashes were falling. The sight of it consoled me, as did throwing Mike's ashes off the bluff. I was releasing him. I was saying "Goodbye."

John, then Becky, then Katie took a turn. John then motioned to the others. A handful of people joined us and saw the butterfly when they approached the bluff. The butterfly stayed with us until we finished. People were leaving and telling us goodbye, but we were finishing the task. Finally, there was one last scoop. I turned the box over and dumped the remainder into Jamie's shovel. She stood poised, and then she slung it out like she had done before. Every bit of it came back into her face. I laughed. She laughed and ran back away from it. We all laughed.

Mike had the last laugh after all.

CHAPTER 31

TATTOOS

I continued with grief group to aid my mourning. I also started to see a therapist who had worked with Vietnam vets and with alcoholics. My husband had been broken. I felt broken. However, I knew I could reach healing and recovery. Mike did not have that objective in mind.

Dr. Kathleen Lewis enabled me to reach insights I would not have otherwise. She helped me to understand that Mike was hurt significantly by the Vietnam War. His work as a medic was traumatizing, but the reception the Vietnam soldiers received when they arrived home was equally reprehensible. She told me she and Dr. Elisabeth Kubler-Ross, the psychiatrist known for her work in near-death studies and for her theory of the five stages of grief, had met with groups of Vietnam veterans in large conference settings and had them stand up at the beginning of the conference. After they stood up, she and Dr. Kubler-Ross applauded them. She told them this is what they should have received when they arrived home from Vietnam. She told them they were heroes.

I continued to cry daily and wondered if the grief attacks would ever cease. Each time, however, after an attack I felt a layer lift away from me, and I knew this was part of the healing process. I imagined it as the peeling away of a layer of an onion. I had attended a Bible study after Mike left me that focused on Beth Moore's studies of the Bible. I felt she was talking to me with every word she uttered. I was now invited to a women's retreat that was arranged by a local church. Again, I felt every word was meant for me to hear.

The leader of the women's retreat had each of us think about a specific time when we felt we were loved unconditionally. She gave examples of being at the deathbed of a loved one or just being with someone and feeling their unconditional love. I closed my eyes and tried to imagine it. No one came to mind. I thought more but still could think of no one. I teared up but fought back the tears.

No wonder I wanted children so desperately. I could not think of anyone before my children were born that I felt loved me unconditionally. Mike was not the only one with the problem of showing love. If I had not felt it from my parents, how could I show it to my husband? I knew it was not my parents' fault. They did the best they could do. They were hard workers, and their work was important. With ten children to support, their survival depended upon it.

The leader talked about affirmations, and I understood how they were important to changing your mood and your mindset. I knew that whenever you remember an event, your brain reacts the same way it did when the event occurred. So, remembering it brings back the same emotional reaction. If an event occurs that causes sadness, then memories of that event will also cause sadness. If we want to change to more positive feelings, we have to recall more pleasant experiences. The brain then reacts as it did when the pleasant experience occurred. This works in the same way with affirmations. If you say a positive affirmation, your brain should react with a positive response.

When I left the retreat, I decided I needed to use affirmations more in my daily life so that I could lift the sad feelings that pervaded my consciousness. I went home that day and walked into my bathroom. I peered into my mirror and said, "I love you, Marti." I started crying and found myself having a downpour. Why was this so hard for me? I realized I did not love myself, and I knew I had to start with me before I could really love anyone else.

I had lost myself over the years, and I had to find myself before I could heal fully and be whole again. I turned inward and searched for me. I had become someone's husband, someone's mother, and I had been someone's child. I read *Women Who Love Too Much*, a book about women who were addicted to men who were not good men and who were not emotionally accessible. I learned to meditate, and I looked deeper inside myself. I took breaks from soul-searching, and I grieved. I took breaks from grieving, and I soul-searched. I knew I had to get through the pain to get to the other side where the blessings flow. I also knew that everything I had done in my life led to this moment. I was not patient, and I knew God had given me an opportunity to learn how to be patient.

As that first year progressed, I found my grief attacks lessening, but I still had them. At first it was daily, then it was every other day. At times I was surprised several days passed. Just before the first anniversary, I realized I sometimes went weeks before I was again attacked by the grief. I decided my daughters and I needed a ritual that would carry us through the first anniversary of their father's death.

I made plans for a trip to the Hilton Hotel in Daytona Beach. I knew it was not the best of locations, but I had a free two-day stay there because their staff had wrecked my car when I had attended a school psychology conference there the previous fall. I decided since the stay was free, I would buy us all a spa treatment.

The girls arrived in Jacksonville on a Thursday, and we headed to Daytona the following morning. I had scheduled our spa treatments, and we checked into the hotel and left our baggage with the desk clerk. We made a beeline to the elevator and down to the spa floor. The mud wrap I had was most relaxing, and I was hoping the girls were enjoying their treatments as much as I was. I needed this.

The girls thoroughly enjoyed their spa time, and after we had lunch, we sat out by the pool and caught some sun rays. Music was playing, and I was surprised to hear every song their father loved playing through the speakers.

"Oh my gosh, girls, this was your dad's favorite song." I must have said that ten times that afternoon. He apparently had many favorites. "Maggie May," "Bad Moon Rising," and "Listen to the Music" were just a few. I sang along to all the tunes as I recalled his facial expressions and movements when we danced to them. How we enjoyed dancing! I smiled and was happy that I was remembering the gleeful moments.

We stayed out by the pool for a couple of hours and enjoyed our time together. We took turns in the shower and dressed for dinner. I had been trying to think of a ritual we could do in their father's memory and was still trying to come up with the perfect one. My eldest surprised me at dinner with her own idea.

"I think we should do something special while we are here in Daytona as a memory maker for Dad."

I looked at her in surprise. I had been thinking the same thing, but I also knew the other two would probably like their sister's suggestion over anything I might propose.

"Well, here we are in Daytona, and you know it's considered the tattoo capital of the world," she exaggerated but continued, "so I think we should all get a tattoo of a bear. I love the diamond necklace Mom had made for us, but I can take it off. I want something permanent, as an everyday reminder of Dad—something I can never take off." She finished, and I looked at her sisters.

They did not jump at the idea right away, and a lengthy discussion ensued. "I just think it is perfect," Jamie said. "I mean, look, here we are in the middle of the tattoo capital … it makes perfect sense."

I was quiet. Does she expect me to get one as well? He left me. I didn't think I wanted a daily reminder. I also knew I might have another relationship one day; how would that guy like looking at a reminder of my first husband stamped on my body? I only hoped my daughter was not including me in this venture.

The excitement accelerated during the course of the meal, and the decision was made. They would all get bear tattoos. They agreed that I would not need to be included. He would always be their one and only father; it was possible that he might not be my one and only husband. We finished our dinner and opted to go back to the hotel room, even though a band was starting to play dance music in the adjoining bar area.

We spent the next day walking through some of the shops in Daytona and then we suntanned by the pool. The music was again from the seventies and eighties, and I listened to song after song that my husband had played on his reel-to-reel. He had albums from Led Zeppelin, Pink Floyd, Lynyrd Skynyrd, the Styx, Eric Clapton, the Rolling Stones, Grand Funk Railroad, Rod Stewart, and others. The music brought me back to an earlier time and engendered a pleasant feeling. He had loved his music. I called each song out to the girls to let them know this was their father's music.

We left the pool to get ready for an early dinner. We had stopped by one of the tattoo parlors that afternoon and scheduled three appointments. While we were at dinner, the girls talked about the types of tattoos they would like and where they would have them placed, and they were still discussing the possibilities when we left for the tattoo shop.

The tattoo shop was housed in a rather large building at the end of a strip mall. Besides tattoos, the shop touted all kinds of tourist attraction items. The girls went to the main counter and looked at bear tattoo options but could not agree on the specific tattoo. Aly finally proposed that since they each saw their father differently, they should each have their own unique tattoo. She wanted the word "Bear" tattooed on the inside of her wrist. Jamie selected an outline of the side of a bear walking on its four legs and planned to place it on her hip. Lindsey picked out a teddy bear outline and wanted to have it tattooed on her hip also.

Jamie was given the "you go first" position and situated herself on the lowered table. I called their Uncle John to tell him what his nieces were doing. The girls were laughing and excitedly discussing the fact they were getting tattoos. I walked away to a distant corner so I could hear John better. He groaned when I told him.

"Marti," he said, "don't let them get tattoos."

"John," I said with emphasis, "it's already done. Jamie is on the table now." I looked over at the girls, and they were beckoning to me and pointing up to the ceiling and looking even more elated. I couldn't hear them—I had walked across to the far side of the big room. I walked toward them and told John they were calling for me. They were yelling something, and I pulled my cell phone away from my ear so I could hear what they were saying.

I didn't even have to ask. I could hear it myself. "Bad to the Bone" was playing over the loudspeaker above their heads.

I could not suppress my astonishment. "Oh my gosh, John," I shrieked. "The song Mike sometimes played out loud for the girls when they rode with him is playing right now. He would open the sunroof in his car, roll down all of the windows, and turn the volume to the highest level." I knew it was a great memory for them. I also knew Jamie had heard it on the jukebox within a week of his death when she had picked out other songs.

"I have to go, John. They are okay, and this song tells me he is okay. I'll talk to you later." I hung up and walked over to them.

"Wow!" I said as I approached them.

"Mom," Aly exclaimed, "as soon as he touched Jamie's skin with the needle, that song came on." I looked at Jamie. She was clearly not liking the sting of the artist's ink. I grasped her hand and told her to squeeze as hard as she needed. Despite the pain, she, too, was amazed by the song.

"He is very happy you all are doing this," I solemnly told my three brave girls. "You have made him very happy."

CHAPTER 32

ILLUMINATION

I called my grief group leader a month into the second year following Mike's death. I thought it was supposed to be easier.

"No," she said, "but it would be harder on you during the first year if you thought the second year would be as hard."

My grief attacks did seem to spread out more after that first month. I felt myself healing, and I started dating. I knew I would have a better future. I knew that guy would come one day and that he would be the love of my life. I met Ben, and I did not think he was the one, but he said he was. I knew I had not recovered fully yet, however, and I told Ben I was not ready to have a relationship. I knew I was not ready. We dated, but I was often busy when he asked me out. I was out with friends a lot, and I was having fun.

I spent at least one night every weekend in either St. Augustine with my school psychologist buddies, Nellie and Tori, or in Atlantic Beach with my good friend Jacquie. Dancing seemed to lift my spirits, and I loved being out with these wonderful ladies. The laughter was endless.

Jacquie was my partner in crime when we headed out to Ragtime Tavern in Atlantic Beach. Ragtime is known for its creative cuisine and expertly handcrafted beers, but we went for the musical entertainment. The bands were great, and when we danced, we felt de-stressed and free. When we received attention from men, we felt flattered, and our self-esteem went up a notch.

Jacquie had a similar experience in her life as I—her ex-husband struggled with pain killer issues and died nine months after Mike. Jacquie and I had a strong bond, and in our grieving over our lost marriages and our deceased ex-husbands, we found opportunities to take breaks from our pain, and we literally danced the nights away. We made each other laugh, and we were happy when we were dancing. We were not looking for men to date or for boyfriends; we were merely girls wanting to have fun.

I knew without a doubt "that guy" would one day come into my life and be the love of my life. I also knew I had to fix a few things in myself before I could be ready for him. Ben had finally stopped calling, and I met a guy named Jack.

A friend introduced me to Jack after he told her he had two tickets to the Andre Rieu concert and needed a date. I accepted the ticket, and we were both fascinated by the stage production and hardly noticed each other. I was not expecting to hear from him again, but he called the next few nights. We talked about his business, his travel, and his desire to preach, with each call lasting nearly two hours. I enjoyed our conversations and getting to know him through them. We went out a couple more times, then he left for two months to travel for business. He was a catalyst for the change I eventually established in myself.

The first time I felt an old pattern was the night before he left. He came over to my house to say goodbye, and we were talking as we sat on the sofa in my living room. "Jack," I said, "I am kind of glad you will be gone this summer, as I have lots I need to do." Although we clearly enjoyed each other on the phone, we had only had a few dates, and I did not think he would be affected by what I was saying.

"You have lots to do?" I saw his reaction and saw a flash of hurt, then he appeared stoic. I felt his withdrawal, and I hesitated. "I mean … it won't be a totally bad thing. I hope you understand what I am saying." I was thinking about the writing I was wanting to do, Lindsey's scrapbook that needed my attention, and the continuation of my healing journey. "I am still going through a process," I floundered, "I need time to get through this." While I was feeling that need, I could tell I was not getting through to him. He had withdrawn from me emotionally, and I wanted his affection back.

"Jack, I just need to take care of some things." Why was he not understanding my need? But then again, why would he? He had no idea where I had been. How could he possibly understand? His face hardened; every muscle was taut.

"Jack." I tried again, "you can't possibly understand what I am saying, as you have not gone through what I have gone through. I just need some time." I also knew I did not want to start a relationship I might not be able to continue. I did not want to hurt him.

Nothing I said mattered. He remained stoic and left shortly afterward. As he walked away from my front door, I was gripped with an agonizing feeling. I had not known Jack that long, but I was aware of our easy conversation—we had talked on the phone close to two hours every night since I had met him—our commonalities, and our attraction to each other. I felt a pain that was more than the situation warranted, and I burst into tears.

I then realized what I had done. I had done to Jack what I had done to Mike a million times (and that is no exaggeration). I had flashbacks of myself doing something to push Mike away, then seeing his rejection of me, and me wanting him back. The fear of losing him or having his attention placed elsewhere was the catalyst for my next move. I would then manipulate the situation, as well as him, to regain his "love." Our relationship was a volatile one, full of drama. Little did I realize how big a part I played in that. I never let him be. I always attacked him with what he should be doing, how he should be acting, what I needed from him, and how I was not getting it. I wanted a relationship with him, but I did not have it. I now realized I was part of the reason I did not have it.

I cried more tears as I thought of Mike and what life with me must have been like. I was never satisfied with him. Only during sexual activity with him did I feel satisfied, content, even fulfilled. I now realize that was the only time we were truly present with each other. At other times I resented past behavior, including earlier transgressions, and I begrudged present behavior of not giving me the attention I craved. I also resented the future, as I had worried he was on a self-destructive path. I saw alcoholism developing, and I did not want to have an alcoholic for a husband.

I realized I was doing the same thing to this man, Jack. I had pushed him away, and when I saw him "leaving" me, it made me want him back. I called him then. I did not know what I was going to say, but I felt so sad. The feeling was inexplicable, and I vowed I would let this unfold. I would not resist, I would not manipulate, I would simply be. Jack was at first distant, and I muddled through my apology and my ignorance. At the end of the conversation he told me he was proud of me. "That took a lot for you to call me. I am so proud of you." Did he know me better than I knew myself?

I had an epiphany on two other occasions. Jack called often while he was away, and during one phone conversation with him, I casually said we had talked so long that I was developing a tumor in my brain. He declared, "Marti, that is the dumbest thing you have ever said." I was struck down by his comment. Of course, I did not mean what I said. I was trying to be humorous. I became quiet. I told Jack how hurtful his comment was. He immediately said he was sorry, but "you should never say anything like that. I would never do anything to hurt you, Marti." I told him I knew that (I thought I knew that), but it hit me deeply. I told him I did not mean what I said, but I felt foolish and stupid. I recognized the feeling and tried to consider where it was coming from. It was an awful reaction, and I knew I needed to explore it further. Jack and I continued to converse, but the feeling stayed with me. After we hung up, I searched for meaning.

What was this feeling telling me?

I did not find the answer until later that afternoon when I was doing my four-mile walk. My father often said things that diminished me: "You are so stupid! I asked you to get the wrench, not the pliers!" One of my older brothers antagonized me and my sisters, then belittled us. Mike had also put me down and ridiculed me in public. I realized this had nothing to do with Jack; the old script needed to end, and I decided to end it right then and there.

The third occasion involved something trivial and downright embarrassing. I called Jack one Monday mid-morning feeling animated and "on a cloud" from our weekend conversations. He did not answer, so I left him a message and knew he would call back when he could. By mid-afternoon, I started feeling anxious. I wondered why he had not called back. He had always called me back within a few hours. By six p.m. I was feeling saddened. I loved hearing his voice, and I wanted to hear from him. By nine p.m. I felt a deep sadness and wondered if he was okay. Had something happened? I could not imagine any reason for his not calling me other than something had happened, and he was unable to call me.

I hesitated before calling him at ten o'clock that evening. He answered in his cheerful manner, but I was spent. I had become so sad and so "needy" that I was upset with myself. I probably did not sound like myself and he asked, "Are you okay?"

"Yes," I replied, "I am just really tired." I felt such strong affection and desire for him, but I was disappointed and hurt. After we hung up, I wondered about my irrational self, and the realization came to me that I had done this a million times with Mike (again, no exaggeration). How many times I had nagged and fussed at him in those first months of our relationship, complaining that he had not called me, whining that he must not love me if he did not want to talk to me, and how I continued to do that throughout our lifetime together. I always interpreted his action or lack of action, and I always applied what I perceived as his motive for doing something or for not doing something. It was my interpretation; I now realized it had nothing to do with him. It was all about my reaction and my assumptions.

It had always been about my obsession with him. I was consumed by my thoughts about him—what he was doing, where he was, how he was, why he was. After the children came, I became consumed by them. Where was I in all of this? I did not exist.

My knowledge of this pattern of behavior had a profound impact on me. The realization that this was an old pattern enabled me to release it. I sobbed that night in my bed, as I realized how I had interacted with my husband of thirty-three years. Again, I realized I had not been able to let him "be." I had never been present with him. I always had the past and the future in my thoughts, and I never focused on the here and now.

As I cried, I felt the release of one more grief layer. I was grateful for the grief thief that kept taking some of my heartache. I recognized grieving as a slow process, but if one encounters it, accepts it, and tackles it head on, it can be conquered. I knew it would always be there in some form or another, but it would no longer drive or rule me.

Three epiphanies. Three awakenings. I was beginning to appreciate when something brought out the "drama" within me. If I felt hurtfulness, sadness, jealousy, anger, or any negative feeling I could not identify, I was learning to acknowledge the feeling, study it, and bring it into my full awareness. I could discover the pattern or script that preceded it, face and embrace that pattern or script, and let it go.

That night I said to myself in disgust, "You can take the woman out of the drama, but you can't take the drama out of the woman." I followed that with, "Oh yes, you can." I felt I had profited from my nearly two years of soul-searching and spirituality grasping, but I still had a long way to go.

CHAPTER 33

OLD INSECURITIES

I continued to talk to Jack by cell phone while he was away on his travels. He suggested I meet him in one of the cities he was visiting, and we made plans for me to fly to Boston and visit him in Manchester, New Hampshire. He bought me a ticket, and we could not wait to see each other.

I got off the plane in Boston and searched for Jack's vehicle. I located it, and a policeman was leaning in toward the passenger window. Uh oh, I said to myself. He is going to have to drive away before I even get there. Jack saw me approaching, however, and waved. He thanked the officer and jumped out and grabbed my bag. He quickly stowed it in the back of his vehicle and gave me a quick hug. He knew he had to hurry, so Mr. Policeman would not come back after him. You are not allowed to park in front of airports anymore, and that can be such a nuisance.

I jumped into the passenger seat and looked at him. I really liked the version of the guy with whom I'd spent hours on the phone, and I now studied him anew. He was nice looking with his square jaw and great smile. He was wearing a baseball cap. I had a vision of him embellished by our long phone conversations but was seeing something different in person—something reserved or guarded.

I had felt this difference the first week I had met him. I had enjoyed our nightly phone conversations following the concert, and I had looked forward to two consecutive dates we had scheduled. But when he picked me up to take me to dinner on the first of the two, I froze in surprise. Maybe it was his clothes (the white, long-sleeved undershirt beneath the short-sleeved, purple polo shirt with raised collar). Maybe it was his balding head. Maybe it was his demeanor—his smile was twisted. Or maybe he just appeared older, as I was picturing a twenty-eight-year-old boy when I was talking to him on the phone. He was so youthful on the phone, and when I talked to him I felt like such a young girl.

He talked incessantly that first night at dinner, and I listened. He was full of expression, and he even got into my face several times to make a point. That made me very uncomfortable—his face took on an eerie expression as he leaned in way too close to me. I was a little frightened. This was not the guy I had been talking to on the phone. *I do not know who this is, but after our date tomorrow night, I am out of here.* He gave me a quick kiss when he left me at the door.

Jack had picked me up the following night wearing a baseball cap and sunglasses, and I wondered what was wrong with me. This guy was darling. He wore a short-sleeved shirt, and his muscled arms were gorgeous. He conversed easily, he seemed comfortable with me, and he never got in my face. I liked this guy.

Now, driving from the Boston airport, I again felt confused. I tried to dismiss any thoughts from my mind. Jack broke into my musing. "Oh," he said, "I have to tell you about the dream I had last night." He waited for my, "okay," and continued. "I don't know where I was or what was going on, but I walked up to a couple of guys and one of them said to me, 'Hi, my name is Chit. Would you like to sit and have a chat?'"

"In my dream, I replied, 'Sure, I'd like to sit, Chit, and have a chat.'"

I burst out laughing. "Really!? You actually dreamed that? Where in the world did that come from?" I could not stop laughing.

"I don't know," he replied. He was laughing now. Neither one of us could stop laughing.

We entertained each other all the way back to his hotel. I shook off the earlier feelings, and I felt his physical presence. I was happy to be beside him. I had talked to Jack many hours, and I *did* like that guy on the phone.

Jack introduced me to fellow employees who were traveling with him. They were scattered throughout the lobby. He walked toward one of the female employees and before he could introduce me to Rebecca, she asked, "Is this our newest hire?" He said, "No, this is my Marti." After that he always introduced me as "my Marti." I wondered how Rebecca did not know that he had picked me up at the airport and how she had not expected me.

While Jack attended to necessary work, I roamed around the hotel. It was a huge facility, and it had all the accommodations. There was a fitness room, an indoor swimming pool, an outdoor swimming pool, and a tennis court. *Nice.*

After Jack finished his work, we went to the grocery store and picked up a few items he needed. He was into nutrition and fitness, and his diet and his body showed it.

We made love that night. I felt the sexual tension growing just after meeting him at the airport, and I knew he did too. We could not help ourselves. It had been a long period of celibacy that had been forced upon both of us. Neither of us had chosen that for ourselves. Our hunger showed, and we were insatiable. I had not felt like this in years. I felt the intensity, the need, the desire, and it consumed me. I lost all fear of intimacy.

The next day started out rather quietly. Jack had a juicer in his room, and he juiced carrots and added beet and barley powder. I was surprised by the immediate euphoria I felt. *Wow. I may have to start juicing.* I had never felt so alert and so alive.

After his morning work, we went on one of the computers near the front desk to look at hotels for our weekend trip to Boston. He was annoyed that he could not get to his work computer, as someone had borrowed it and had not brought it back to him. I made a casual comment about the available hotels we were reviewing, and he snapped at me. His tone was harsh, and I looked quickly at Rebecca who was at a nearby computer. She turned away and appeared embarrassed for me. I did not say anything, but I took note. Jack later apologized.

"Marti, I am sorry for the way I talked to you when I was on the computer earlier."

"Oh, you even noticed that you snapped at me?"

"Yes, and I am sorry."

"Jack, you have done that at other times."

"I have?" He was incredulous. "No, I have not."

"Yes, you have. You have snapped at me several times. You use a certain tone, and it is not pleasant." I had only started to notice, but I had encountered his impatience and that tone twice before. "I will let you know when you do it," I offered. I did notice that he could only do one thing at a time. If he was busy on the computer or setting up his juicer or steamer, he could not deal with me talking to him. He was a single-tasker and when I made a comment about it, he made a derogatory statement about women multitasking and being scatterbrained. I really was starting to see a side of him I did not want to see, but I was glad I was seeing it.

As the next few days passed, I noticed Jack becoming more and more direct with me, telling me to "move to the right" as others were approaching us, as though he assumed I was going to walk right into them. What was he thinking? Just as I was about to move over to the right, he directed me to "move over to the right." He did this another time. I was about to hold the door for a couple of people and before I could, he told me to "hold the door for them." Did he think I was an idiot?

I also noticed that he was very attentive and tuned in to me when we were in bed, but he tended to ignore me any other time. I knew he was preoccupied with his work and thinking about his schedule and what he was about to do next, so I had abandoned any thought of communicating with him when he was working.

We were eating lunch near the outdoor pool one day, and I made a pleasant comment about the young Down syndrome couple playing on the slide in the water. He made no reply and said something about what he had done earlier in his work. I started noticing that more and more. He did not seem interested in finding out anything about me or discussing my initiated topics. He always talked about what he was doing or what he was thinking. I was starting to lose myself, and I had to take a step back and take note.

By the end of three days, I had taken lots of notes. I felt I was back with my husband! Mike and I had enjoyed our bed, and at other times he ignored me. He had no conversation to offer, he did not want to do any activities with me, and here I was again feeling neglected.

I saw lots of parallels. Jack showed little interest, unless he wanted to hear what I had observed about him and the people with whom he worked. I felt an insecurity rising in me that I had not felt in a long time. No, this was not going to happen. How many times did Mike make me feel insecure, and the more insecure I felt, the more I wanted to cling to him. And the more worried I became about our relationship or the lack of it.

I was not going to engage in this pattern again. The more resolve I felt, the more I saw it happening: Jack's negative comments about the "doll" female commentator on the sports network, his lack of interest in what I might want to do in Manchester, his stoicism and unresponsiveness to me at times, and his making fun of me when I had not heard all he said. And then telling me my response was "stupid." This was not good for me, and I did not like how I was feeling around him.

I talked him into taking me to Portsmouth on Friday night. He probably would not have, but I told him in front of some of his coworkers that I would really like to go, and they told him he should take me. It was late when we left the hotel, but we were able to spend a couple of hours in Portsmouth. I went into a corner coffee shop to use the restroom after we had been there for an hour, and when I came out, I did not see Jack. I took a few steps in one direction and then turned back in the other direction. I saw him out of the corner of my eye, leaning against a lamppost on a dark corner of the street. He was watching me. He seemed to enjoy my being lost—another stab at trying to make me feel insecure? Or was it my imagination?

After we went back to Manchester, Jack worked Saturday morning, then returned to pack and get ready for the train trip to Boston. I was ready, but I did not know he wanted me to pack his things for him. I added something to the bag we were sharing, and he used that mean and derogatory tone I hated and said, "Don't put that in there like that!" I walked away and turned my back to him and placed my hand on my heart. Ignore that, I said to myself. Get lighthearted.

He grabbed my arm and pulled me back. "I don't like you distancing yourself from me like that."

"I am not—" I was cut off.

"Don't interrupt me. I don't like you distancing yourself. That is not a good thing to do."

"Jack," I tried again, "I am not distancing my—"

He cut me off again. "You were too!"

Oh, what is the use? I can't talk to this man. What happened to that great guy on the phone?

My therapist had warned me before I left to stay lighthearted while I was in New Hampshire. She had asked me if I ever noticed feeling heavyhearted. I was not sure what she meant, but I told her I sometimes felt that way at night time. I thought she meant about my sadness over my husband. She told me to put my hand over my heart when I felt heavyhearted and let myself lighten up again. How could I explain all of that to Jack? Apparently, I could not. He would not let me.

We took off to the train station, and I was afraid we had waited too long. Jack was even later than I was. No one I knew would believe that.

I anticipated a nice dinner in Boston as well as a fun tourist outing. We arrived at the hotel, dropped off our bags, and headed to Park Station. From a distance we could see that festivities were wrapping up in the park. There were a few food vendors left, and they were packing up slowly and apparently hoping for more customers before they completed their night.

"I am so hungry," Jack exclaimed, as he walked toward one of the vendors. I followed him. I had been doing a lot of that. He had long legs and tended to walk faster, and I sometimes had difficulty keeping up with him. I did not mind it so much at the hotel in Manchester, as he knew his way around there, and I had no choice. I did not like the way he did it, however. He never looked back to see if I was still with him. It reminded me of my husband when he was irked (such as when I made him accompany me to go Santa shopping for the girls, and he headed toward the toys section on a mission, and I had to follow him).

"These beef empanadas look great," he was now saying.

I peered into the container. They did look good, but I had hopes of a nice, quiet, romantic dinner. We were going to eat festival food?

"I will take three," I heard Jack saying. Well, I guess we were. I did not feel I had a choice, so I accepted what he gave me. We sat on a park bench and ate. We had been in Boston for two hours, and I had not seen any of the sights. He did not appear to be in a hurry, and he stretched out after he ate. I was getting restless. I wanted to see the city, and I thought Jack did too. I thought he'd said he liked history. After he got up, we walked toward the Boston Common. He did not look at any of the memorials we passed unless I encouraged it. He did not appear interested.

We finally found the John Hancock Building, but they were not allowing anyone to go up to the observation floors and had not since 9/11. We walked over to the Prudential Tower and rode up to the fifty-second floor. When Jack saw the charge for the view, he said, "Why would anyone want to pay eleven dollars to go see a view? I don't want to. Do you?"

I was stuck. How could I say I wanted to? I realized he did not want to spend the money. I did not want to spend his money, so I agreed with him. I later wished I had said, "Yes, I do. So I will pay for my ticket and meet you after I finish." It would have been very interesting to see his reaction. I did not think of it then, and I lost my opportunity to see a panoramic view of Boston.

Jack had mentioned having a beer when we were eating, and I was now ready for one. He had not mentioned it again, so I did. "Sure," he said. We went into several bars and outdoor café-type places. Most of them were full and had forty-five-minute wait times. We finally ended up at a sports bar.

As we were seating ourselves at the bar, Jack noticed the glasses being returned to the bar. "They did not even wash those glasses. Look at them. They merely rinsed them. We are going to have to drink our beer with a straw."

A straw? Surely, I had not heard him correctly. Drink a beer with a straw? Again, I was faced with a decision. I did have a choice, but I did not want to make waves. After all, I was far away from home with this person. I just wanted to get back home.

I took up the straw Jack handed me and proceeded to drink my beer. He took a sip through his straw and turned to the guy on his right. I could not hear what they were saying, but it sounded sports-related, and they were looking up at the TV screen to their right. I looked to my left. Two guys were sitting next to me at the corner of the bar and were talking in a foreign language. I thought about asking them what language they were speaking, but I did not.

I sipped my beer through the straw. I noticed the guy sitting in front of me at the far end of the bar. He kept looking at me, and I mused that he was probably wondering what I was doing with this guy who was engaged in constant conversation with his neighbor.

I continued to sip, having no one to talk to, wondering what I was doing there, and started to feel insecure. Stop, I told myself. I looked around. The gentleman in front of me kept looking at me. I looked behind me and saw another guy watching me. That made me feel better. I flirted with my eyes and laughed to myself. I was so over this guy sitting next to me. After I finished my beer in solitude, I leaned over and said, "I am going to the bathroom." I knew he probably had not heard me, so I left him sitting and talking to the guy seated next to him.

When I came out of the ladies' restroom, I saw the gentleman who had been watching me, and he smiled at me. He was headed toward the men's room. I smiled back and then saw Jack behind him.

"I didn't know where you had gone!"

"I told you I was going to the bathroom, but you weren't paying attention."

"I'm sorry I was talking to that guy so much," Jack said. "He kept talking to me, and I could not get away from him."

Bullshit, what a lame excuse. I looked at him. Did he really think that was acceptable? "Jack," I stared at him. "No one, and I mean no one has ever ignored me like that, sitting with me at a bar, and ignoring me the whole time. No one."

"I told you I was sorry. ..."

I was quickly learning volumes about this guy. Could he not contain this rude side of himself for just one week? How bad could it get if this is what he was manifesting after such a short encounter? I was really having second thoughts about this man's presence in my life.

CHAPTER 34

BREAKING PATTERNS

Jack and I saw a few more sights around the Common area after our beer and headed back to our hotel. He was sweet and attentive, and he seemed completely different from the guy out on the Boston streets. I wanted to know who he really was. "Jack," I tentatively stated.

"Jack," I tried again, "sometimes ... sometimes ..." I could not get the words out. I tried again. "There's the guy on the phone and the wonderful guy who is great with kids." I had seen him interact with the children of his coworkers.

I was sitting on the bed, and he was standing across from me at the desk, and he slowly turned around and looked at me. He had the worst expression on his face. I had not really said anything yet, so I stumbled on. "And then I am with you in your car, and you're fussing at people and calling them idiots, and you sometimes seem so negative."

His expression changed and was growing meaner by the second. "And there's that guy ..." He was beginning to look evil, and I was getting scared. Why couldn't I stop? "And there's this amazing person with whom I love talking on the phone."

He looked at me in disgust. "I am not three persons, Marti. I am one person." Of course, I knew that. He could be so literal at times. His face had the meanest look on it. I felt his negativity.

"Marti," he hissed, "why are you bringing this up during our Boston weekend? That is bad psychology, Marti. That is psycho!" He was yelling. "That is stupidity!" He yelled the last even louder.

Okay, I did not know what this was, but I knew I had gotten a reaction that went a lot deeper than what my comment had warranted. Somehow, we both went to sleep that night, but he was steaming.

The next morning, Jack had his back to me, and he was obviously not speaking to me. He was trying to figure out how to get me back to Florida, though, as he asked, "What all do you have back in Manchester?"

"Well, I have everything, Jack. I brought very little to Boston."

"Well, I need to get you back to Florida, and the sooner the better."

He added, "I am so grateful, Marti. I am so glad that happened last night, so I can see you for what you are. You act like you have this perfect, positive world. You think you are so perfect. You are the queen, and you are waiting on the perfect prince. You know I am striving to be perfect, but I am not there yet!"

Oh my gosh, what is happening here? He was the one that reacted so vehemently last night. Why was he trying to put all of it on me? Granted, my comments to him were probably weird, but I was trying to get a grasp on who he really was.

"What you initiated is unforgiveable. Making accusatory statements that I am negative, blasting my character."

Okay, now he is really moving into uncharted territory. What is he talking about? I had never accused him ... well, maybe I did.

He went on, "I would not trust you. I would not trust you with my car keys!"

I just wanted to go home and get away from him. I was so glad to see this. I knew I did not need this in my life. However, we had made plans to go to a Red Sox game, and I had bought the tickets. I wanted to go, and I did not care about him or what he wanted to do.

A few minutes later I said, "Jack, I know you hate me, but we have tickets for the Red Sox game. I think we should go."

"I don't hate you, Marti. I can go to the game with anybody." My feeling exactly.

Somehow, we dressed and prepared to leave. After he checked out at the registration counter, I asked the attendant about rooms. I had decided I would spend only one night in Manchester, pack my things, and catch the train back the next day before flying out on Tuesday. Jack walked back up to the counter. He was no longer in control. I could feel his concern that I was taking the initiative to leave. "Let's worry about this later, Marti."

We made it to the subway, and he looked down at me. "What the fuck were you thinking last night?" I was shocked by his swearing. I thought he was this super nice guy. I had been misled, and I had been deceived. I pondered my answer. What was I thinking last night? I should have been thinking how stupid I was for not seeing him as he was and for thinking he was such a nice guy, and I said aloud, "Stupidity." He looked satisfied. Did he really think I was serious? Was he really used to women falling all over him and giving in to him like he was assuming I was?

He remained stoic and wore his ego on his shirtsleeve the rest of that day. We both enjoyed the game, but we did not enjoy each other. Later, on the train he was talking about something. I was not really listening. I was just trying to get through the evening and then the next couple of days so I could leave. I heard him saying something and thought, *Did he really just say that?* What I thought I heard was, "The next time you are at home and feeling so smart, just call me and I will tell you how stupid you are."

I was also noticing Jack's evident need to be important. The Red Sox game had tied at the end of the ninth and had gone into the thirteenth inning. We had left before the tenth inning. No one on the train knew the score. Jack's dad was watching the game, and Jack told me he would call to find out the score and let everyone know.

We were moved to another train car before he could make the call, and a man in that car was talking to his mother and was getting the details. Jack asked him what he had found out and told me he was going to let the other car know. I could tell he loved the idea of carrying the news to them. Unfortunately, the guy's mother had it wrong, and Jack carried incorrect information to the other car.

So, after all of that, why was I responding to his physical presence? Why did I continue to feel chemistry? This was a pattern, and I recognized it. Mike would belittle me in those first few years, and I would feel insecure and humiliated, and we would later have great sex. Apparently, I had felt I deserved that treatment. I was in a similar pattern with Jack, and I had to salvage myself.

Somehow, I got through the next day. On Tuesday morning we picked up food from an outdoor event near his hotel and planned to eat it at a stop on the way to the airport. We carried our plates and walked across the lawn to Jack's car, and he marched on ahead of me. I struggled to keep up with him and called to him that I had heels on and not tennis shoes, and he said, "Oh, I forgot you had heels on." He never slowed down. It was humiliating. I recognized the feeling, and I vowed to get away from this man.

While en route to the airport, Jack made a wide turn, and I adjusted my knees so I would not spill the plates of food resting on my lap. He noticed and made a comment.

"You did not spill any of that."

"Of course not. Why would I spill it?"

"Well, any other woman would have let the beans fall into the door." He had made similar comments at various other times, and I was getting tired of being compared to other women. I knew I had talents and skills. I knew I was smart. I also knew I was fun and cute. Had he not commented on the phone about my cuteness? He was not going to take me down. No man would ever get away with that again. I had committed to my husband, and he had not shown that other side until after we were married. I was fortunate to see this side of Jack early on.

I turned to him now. "Did you date a bunch of blondes?"

"Of course!" he replied. What was that supposed to mean, I wondered? He preferred blondes. Was that supposed to make me feel bad?

"My mother loved to make blonde jokes," he added.

"Your mother is a brunette. Why weren't you dating brunettes?" I saw the look on his face like this was getting annoying, and he immediately changed the subject.

After I returned home, I saw my therapist who could not believe I would talk to Jack after the Saturday night episode, much less continue to stay with him a few more days. "I know," I told her. "I am sick." I did not feel like myself, and I hated the feeling. I was determined not to repeat this pattern. I also knew I had been afraid of what he might do had I told him I was leaving his hotel early.

Jack called me the next night, and I told him I had not been able to communicate to him what I was trying to say on Saturday night. He said it was too late, and he needed to go to bed. I said, "I know. It is never a good time."

He called the next day and left a message: "I talked to you all night. I talked to you all day yesterday." I did not know what this part of the message meant. He was talking to me in his head?

He went on, "I hate discord. I hate disunity. It is the enemy. That's why I am a real good businessman. I maintain the unity. Without unity and harmony, there is nothing. Neither one of us have the right to challenge that or to take that away. My initial reaction is just to remove myself from discord and harmony. I wasn't raised with drama. I do not like drama. I am not used to drama. I don't perpetuate drama. It is not natural for me to continue to stay in these types of things you have initiated." He ended the message but called back and identified his call as message number two.

"I seem to recall that you suggested I slap you the next time you do that. That is what you said to me, and I said, 'Oh, yeah, I look forward to that.' I really want to talk to you. I am pretty busy, but I will always have time for you." Little did he realize that I was not wanting him to literally slap me. But it was my way of saying to stop me next time I do something like that because your reaction is so out of proportion, and I don't need or want to be with you at all.

He called the next night and I told him, "I can't do this, Jack. This is not good for me." He sighed and said, "Well, the best to you."

I replied, "The best to you, Jack, and I really mean that."

"I know you do, Marti." He hung up.

He left me a message the next day. "I want to tell you how I finally got some peace. The Lord gave me Romans 28, and he will work it out for my good, for our good, one way or the other." I caught his slip-up here and thought, yes, Jack, you did a similar slip-up when you said, "I love this," during an intimate moment, then quickly recovered, "I mean you … I love you."

He went on, "He was encouraging me. I was grateful. We are still struggling—I am arguing with you all the time." Who was arguing? I was not arguing with him. I was done.

"I don't have a right to react this way. I am supposed to take it. I don't think we can divorce. I feel wrong walking away. Wrong, wrong, wrong. I am committed." *Divorce*?

Jack called many times and told me he could change. He again said neither one of us had the right to divorce from the situation. He was committed. I knew the situation with him was not good for me, and I reiterated that statement. I had to talk to myself a lot, however, as I felt a certain thrill when he called, and I knew deep inside that I wanted him to call. I had to remind myself this was a familiar pattern, and this was not good for me. Still, the thrill was there. I found myself very attracted to him, and I knew why. He was not available to me. He was simply not emotionally available. My father had not been. My husband had not been. Here was a chance to break the pattern, and I finally did.

How freeing and empowering! I knew I would never find myself in that trap again. I somehow knew, though, that I had to place myself in that same situation to undo it. Unfortunately, I had placed myself with a crazy person.

CHAPTER 35

A PAIN IN THE ASS

I still cried at times over my deceased ex-husband's sadness and ultimate death, the ultimate that had happened fifteen months previously. Mr. Grief's visits were less frequent, and after each visit, I felt another layer peel off. I came home from a solo visit to Mount Nebo, and I wanted to continue the writing I had started. Yet, I couldn't seem to get to the computer. My life had become cluttered with activities that did not fulfill me.

But something stupendous happened while I was on the mountain that filled me with joy. My college roommate and good friend, Frances, came to the mountain to spend a night with me. I left my writing and enjoyed the time with her. We always picked up where we left off. She was that kind of friend. We decided to make the mountain margaritas, a special mixture that was only made and consumed on Mount Nebo, and we took them and our cameras to Sunset Point.

We sat on a large rock on the bluff and watched the bright orange sun as it moved down toward the horizon.

"I want to see a bear cloud." I looked at Frances. I had told her about the one that appeared over the Office Depot store. "I want to see a bear cloud," I said again. "I want to know this all has meaning, and this is what I am supposed to be doing … I am supposed to write this book and do something for the military … and do something for other people."

She smiled at me but said nothing.

"I need a sign. I need a bear cloud," I said emphatically.

I watched the bright circle of sunshine as it slowly dropped down toward a cloud formation that was hovering above the horizon. I watched the cloud and saw it change shape as the sun rays hit it. I snapped pictures. The sun lowered behind the cloud and just as it was about to disappear behind it, I saw the bear. It was a cub. It was illuminated by the sun peeking out from behind it, and it glowed with an orange, pink, and yellow radiance. It was breathtaking. I captured it on my camera. I was amazed, and I was filled with hope, peace, and assurance that all was well, and I was doing what I was supposed to be doing. I watched the bear as it slowly disintegrated; it turned into various shapes and at times resembled a dragon or a dinosaur or some alien creature. It finally disappeared entirely.

I turned to Frances. "Wow," I said. She saw it. When I showed the pictures on my camera, she said, "Oh my gosh. You got it." She took it in stride. We acted as if we asked for and saw requested clouds every day. No big deal. It was a huge deal, however. I knew this was my God-touch, and I knew He was watching over me.

I was filled with joyful hope the remainder of my time on the mountain. Once I returned home, I wanted that feeling to stay with me. I also wished I could get back to my computer and my writing.

I met Brent several days after I returned from the mountain. I walked into a restaurant with my two friends, Barb and Joan. We were celebrating Barb's birthday. As we followed the hostess who was leading us to our table, my eye caught the eye of a gentleman sitting at a table to our right. I was in the middle of a sentence, and as I completed it, I was suddenly aware the gentleman and I were staring at each other. He smiled and said, "Hi, how are you?" I did not alter my pace, and as I walked by his table I answered, "Hi, I am fine, thank you."

Barb, Joan, and I had a wonderful lunch, starting with a lemon drop martini. It was a birthday celebration after all! Halfway through our meal, I noticed the table where the gentleman had been seated was vacated. A few minutes later, I heard at my left side, "Excuse me, ladies."

I looked up and saw the gentleman. "Excuse me. I just had to do this." He set his business card down on the table and turned and walked away.

The girls (as I consider them, even at our ages) looked at me.

"Look at that," Joan said, "and to think it started here. We are witnesses."

I laughed. "Nothing has started," I replied. "But that is very interesting. It has me a bit intrigued."

I emailed Brent a few days later. "Excuse me, Sir," I wrote, "excuse me but I just had to do this. I had to send this email. I met you a few days ago at Maggiano's." Short and simple—much like his statement to me.

He replied to the email, and he called me a few days later. He called me several times more, then asked me to meet him for lunch. We met a few days later, and he was friendly, personable, energetic, and I liked him. He left for San Diego the next day for a week-long training. We texted each other and sometimes he called. It was nice talking to a normal man again.

When Brent returned from San Diego, I did not hear from him for several days or even weeks, then he would text or call. I liked that he was busy enough. He asked me to meet him a few times, but I always had plans (with girls). I finally was able to go to dinner with him. Again, he was pleasant, friendly, and was enjoyable company. We talked through dinner, and we talked through the after-dinner glass of wine. He hugged me when I told him about Mike. He kissed me on the nose when he left me at my door. When he said he would see me soon, I answered, "I will probably see you in a month—that seems to be our pattern." I laughed as I said it. It was fine with me. He laughed in return and left me at my door.

I did not see Brent for over a month, though he texted or called sporadically. He had a busy schedule, as did I, but I could not help but wonder if he had a girlfriend or if he was married. He had denied the latter when I had dinner with him. I had wondered, as he called or texted me a lot when he was out of town, and I did not hear from him when he was home.

The months passed, and I attended the school psychologists' annual state conference during the last week of October. The conference itself was informative, and I enjoyed all the sessions I attended.

I saw Dale, and he was no longer separated from his wife—they were trying marriage counseling. He and I had stopped our friendly communication a month after my divorce was final. At that time, he had said he understood my need to have fun, get out with my friends, and dance. I was glad he and his wife were trying to resolve their issues, and I was glad he was a friend.

The nights at the conference were always fun. Our school psychology group is tightly bonded, and we enjoy being with each other. We laugh a lot. No matter what we are doing, we share a great camaraderie.

When I returned home after three days of education, fun, and frivolity, I felt a sadness when I entered my house. It is difficult to come home to an empty house after such a fun-filled experience. I shook it off and made preparation for a shrimp boil I was planning the next weekend. I talked to one of the other girls who had gone to the conference and found that the three of us who were single felt the let-down. We felt a sadness for an entire week that others did not feel.

The melancholy lifted for me during the shrimp boil preparation. Brent called a few days before the weekend. I had not heard from him in months, so I was surprised. I asked him if he wanted to meet me at Safe Harbor Fish Market, where I was planning to pick up the shrimp for the boil. He agreed. We would have a beer there and go our separate ways. I had a lot to do that evening to prepare for the next night's shrimp feast. I also found myself struggling through what I had assumed was another Mr. Grief attack. Meeting him would be a diversion.

Brent showed up within minutes after my arrival. I ordered four and a half pounds of shrimp and went out to my car to get the Styrofoam ice chest. Brent got us a table and ordered two beers.

I went to pay for the shrimp, but I realized I had not asked them to separate the half-pound I needed for a shrimp dip. I had no idea how many shrimps were in a half-pound, and I asked the cashier if she knew. She had no idea and directed me to a worker standing behind the fish counter. I walked over and asked him. He did not know either. I was taken aback. Surely, he had some idea. I needed four pounds for the shrimp boil, so I only needed to separate out the half-pound. He said he would measure it out for me, and he would do that after he finished with a customer.

I walked back to the cashier to get the bag of shrimp I had left there and stopped at the table where Brent was sitting. I looked at him and said, "He has to measure out a half-pound for me—I forgot to ask to have it separated out."

Brent looked at me and said, "He must think you are a pain in the ass." Brent had used "ass" before in conversations with me. And while I am not a prude, I would think that a guy would be on his best behavior in the beginning of whatever this was. I could not use the term relationship, but friendship at least seemed to apply. I was surprised to hear those words, but just made light of it, made a face at him, and walked away smiling.

After the half-pound of shrimp was separated out, I placed the two bags of shrimp into the ice chest. I halfway wondered if Brent would jump up from the table and help me carry it out to the car. He did not. Maybe he was not the gentleman I first labeled him to be.

When I returned, we made small talk. We drank our beer and departed. He gave me a hug when I left, but I knew I was over it. This man must see women as pains in the asses, I told myself. That has nothing to do with me—he has been hurt or been in relationships or a relationship that was not fulfilling. I know women can be a pain, but he did not know me, and I did not want to be judged from his smoke-colored viewpoint. I thought I had left the pain-attraction behind me. I just wanted to live in the present and accept what life was now handing me. I also just wanted to be accepted for me, not lumped into someone's negative perception of women. I am not a pain in the ass, but I am sure I have been, I told myself. *This is not good for me*, I thought as I drove away.

I was never stressed that night while I was making the preparations. I played music and thoroughly enjoyed setting my table with lighthouses, shrimp boats, shells with tea lights in them, and netting.

The evening of the dinner I put on my overalls in Mike's memory—he wore overalls frequently when we were married and while he was in college. I was having a Lowcountry shrimp boil, and I was dressed the part. I welcomed my six lady guests and showed my appreciation for the friendships we had developed over the past two years.

When I dropped the seasonings into the boiling water, I knew I was going to burn my guests' eyes. This was Mike's recipe, and we always had to open the windows in the past. We had finally bought an outdoor cooker, but I sadly did not know how to use it. My guests had to retreat to the Florida room to get away from the stinging fumes. I could see the trepidation on their faces.

I laughed, "Don't worry. It will be delicious, I promise you." Mike had never failed it, and I wasn't going to either.

After the potatoes and corn cooked, it was time to drop in the shrimp. Somehow, I felt Mike's presence. I felt it in that moment like I had the night before as I busied myself and recalled the nights he and I had undertaken the shrimp boil preparations together. My friend Dawn walked up right after I dropped the shrimp into the water. I knew Mike had always said they only needed to cook a minute and that three minutes was too long. Everyone made that mistake he had said. "As soon as they turn pink, they need to come out." That only took seconds. I grabbed the pot holders and prepared to lift the cooking pot and carry it to the sink where I had two large strainers waiting.

Dawn said, "It needs to cook for three minutes."

"No," I replied, "you should take it out when it turns pink."

"It needs to cook a little longer," she said emphatically.

"No, really. That is when it gets rubbery." I kept hearing in my head, "Take it out!" Mike had told me about the one-minute cooking rule the first time we made our experimental shrimp boil. He had gotten the recipe from a man who had told him it was done when it turned pink. I had only just put it in that first time, and I had always been told to cook it three minutes. "Take it out," he kept saying. After less than a minute that first time, I had relinquished. It was perfect then, and I wanted it to be perfect now.

Take it out, I heard again in my head. *Take it out*! Dawn was trying to stop me, and when I heard "take it out" again, I quickly whipped the pot off the stove and tossed the contents into the strainers sitting in the sink. I felt immediate relief, and I knew I had grabbed it just in time. Again, it was perfect. I knew Mike wanted it to be a successful dinner, and I knew he was helping me. After all, I had asked for his help the night before.

Interestingly, when another friend left later that evening, she said to me, "Mike is so proud of you. I feel his presence tonight, here in your house, and he is so proud of you. You did a great job, and everything was perfect." It was nice to hear expressed by someone else what I was feeling inside. Mike *was* proud of me. That friend had lost her daughter to brain cancer, so she was more open to the possibility of our loved ones' spirits being around us.

Brent texted the following day and asked how it went. I texted him back and told him it went very well and that I had shrimp for him. I offered to meet him halfway. He had told me the day before that he was going to get his children later in the afternoon, so I had offered to take shrimp to him and suggested the possibility of a picnic. I had not meant "picnic" in the total sense of having a basket and spreading out a blanket, I had merely offered him food. However, he texted that he needed to go get his children earlier and would not be able to meet me. I thought it was his loss, as the shrimp was delicious. I did not really care to see him.

I never heard from him again, and it was just as well, as I was questioning who might be the real pain in the ass.

CHAPTER 36

TREATS FOR VETERANS

Thanksgiving and Christmas had come and gone. Eric and Jamie joined Aly, Lindsey, and me at Thanksgiving, and we truly loved being together. Eric admitted to having anxiety attacks, and we talked about what that might mean. I told him anxiety was sometimes a manifestation of repressed memories and that I had a theory about anxiety. What if we had anxiety because we knew somehow on a deeper level something bad was going to happen in our lives, and the anxiety was there as part of the repression of that knowledge?

I told Eric and Jamie about a speech and language therapist I had worked with seventeen years ago. Janet told me she sometimes felt this wave of panic and anxiety when she was sitting in her den with her husband, watching TV. She would jump up at these times and wring her hands, "What is this!?" She would tell her husband about the anxiety attack and be bewildered by it. As far as she knew there was no reason for it.

Just within six months of telling me this, Janet's husband was in a critical car accident. He was left a quadriplegic.

I related my own story to Eric and Jamie. I had felt anxiety and sometimes panic attacks over the years. I felt my first anxiety within months of marrying my husband. Every ten years I would go through a period of several weeks of extreme anxiety. When my father died in February 2004, I felt heightened anxiety during the days I was with him. I had been by his bedside for the first two days after I flew into Arkansas from Florida. I felt a spiritual connection with him that I had not previously experienced, and I had a distant, obscure sense of the other realm to which he was about to return. I did not sleep the two nights I was in the hospital, and I went to my mother's house to rest on the third day.

During the hours he lay dying, while I was away from his bedside, I felt my anxiety peaking. I did not know he was breathing his last breaths. The family tried to call me but could not get through. I, in the meantime, was trying to let him go. I finally managed to do that. I received a call from my niece an hour later, and she told me Dad had "passed an hour ago." They had tried several times to call me to let me know he was dying.

I had not felt that heightened anxiety since then. I did feel anxiety regarding my husband's leaving me and the ensuing events, but I knew something was unfolding that I had no control over, and I had to let it happen. I may have been anxious, but the anxiety was lessened because of my experience with my dad, and a deep sadness had replaced it.

Eight days after that talk with Eric and Jamie, Eric's father was killed in a car accident. He had a heart attack. It was a complete shock to all of Eric's family, and Eric was devastated. He had become very close to his dad, and he was not prepared for such news. Jamie and Eric left for Dallas, Texas the next day.

While they were in Texas, Jamie received calls from many of her friends: "What the hell, Jamie!? How does this happen?" "How many twenty-nine-year-olds lose their fathers?" "For you both to have lost your dads so early in life …" Everyone was echoing these sentiments. My heart was broken for my daughter's boyfriend and for what my daughter was facing once more in her young life.

I mentally reviewed the sad events of the recent past. First my dad, Jamie's maternal grandfather, died in 2004. Then Mike's dad, her paternal grandfather, died in 2005. Then Mike, her father, left me in 2006. Then he died in 2007. Now, Eric's dad was deceased in 2008. I was bewildered. I had no idea what my daughter was feeling. I did know, however, that Eric was lucky to have her by his side. She knew what he was going through. She had been through it.

Christmas had been a quiet one. Jamie and Eric returned to Dallas ten days after Eric's father's funeral to have Christmas with Eric's family. It was a very sad Christmas for them, and Jamie's cell phone text messages to me indicated that.

A few days before the official start of the school holiday, it occurred to me that we did not have to wait to have a foundation before we did anything for the military. The girls and I had been talking about starting a foundation after their father died so that we could possibly help other soldiers who were having symptoms of post-traumatic stress disorder and feeling the woes of depression and alcoholism. We were hoping to prevent others from going down the road to suicide. We saw suicide as a particular issue for the military.

What about holiday gift bags with home-baked goods for the soldiers? I was struck by the thought. The girls were consulted and thought it sounded great. Lindsey came home from FSU for the holiday, and she received her first assignment as event planner and fundraiser designee. She made the arrangements, and the project was on.

Before I left school for the two-week holiday, I sent an email and asked teachers not to throw out any baked goods or candy. I would take them off their hands. I told them what we were doing. The response was gratifying. We had a huge box full of chocolates, Hershey kisses, candy canes, and other great filler items to go with the baked treats. Another teacher offered me baggies and lunch bags. She had more than she needed, and I took them gratefully.

Aly, Lindsey, and their friends decorated brown lunch bags the weekend before Christmas. We planned to distribute them on Tuesday, December 23. While they were busy with their project, I started making candies and cookies. I made three batches each of four different kinds of holiday treats. After twelve batches, I thought, *I need help with this.* My goal was to have two hundred holiday bags. At this rate, I would be lucky to have one hundred.

I sent emails to my bridge group and my book club. I wanted to send emails to my Bible study group, but I did not have their email addresses on my home computer. Three individuals replied and brought more goodies. I put a copy of the email into five of my closest neighbors' mailboxes, and two responded. The holiday treats were multiplying in front of my very eyes. I was joyful.

I went to Winn Dixie and Publix supermarkets and asked for donations, and they both donated twenty dollars to the cause. That helped with some of the expenses of the ingredients needed for baking, and it enabled me to buy more "filler."

The night before the big day, I had help from two of my neighbors who were stuffing bags, while the girls plodded on with decorating the holiday treat bags. I have to say they were quite artistic, and the bags were festive. After adding home-baked goodies and the filler items, we added a note, "Thank you for all of your sacrifices. You are our heroes."

Lastly, we added red or green Christmas tissue, which stuck out of the top of the bag.

Jenny, for whose children Lindsey babysat, called and said she had cookies for us. We had filled 140 bags, and I thought it was over. It was after ten p.m., and we were due at the VA clinic the next afternoon at one o'clock. I drove to Jenny's house the next morning and found to my surprise a large garbage bag full of cookies already packaged and ready to go. That was from Jenny's neighbor, and Jenny also had a large supply of brownies. I rushed home with my treasures.

It was eleven a.m., and we wanted to leave at twelve o'clock to get to the VA clinic on time. The girls were instructed to decorate more bags—I had called them when I saw the amount Jenny had for us. Aly, Lindsey, and Lindsey's friend Casey were busy with the bags when I arrived home. I started filling the decorated bags, knowing we were racing the clock.

A friend of Jenny's came over, who was planning to play the guitar and sing Christmas songs at the clinic while we handed out holiday bags. He joined in and helped fill more bags. Finally, at ten after twelve I said, "We have to go." We gathered up all the shopping bags and boxes filled with goody bags, and the girls brought their supplies to continue decorating bags and filling them with the brownies and cookies that were left in the garbage bag.

It was a forty-minute drive to the VA clinic, and they were able to finish. When all was said and done, we had about 180 or more festive treat bags to hand out. A golf cart pulled up to our van just after we parked in the VA parking lot and offered us a ride to the door. Somehow, we managed to put all the bags, the guitar, and ourselves into the cart. We were all giddy by then, and we felt good about what we were doing.

I spoke to the VA clinic representative that Lindsey had contacted, and she voiced her appreciation of what we were doing. "You know, people used to do this all the time. I am glad to see it is starting up again." I vowed we would do it again next year.

We were directed where to go, and the girls offered the colorful Christmas bags to all the service members seated in the waiting room. Aly started giving bags to the workers, and more workers came for them. A lot of the workers were military veterans, so we were happy to give them treats. Several people asked us who we were with. I was glad we were not with any organization. We simply told them we were an American family, wanting to show our appreciation to the military for what they had done for us. The girls were quick to tell the veterans who thanked them, "No, this is our thanks to you. Thank you for all you have done for America."

An administrator walked out and told us, "All the veterans here are in need of medical care, but what they really need is what you ladies provided today and that was to know that people care."

My heart was swelling with pride for how my daughters were handling this. I thought they were Santa's helpers that day for sure. One of the nurses walked out of a room and corrected what I was thinking. "Look at all of the angels," she said.

CHAPTER 37

SEARS SOLDIER

Earlier in the month I had made a trip to Sears to exchange a camera, and I found myself engaged in a conversation with a soldier who had been to Iraq four times. His PTSD symptoms were evident. He confirmed for me that our foundation was needed, and we had to help these American heroes.

I met Jason on December 12, 2008, when he was working the cash register at Sears. I don't know why I asked him if he was a soldier, but he confirmed that he was, and then he told me about his four deployments to Iraq. I asked him, "How are you doing this? How are you here with shoppers all around you and what appears normal but for you so very different from that experience in Iraq?"

He looked at me. His face remained expressionless.

I asked again, "How are you doing this?" I waved my hand around the department store and pointed out the shoppers who were doing their normal—picking up a piece of merchandise and looking at it and setting it down, then picking up another one and so on.

I continued, "I can imagine you doing the army crawl across a sandy desert land, lugging your gun beside you, dragging your body along the ground with your heavy backpack on top of you, swatting at the bugs and desert creatures that were trying to make a home on you, and sweating profusely." I asked again, "How are you doing this?"

Jason told me how he was doing this. He described symptoms such as not being able to sleep, feeling jumpy and over-alert, being always watchful of people around him, and the list went on. His descriptions suggested a general hypervigilance. I talked to him about PTSD and that what he was describing sounded like symptoms of it. I added, "You guys were over there in a war zone, with military fatigues and guns all around you. You come home, and people don't understand what you just went through. You feel different—you don't even know how to act."

He said, "Yeah, when we set foot on American soil, I looked at the guys around me and said, 'What do we do now?'" It was a rhetorical question. He did not expect an answer.

Jason told me that right after he came home was the worst time. Sleep problems were worse. He said, "It has gotten better, but not completely better." He told me it had been two years since he had left Iraq, and he still did not feel right. "I have memories I try to keep out of my head, and I do okay when I am around people at Sears, but it is worse when I am at home." I found out he lived alone.

"I bet you have the TV or music on all of the time when you are at home so you can keep those thoughts out." I looked at him. He looked at me in wonderment, as he sensed that I understood. I was merely putting into words what I thought he was feeling. I had not been there—how could I possibly understand?

I told Jason about my husband. I didn't bother to say he was my ex-husband. I told him Mike had come home and had turned to drugs and alcoholism as an escape. He would not talk about his days in Vietnam. He had been a medic, and he had seen the worst. He interjected, "Yeah. You would not believe the things we saw." He shook his head ruefully. I told him my girls and I wanted to help vets when they returned home.

"What happened when you first came home?" I asked, speaking softly.

"Well, they talked to us, and they gave us a phone number to call if we felt we were feeling …" He could not say the words.

"Have you called it?" I asked gently.

"No," he replied. "I don't even know if I still have it."

"Didn't they talk to you about what to expect? How you might feel?"

"No, they never told us any of this stuff." He was referring to the PTSD symptoms he was experiencing.

Maybe they had told him, but he was still in a fog when he came home, and he had left a part of himself in Iraq. He could not process everything he was encountering once he touched American soil. How could he leave that war-filled territory and enter "normalcy" as he had known it? I told him he was experiencing a loss, and he was grieving. "You lost a sense of what you had before; your view of the world as you had always known it had changed. You were around killing and things that were not previously a part of your view of the world—it was hard to come back to this."

I waved my arm around the Sears store and the people who were walking around. Shopping for God's sake. How discrepant was that from what he had experienced in Iraq?

He fixed his empty eyes on me. I felt an urge to help him but didn't know how.

"So, what did you need when you first came home? My girls and I want to help. Did you need money to buy clothes to wear on a job interview? Did you need money for the first month's rent? What did you need?" I asked again.

He answered slowly and seemed to have trouble talking and responding, as though he were in a fog. Or on drugs. "They give you a sum of money, and you walk around in a haze until all your money is spent."

He looked at me, still trying to comprehend what he was seeing and hearing. "What about you? Are you okay?" I ignored his question. This was not about me. I told him my husband had returned from Vietnam and had tried to manage for thirty-six years, but he just could not do it anymore and died at his own hand.

The Sears soldier did not react to what I said. Maybe he did not understand what I meant. I said, "At least your group was not ridiculed. The Vietnam vets were laughed at and ridiculed. No one was at the airport to applaud them."

"Yeah," he said, staring off. "That was strange. Being in the airport and people walking around as though nothing had happened."

"I hope people applauded you," I said. "I tried to do that one time, but one of my kids stopped me and said, 'Don't. That's embarrassing.' I said to her, 'No, we should applaud them.'"

He said, "A few women clapped when we walked by, but I think they were military wives." I wondered how they would have felt if civilians who did not have a personal interest applauded them. What an impact that would have made.

"Did your husband talk about it?" he asked me.

"No, I tried to get him to, but he said I could not possibly understand, and no one could possibly relate to what he had seen and done. 'You have no idea,' he said to me. He would not talk about it. He went through life unhappy and depressed, he turned to alcohol, and he eventually killed himself." I thought I needed to be more straightforward with Mike's suicide, but the soldier still showed no reaction to what I said. I left it alone.

I asked him, "Would it have helped you to talk about it with other soldiers who had been through the same thing?" He did not answer. He was staring off again, and he just seemed to be in a fog. I did not want to trigger any memory that was too painful.

"I don't want to scare you," I said, "and I know you are okay." I repeated with emphasis, "You are okay." I added, "You guys are so strong, and you did so much for us and for our country, but trauma can change the brain, and PTSD is not a sign of weakness. Your brain actually changes, and you really have to process it. It is still in there."

I was thinking that he does not know what feeling happy is like anymore since he does not feel happiness. He looked lost. I knew he needed help. I asked for his phone number, and I asked him to call that number he had received. "It could be a military guy on the other end of the line who has been through what you have been through, and you might be able to talk to him."

"What would have helped you or what has helped you since you have been home?" I asked.

"You want to know what has helped me more than anything this two years I have been back?" He jabbed his index finger onto the countertop and tapped it once for each of the next three words. "This right here." He leaned over the countertop toward me and said, "Your talking to me and telling me what you just told me. I have not talked about this to anyone, and I have said more right now than I have ever said to anyone."

I was stunned. Speechless. I looked at him, but no words came to me.

I knew he had a lot inside of him that needed to get out, and I wondered why he had not sought help. It seemed he did not know that what he was feeling was a natural reaction to an awful, traumatic experience.

Finally, I said, "You know what I hope to see? A psychologist or a therapist who does successful post-traumatic stress disorder treatment with soldiers, standing in front of an audience of soldiers who have just returned from deployment and doing a presentation that talks about what could help them."

He jumped onto my words and became animated. "I think *you* can do that! I know how you can reach a large number—at Mayport Naval Base and Norfolk Naval Base. Lots of soldiers come home and land there. If you had a presentation set up, they could come in and hear it. You would reach a lot of them."

This was out of my league. Surely the military does this debriefing when the soldiers come home. I knew they did, but the newness of being back in America was too much. I imagined that returning soldiers had difficulty processing their first encounters with U.S military psychological exercises and needed those presentations repeated often. I was sure they were repeated, but somehow Jason had gotten lost.

I wondered if the vets would benefit if a small group of them with like experiences gathered together with a vet volunteer who could facilitate discussions and allow them to talk about their time in the war. They could also talk about their experience since they returned from the war. Talking about it could maybe help them become whole again. I could see this guy was feeling fragmented.

I tried to figure out what I had said or had done that had helped him. Seeing someone who cared and who wanted to reach out to him? Hearing terminology for feelings he was experiencing and realizing he was not going crazy—that these were a part of a normal reaction to what he had been through? Hearing in words the dichotomy between where he had been and what he had seen compared to where he was now and what he was seeing—two separate worlds that his brain could not wrap around?

As I walked out of Sears, I thought back to my long drive to the mall where the Sears store is located. I was juking to music playing on the car radio, and I was feeling happy aa I thought of Mike. "You know I miss you, Mike," I had said aloud, perhaps feeling a little guilty that I could feel happiness. I then thought it would be nice to get a message from him through a song, but immediately dismissed the thought. My attention was alerted, however, when I heard the first few words of the next song. I usually never hear the lyrics—I only hear the music—but the words of "Babe" by Styx drew my attention. I knew this song was meant for me, but as I listened, I wondered who was giving whom "the courage and the strength."

After the song ended, I thanked God for sending those words to me. I had felt they were words Mike would have wanted me to hear. I had carried those words with me as I stepped out of my vehicle and headed toward the Sears building. It was only then, as I was walking through the front door, that I realized he and I were giving each *other* "the courage and the strength."

Now, as I got back into my car, I wanted to hear another song confirming what had just occurred. I did not give it a lot of thought (as had happened before), but I was again drawn to the next song that played on the radio and particularly the words that involved saving a life.

When I told my daughter Jamie about my whole experience with the soldier and the songs, she said, "Mom, maybe he was thinking about suicide. Maybe you saved him from that. You gave him hope. You showed you cared. You talked to him about it where no one else ever has. You will probably never know how much you helped him."

"I don't know about that," I said, "but that song did come on right after I left him."

I thought for a few seconds then said, "You know what? It starts with the small things, Jamie. We have talked about so many things we want to do. We see the big picture and the ultimate organization, but how does it all begin? I have wondered about that. Well, it started tonight. If we have helped just one, we have helped one. That is more than what would have happened if your dad had not gone through what he went through and left us with this to do. We have made one small start."

CHAPTER 38

THE BEST YEAR EVER

I continued to feel the joy I felt during the holidays while baking goodies and assembling Christmas treat bags and delivering them to the vet clinic. I was glad we were able to show our appreciation to veteran soldiers and let them know we cared. I took a prettily wrapped plate of goodies to Jason, the Sears soldier, but he was not there. I left it for him. I was told he would be back the next day, Christmas Eve. I tried to see him the first week of January, but he was not there then either. I wished I knew how to eradicate his PTSD and give him back his life.

A wonderful New Year began when I went with my friend Jane to a New Year's Eve party. I found I was very comfortable with everyone. Some of the couples had been friends of Mike's and mine just after we moved to Ponte Vedra Beach in 1991. One couple had moved away five years before and had just moved back. The wife gave me a hug. She told me how she had remembered Mike's smile and his sparkling blue eyes, and when she heard how he left me, she said she told her husband, "Something is wrong. He is sick. He would never leave Marti. He loved her and those girls." We talked about that, and I was glad to see there were others who saw his sickness as well.

Most of Mike's golf-playing friends were mad at him when he left me. Even though they saw a change in him, they thought he had control over what he was doing. They only saw how really sick he was when he committed his last act. Others saw it at the outset. I had seen it before he even left me. I knew some of them were carrying guilt about how they reacted to him, but I also knew there was no way they would know how broken he was. There was absolutely nothing any of them could have done that would have made any difference. I had held conversations with some of them after Mike's death, and it always made me sad to hear them say how bad they felt. They wished they had reached out to him. I pray they can find their peace with all of it.

It was a new year. I declared to my three daughters that this would be our best year ever. I made plans to spend Valentine's Day in Chicago where Jamie and Eric lived. I had a free companion ticket and was planning to ask a friend to go with me. She and I had gone to dinner the last two Valentine's Days, so it was only fitting to ask her.

Eric called after I told Jamie I was booking a flight and said, "That is great, Marti! You can come to the party I am throwing after I take Jamie out to dinner and ask her to marry me."

"What!? Oh my gosh, Eric. I'm ecstatic! Of course, I want to be there!" I started to say more, but he was at work and needed to go. The engagement and party were to be a surprise for Jamie.

Eric had already told me the previous summer he was going to ask Jamie to marry him, and he did not really need my permission. I told him I was happy he would be my son-in-law. I did not know when the engagement would take place. He didn't either at the time.

After I hung up, I thought to heck with my friend and immediately called Aly, who would take the companion ticket. I called Lindsey, who also wanted to go, and I called Jamie a few days later. "Hi, honey. My friend had a conflict at the last minute, so Aly is coming with me."

Jamie asked, "What about Lindsey? She might want to come also."

"Oh yeah, I probably should ask her," I said.

This was turning out perfectly. Jamie suggested Lindsey should also go, and I knew Jamie would have no idea we had all already made plans to be there. This would be our first celebratory family event since Mike's death. Jamie had no idea—she thought we were simply spending Valentine's Day with her.

I called Jamie a week later and told her Lindsey was flying with us. Jamie suspected nothing. The trip just evolved.

We spent the first day in Chicago with Eric; he took us to Millennium Park and we snapped pictures under Cloud Gate, the mirrored sculpture that is shaped like a bean. We marveled at the faces on the tall, glass block towers at Crown Fountain and laughed as the water spouted from their open mouths.

Eric took us to a late lunch at The Signature Room at the 95th atop the John Hancock Center. The view was spectacular, and the food was delicious. We had lots of laughs, and we acknowledged a shared excitement about the upcoming surprise.

Jamie joined us that evening. She had been working out of town. Eric was a great host; he was entertaining and considerate, and he was wanting all of us to have a good time. He took us to a pool bar down the street from his apartment, and we played pool and danced to the music playing in the background. It was ironic that Beyonce's "Single Ladies" played on the jukebox several times. All three girls did the up and down dance motions each time that part of the song played.

We relaxed the next day and enjoyed our time together. There was lots of laughter. Eric told Jamie he wanted to have a private Valentine's dinner, and he sent Jamie's sisters and me to Carmine's on Rush Street.

Jamie told us later that Eric had made previous arrangements with the waitstaff, and they all knew he was going to ask her to marry him. They were witnesses, and of course, she said "yes." There was applause all around. The evening was flawless. The engagement party was held in a section of a very elegant bar, and it was a true celebration. Eric had invited approximately thirty guests, including the three of us, and Jamie was beside herself with excitement. She wanted that commitment from Eric, and she was thrilled to be engaged.

Plus, she was now eligible to accompany him to Cabo San Lucas, Mexico. He was awarded a trip to Cabo every spring, and he was only allowed to take a wife, parent, sibling, or fiancée. She thought he was taking his sister on the March trip, and she was not happy. She did not know he had already planned to make her his fiancée, and he was taking her. We celebrated into the early morning hours. It was the first of one of our happiest times since their father's death.

The next few months passed, and we found ourselves facing the two-year anniversary of Mike's death. All three of my daughters came home, and we spent an enjoyable weekend with each other. We rode bikes in Jacksonville Beach, reminiscent of the days following Mike's death when we all rode bikes down the streets in Jacksonville Beach, not knowing what else to do with ourselves the day after Mike's funeral. We dined out, laughed together, and tightened the bond that encircled us.

Another month passed. Eric gave Jamie a puppy, an English bulldog, and Jamie fell in love with her cute pug-faced Jamieson. Jamie was excited to be accepted into the Kellogg School of Management at Northwestern University. She was happy to be getting her MBA.

Aly passed a telephone interview and accepted an internship position with the Baltimore Ravens. She was near the end of her post-graduate coursework in athletic administration, and she was excitedly making plans to do an internship in Maryland for six weeks, starting mid-July.

Lindsey accepted a twelve-week internship with a nonprofit organization in Tallahassee and started work immediately. She told me a former pro ballplayer gave a presentation during a staff meeting, and after she made a comment, he walked over to her and told her she was very intuitive. I was not surprised, as she was my "in the moment" daughter. Her supervisor and several other staff members told her they wanted to meet her mother. I thought that was odd, but when I did have a chance to visit Lindsey in Tallahassee, she took me to her office.

Staff members were leaving their offices to come out into the hall to greet me. I felt like a celebrity's mother. One of the administrators took me aside and said, "We love Lindsey. She is nice, she is cute, and she is capable. We have never told an intern before that we wanted to meet her mother. We have been so impressed with her, we just had to meet the mother who raised her."

I was flattered … every mother's dream.

Aly was able to find a lovely couple in Westminster, Maryland, who was more than happy to rent an apartment to her for the six weeks she would be there. Mr. and Mrs. Johnson were avid Ravens fans and were delighted to rent space to an intern who would be working at the Ravens' training camp. They told her if she ever needed anything while she was there to let them know. That certainly made me feel better about her being that far from home.

Yes, it was turning out to be our best year ever!

I saw Jason, the Sears soldier, again in August. I told him about the Wounded Warrior Project, a veteran service organization that was founded in 2003. He did not know about it. I also told him the Veterans Administration offered help, and he said he went to the VA for his medical needs. I was glad to hear that. Maybe they would see his PTSD symptoms and make recommendations. He told me he would investigate the Wounded Warrior Project. I prayed he would get the help he seemed to need.

Later that summer I met a new hire, Michelle, who joined our group of school psychologists. I did not find out until the fall that she had been married to a service man who had been deployed to Iraq during their first year of marriage. He was killed days before he was to return home. They were only married one year. I could not imagine her grief, but I had some knowledge of it. I thought of all that she had lost—her future with him, her dreams of having his children, her vow to have him in her life forever for better or for worse. My heart ached for her. She was only twenty-nine years old.

Michelle and I had many conversations. We seemed to feel the other had some understanding of our individual grief. I told her there would be a day when she did not feel the pain she was experiencing, and she had to believe that. "One day you will look back on all of this, and you will be amazed that you are as happy as you are. You will have someone else in your life, and you will have a family. You have to believe it will not always be the way it is now."

I knew those words were true for me, and they were true for her if she believed them. I knew I would not be having children with someone else, but I would embrace his family.

Michelle accompanied me to an Out of the Darkness community walk in Jacksonville Beach later that fall. I was so grateful for her friendship. I was astounded by the number of people who showed up who were survivors of suicide loss. We survivors were given specific tags to hang around our necks. Others had tags that showed they were friends of survivors. Michelle was given the "friend" tag.

The objective of the Out of the Darkness community walks is to raise awareness and to also provide funding to the American Foundation for Suicide Prevention. The monies are used to fund new research, create educational programs, and advocate for public policy. Funding is also used to support survivors of suicide loss. One of the goals of the AFSP is to reduce the annual suicide rate. I was happy when my daughters told me they participated in an Out of the Darkness community walk a month later in Chicago.

Another December was soon upon us. My daughters, Jamie's fiancé, Eric, and his sister were spending Christmas in my home. We again made plans to take Christmas treat bags to the VA clinic. We made a change from brown to white lunch bags. I approached the staff in my three schools where I was providing psychological services at the time. Some of the teachers were looking for projects and volunteered their classes for decorating the bags. The middle school became involved in the bag decorating as well, thanks to my friend, Jody, who was a teacher there. It was quite a project.

Aly and Lindsey came in from Tallahassee and Orlando, respectively, the day before we took treat bags to the clinic. They helped with the cooking, baking, and filling of bags. Friends joined us, and by the end of the night, we had 240 treat bags ready. Jamie flew in the morning of the event, and we carried the decorative bags to the clinic. Once again, we were honored to show our appreciation to our wonderful military men and women. Once again, we were overjoyed.

I did not realize the impact of our small act of appreciation until I saw the following article in *The Florida Times-Union*, a Jacksonville newspaper:

Children a Blessing to Vets

Raves to the dear public school children in the area of Ponte Vedra. They individually decorated lunch bags with holiday messages for the veterans, filled the bags with homemade cookies and candies and had some volunteers walk this morning through the waiting room of the veterans clinic in Jacksonville. You should have seen the smile on some of the pain-filled weary faces of our veterans as they were given a bag. A little note inside thanked the veterans for what they had done and believe me (as a veteran's wife), this meant so much to my husband. To think of others is the greatest measure of a civilized society.

The article made my heart sing. We were making a difference for our wonderful service members.

I had planned a party on December 27 for my daughters, for all the successes they had achieved during the year and for Jamie and Eric's engagement. It had been a wonderful year, the best year ever, and we needed to celebrate it. A friend knew a chef who catered. I hired him, and he did an excellent job. The food was incredible, and the party was a success. While I was celebrating all of them and their achievements, I was also celebrating the fact that the four of us were healing.

CHAPTER 39

AND THE BLESSINGS FLOW

As wonderful as 2009 had been, I knew that 2010 was going to be even better, 2011 better than that, and so it would go. I was at peace. I do not know when it happened, but I felt an inner excitement that was inexplicable. It followed me and hinted at great things to come. I anticipated wonderful blessings, and I looked forward to each day.

One of the first blessings occurred when I was able to attend my beautiful mother's ninetieth birthday celebration. She had a birthday full of surprises, and all ten of her children were there to celebrate it with her.

The following month yielded other celebratory events. Jamie was honored with two bridal showers, and she had her bachelorette party in Miami. I attended all three events, and I was always amazed at the happiness. It had been three years since Mike died. His death was tragic, and I had been told by several therapists that it takes five years to get over a suicide. I had worked hard, and I had grieved hard. Now I was glad there was so much to be happy about.

I felt the pain again on the anniversary of Mike's death, but three days later I was again experiencing an inner excitement that I could not explain. I wondered if "the one" was soon coming into my life. I decided I did not have to have that grand romance yet—I just wanted a boyfriend.

A week later I understood why I had been having the sensation of inner excitement. I met the love of my life, Jim, on May 29, but that is an entirely different story.

Three weeks after I met Jim, Jamie and Eric had their wedding in Lake Tahoe. It was the second family celebration without my daughters' father. It was a happy, joyful occasion, and I felt both fathers' ghostly presence during the wedding ceremony. I knew Eric's dad and Mike wanted us all to be happy.

The reception was enchanting, and when it was time for the father-daughter dance, the beaming bride led her sisters and me to the dance floor. We did not know what to expect—we only knew we would be having a family dance—but when we heard the opening guitar riff in "Bad to the Bone," we all looked at each other and laughed. Granted, it was not an easy song to dance to, and it was long! When the song finally ended, we hugged each other gleefully and laughed all the way back to our respective tables.

The blessings continued, and in the late spring of 2011 Jamie and Eric announced they were going to have a baby in December. We awaited the arrival of the first little baby in our small family. The day arrived, and Jamie and Eric were the proud parents of a sweet baby boy, my first grandchild. My daughters and I were all starting a new chapter in our lives, and we were adopting new roles: mother, aunts, grandmother.

We took a picture shortly after Jamie and Eric arrived home from the hospital, and in the picture my girls and I are all surrounding this little one while Jamie is cradling him in her arms. The joy on our faces cannot be denied. Somehow, when I look at the five of us in that picture, I feel we have come full circle; the ends of the circle have reconnected.

I continued to feel the blessings, and life was wonderful. I had never felt this way before. Six months after my grandson was born, we had a small reunion at the cabin on Mount Nebo. All three girls, along with their boyfriends, husband, and baby, were able to be there. Jim was with us—he and I had been together for a little over two years. The guys met both grandmothers and lots of aunts, uncles, and cousins. It was a joyful family gathering.

Jamie, Eric, the baby, my sister Carol and her husband, Norman, stayed at the cabin on the evening of July Fourth, while the rest of us went to Sunset Point to catch the sunset. I had begged Jamie and Eric to go with us, as this was a traditional ritual. I prepared the customary mountain margaritas, and the rest of us took off in Jim's SUV, with margarita glass in hand. We witnessed a wedding proposal on the south bluff as we were getting out of the SUV, and I knew Jamie and Eric would be disappointed when they heard what they had missed.

When we arrived back at the cabin, we found out they had a bear encounter! The bear ambled behind the cabin and crossed the area of the bluff where we had thrown Mike's ashes nearly five years earlier. As it entered the adjoining yard, it turned and looked back at the cabin. It then took a running leap and jumped up into one of the trees in the neighboring yard. Jamie said it was awesome. She knew she was supposed to see the bear instead of having gone to see the sunset. She knew the bear was meant for her. She knew her dad was at peace. Aly and Lindsey were upset they missed the bear, but they understood the significance of what had occurred and were able to draw from Jamie's experience and feel peacefulness.

Four years later my nephew visited me in Florida, and he asked me why Mike had not had the honor guard service. I did not know the answer, and that fall I made several calls to the Little Rock Air Force Base and found out it was doable. I completed the application and set the date for the following spring. I called the Veterans of Foreign Wars organization in Fort Smith, and they said they would be happy to do the gun volley at the honor guard service.

My children's father finally received the honor he deserved for his service as a medic in the Air Force and had an honor guard ceremony at the Fort Smith National Cemetery on May 19, 2017—ten years to the day after his death.

The two honor guard representatives were wearing meticulously clean Air Force uniforms, and they appeared very serious and very somber. They walked with slow, exacting movements, and every gesture was precisely made. They pre-folded three flags before the service and prepared to present one to my daughters. I was planning to give Mike's brother one of the flags. My two youngest daughters would keep the other two. Jamie already had the flag that was given unceremoniously to me at the funeral home days after Mike's funeral. Now, all three girls would have flags.

Mike's brother, John, started the service with a prayer, followed by the honor guard representatives who took the flag that was to be presented and again with slow, precise movements, they unfolded and then refolded the flag. One of the honor guard participants remained in front of the gathering with the folded flag laying on his outstretched hands. The second one walked slowly to the side with much pomp. Three uniformed VFW representatives then performed a three-volley gun salute. After the salute, the honor guard participant, who had been standing to the side, brought a bugle to his lips and played "Taps." His skill was incredible, as the piece was perfectly executed and beautifully played, and the melody brought tears to many of us. It was a very touching ceremony.

After "Taps," the honor guard participant who was standing in front of us carried the flag to my daughters and bent down with one knee. I noticed his knee did not touch the ground. He was in front of the middle daughter who was flanked on either side by a sister. I had informed him that although he would be presenting the flag to one person, the sisters beside her would extend their hands as well so that they all received the flag. They were all tearful when he placed the flag on their hands and looked into the middle girl's eyes and said, "On behalf of the President of the United States, the United States Air Force, and a grateful nation, please accept this flag as a symbol of our appreciation for your father's honorable and faithful service."

After he stood up, I whispered to my daughters to keep their position as I knew the VFW member would place three cartridges into the flag. The VFW representative walked toward them and stood in front of them and said, "I am sorry for your loss." He then presented the three cartridges that symbolized the three volleys that were fired during the ceremony and said, "I present three fired rounds in honor of faithful and honorable service." He then leaned down and inserted the three shells into the back fold of the flag that rested on my three daughters' hands. He straightened and walked away.

I watched my daughters' luminous faces, and I saw their proud acceptance of these tokens that represented their father's honorable service. I also discerned in their acceptance of the tokens, they were accepting the connection between his faithful service and how he lived his life afterward. I could not have been prouder of his and my three remarkable daughters as I sat and witnessed their ability to accept, comprehend, love, and forgive.

The memorial director stepped up and stated, "That concludes this service."

I called the VFW representative later to ask about the symbolism. He told me the firing of three volleys was representative of traditional battle ceasefires where each side cleared the dead, and the firing indicated the dead were cleared and properly cared for. "Taps" was originally composed to signal lights out and was a traditional way to honor service members. It was played to honor the extinguishing of a life.

After the ceremony, I told my daughters a memorial stone would be placed in the memorial section of the Fort Smith National Cemetery. Mike was born in Fort Smith, so it was a fitting resting place for his memorial stone. The stone would include his name, rank, service, place of service, date of birth, and date of death. They were charged with identifying the last two lines to be engraved that would be special or meaningful to their father. They could not use punctuation.

The girls tossed ideas back and forth the day after the ceremony. We were staying in a spacious rented cabin on Mount Nebo, and John and Becky were at the family cabin. I let John know about the engraving and told him to send his ideas. He told me the girls could handle it, and they finally came to an agreement.

I was sitting in a rocking chair on the back porch of the cabin when Lindsey approached me. Her sisters were behind her. "Mom," Lindsey said, "we remember how happy you and Dad were when you danced together." Aly added, "That was the happiest I have ever seen Dad, when you were dancing in the street in Key West that summer, he was so happy!" Jamie agreed and said, "He loved to dance. Whenever we were all together at a party, he danced with each one of us. He loved twirling us around."

I smiled at the memory of their father dancing with me. Those were our better moments. He and I always had fun when we were able to do our version of a rock 'n roll/jitterbug mix. My smile broadened when I recalled each daughter's happy face when her father took her by the hand and led her to the dance floor at a wedding celebration or an anniversary event.

The girls told me what they decided, and my smile widened even more. The inscription on the memorial stone reads:

Keep on Dancing
Bear

CHAPTER 40

A DECADE OF DISCOVERY

I made it. And I now reflect on the last ten years and the circular route that I have taken to get to the point at which I believe I was always destined.

I am here at that chapter in my life that I started journeying toward ten years ago. I have spent a decade of my life, searching, yearning, believing, and eventually coming to this altered station in my life. All my life events have brought me to this place, and I would not be the same person without them. I can only credit my faith, my belief in a higher power, and my unwavering persistence as partial factors that guided me and enabled me to reach my destination. Additionally, I have talked to therapists, and I have read books that focused on relationships, grief, spirituality, and the Vietnam War so that I could glean a better understanding of myself, my marriage, his life, and my life while I walked down the crooked, thorny path of resolving my grief.

The first three years, when grief took over my life, were the most horrendous. I was initially in shock, and I was hurt. I became fragmented, and I became desperate. Thank goodness for girlfriends. I had an event in my life that was insurmountable, and I needed the companionship of other women. This was a time of need for me, and, although it was not intentional, I frequently surrounded myself with women. Women are wonderful caregivers. My good friends allowed me to express my feelings, and they gave me the support I needed. I could not have managed without them.

After I weathered those first years for which I was not at all prepared, I was intent on growing and becoming that improved person that was touted in the grief books I read. Between the covers of those books, I was given hope when I read that I would eventually make sense of my ex-husband's death and find meaning and purpose for an improved life, a life in which I would be a better person. I would be kinder, nicer, extra thoughtful, more real. I knew I had a long way to go, if I could even reach that point, and my therapy sessions with Dr. Lewis were invaluable.

I have learned so much. Dr. Lewis had asked me toward the end of our sessions, "What have you learned?" I went blank when she asked me, but I now know I have learned lifelong lessons.

Even now, I try to capture all that I have learned.

Life *is*. I had never accepted my life as it was; I always resisted what is. I resisted my job at times. I resisted my husband at all times. I even resisted the stage my children were in at the time. I could not wait until they reached the next stage, which I foolishly convinced myself would be a much easier stage for me to handle. Resist … resist … resist. I find I still have to constantly remind myself not to resist what is, and I keep working on accepting what is. "It is what it is." At the same time, I try to follow my mother's motto, "We make the most of it."

Live in the moment. I have finally learned to be present and to be in the moment. I find when I tune in to what is happening *now*, I am much more content and satisfied. I can complete a task and move on to another without the undue stress and strain to which I was previously accustomed. I can see the stack of incomplete work and know it will be done in due time. All I need to do is focus on the task at hand, and it gets done. I am probably more productive than I have ever been. That is hard to imagine, as my German heritage has always been in the background pushing me to be a hard worker.

People are who they are. Who are we to judge them? We try to judge them, and at times we hope to change them, but we should realize that we cannot change them into being what we want them to be. They simply are.

We are constantly trying to change another human being when we try to tell them to do things our way. If it is truly important to us and they don't make the attempt to make a change, we wind up hurt, and we do not feel they truly love us. We don't really see them as separate entities. We see them as extensions of ourselves, and we expect them to behave as we would in any given situation. That is insanity. They are who they are. They are not us.

I did this not only with my husband but also with my daughters. I saw them as extensions of myself until the day I finally cut the apron strings. After my eldest daughter's wedding in Lake Tahoe, I knew it was time to let all three of them go. I can now let my three daughters make their own decisions without my hasty intervening. We can discuss matters without my thinking I know what is best for them. I know they are all on their own paths, and I know they will fall and pick themselves up at various intervals without my having to carry them. I let go of them without anyone telling me I needed to do that.

Some of us think we need to please—we seek approval and strive to live in a way to please others and to not hurt anyone. In all actuality, however, each of us has the freedom to do whatever we please. The truth of the matter is, we cannot hurt another person by our words or by our habits, and they cannot hurt us. I went for years feeling hurt because my husband did not live up to my expectations. He did not treat me the way I thought a husband should treat his wife. I made the choice to be hurt, and at times, I chose to hurt him in return. It was my decision. It was my choice. It really had nothing to do with him. The choice to be hurt was mine. Paradoxically, his behavior, his words, and his habits had nothing to do with me. They merely reflected his way of being.

When my husband of thirty-three years left me, it was his choice. I had no say in it. He was free to do whatever he wanted, just as I was free to do whatever I desired. Who gave me the right to be mad at him for the choice *he* made? What made me think I owned him? What made me think I could tell him what to do? I could not accept who he really was, and I resisted.

I now realize that not all men are alike. I was previously, and had always been, attracted to the man who met the need I had in myself: to be needed. I was also attracted to the unavailable man, the man with whom I did not have to worry about having a real relationship. I did not know what a good relationship looked like. I did not see it in my own parents. I had not experienced it myself in my marriage. The physical attraction was important and necessary, and at one time it was all I could relate to. How many times did I say, "You are too nice," during my dating years in college? I rejected the nice guy and sought the guy who apparently was more in tune with my view of myself: my poor self-esteem, my need for drama, my emotional ups and downs. Likes attract likes. As I write this, I don't even recognize the person I was.

Somehow, I have weathered a severe storm in my life (okay, maybe more than one), and I have come out of it more enlightened and more "real." I now know what is important in life. People are important. However, we also have a need to be true to ourselves. Trying to please others and trying to be for others what they may expect from us is not the way to travel. This behavior contributes to a false self-concept. Being true to ourselves is the most important. Being ourselves. Taking care of ourselves. Everything else will fall as it is supposed to. It will simply be. I have felt a greater connection to others during this process, as well as a greater connection with nature. I feel peaceful when I am out in nature. I feel peaceful when I remember my true self and my connection to all that is.

At the beginning of the tragic events I found myself facing ten years ago, a friend gave me "Symptoms of Inner Peace" by Saskia Davis. I was surprised that I did not have any of the twelve symptoms in my repertoire. I tackled each one, and I was determined that I would exhibit them all. However, I slipped very easily, and I had to remind myself more than I would like to admit. I still find myself resisting, but I am learning to let go and let life unfold as it should, without my opposing or trying to manipulate it in a way that fits my perception of how things should be.

I am codependent. I tend to take care of everyone else and lose myself in the process. However, I have often wondered who would have attempted to keep Mike on the right path if I had not kept trying. Maybe you find yourself in a similar situation. You love your partner, but you find yourself feeling frustrated time after time. You think he has a problem, and you try to help him, but he does not change. He keeps repeating the behavior you would like to see changed, a behavior that may mask even deeper issues. He fails to fulfill you, but you love him.

But, do you love him enough? Do you love him enough to stay with him and lose a part of yourself? Enough to sacrifice yourself for him? Are you able to forget about *you* and take his hand and walk with him through his hell? Can you love him that much? Your needs will be secondary. He needs you more. Even if you do love him enough, can you stay with him and be miserable? Aren't you supposed to be happy? But, how do you walk away and know what he may do to himself if you leave him? How do you live with yourself?

Can you ask him if he loves *you* enough? Does he love you enough to go on and let you be, to leave you alone?

You have a choice. You can continue to care about him, be there for him, and lose a part of yourself in doing so. If you decide to continue to care about him, it will take self-sacrifice. But, does it have to? Can you live with him and take care of *yourself* and let go of him?

Alcoholism is a disease, and it is progressive. It requires treatment just like any other disease. Can you perceive and accept his alcoholic demeanor, his alcoholic stupor, his disappearance into the alcoholic world, and insist he pursue treatment? Can you get your loved one back? You don't think you want him back, but you forget what he was like before the alcohol stripped him. You forget his mental suffering and what he was exposed to in his younger years. You forget the young, handsome man you dated and to whom you were engaged. You forget how truly crazy you were about him. You forget *him*. He has been replaced with someone you do not like. Can you allow him back in your life if he undergoes the proper treatment?

You have other choices. You can accept him and love him the way he is and quit trying to change him, or you can decide that he is not good for you, and you can walk out. You will have to decide. But first, you may want to try to reach him and convince him to seek help. He has buried his weaknesses, his traumatic witnessing of the unimaginable, and his vulnerability. He tries to be stalwart and manly and even macho, but he cannot keep up this pretense forever. You can help him but only if he wants to help himself. You can give up on changing him otherwise. In giving it up, he may decide to change on his own.

In Daphne Rose Kingma's *Coming Apart—Why Relationships End and How to Live Through the Ending of Yours,* these words were meant for my eyes to see and my soul to hear: "… it is only when we truly understand the meaning of our relationships—the tasks we undertook in them, the gifts we received from them—that we can survive their endings with our selves and our self-esteem intact." I was told by a wise, intuitive woman that I had been given a gift. I had been given a gift of love for Mike, and I had been able to see beyond his physical form. I agreed. I saw into his sorrowful soul. Even though I was not responsible for him, I know why I took this on.

I remember the overwhelming feeling of love—the recognition and the knowing—when I first gazed upon the face of each of my newborn children. I felt a deep and powerful connection, and that feeling has stayed with me with each of my daughters. It was there with Mike. I think that is why I stayed with him for as long as I did. I felt I saw his buried goodness, his shattered soul, and I had an otherwise inexplicable love for him. It was always there, even in those moments when I did not like him. I lost myself over the years while I was immersing myself into his life and while I was focusing on keeping him off the alcoholic path.

Although I had lost myself for a time, I have found myself again. I have dealt with the pain, but I have also dealt with myself. I have searched for me, and I have found me. I have learned to love myself—I knew I had to accomplish that before I could be open to accepting a real, loving relationship into my life.

I know who I am, and my identity is my own and not someone else's appendage as spouse, partner, or even girlfriend. I am who I am, and that goes way beyond my outer appearance and my thoughts. Who I am is deeper than that. It is the part of me that is eternal, that will go on even as I die. It is the true me that is full of love, joy, and peace as God intended for me to be. For the first time, I can finally and freely—without resisting or manipulating—embrace life.

The Four Seasons
(Haikus)

A shower of drops
Spring bursts into colored life
And the birds sing on.

The sandy seashore
Speckled with silvered sea-drops
Awakens to life.

The brilliant colors
Making a kaleidoscope
Of God's dying world.

The drifting snowflakes
Teasing the children with warmth
Of cold days ahead.

EPILOGUE

I was married to a Vietnam vet. Somehow, I forgot that over the years, but I do know that my husband would not have committed suicide if he had not gone to the Vietnam War. My children do not have depression or mental illness in their family lineage. What they do have is a war hero, a war hero who encountered experiences none of us can even remotely understand.

The Vietnam War was a horrible war. It was one of America's longest wars, and it was known as the war of attrition or "body count" war. The American military fought the Viet Cong relentlessly during that war, assuming if enough Viet Cong were killed, North Vietnam would surrender. At the same time, the Viet Cong leaders sent in endless numbers of troops and continued to fight, thinking the citizens of the United States would not be able to tolerate seeing the return of American soldiers in body bags for very long. The killings continued, and the casualties multiplied on both sides. The United States had more than 58,000 soldiers die in that war, and over 300,000 soldiers were wounded.

Mike was stationed in one of the base hospitals in Vietnam, and he attended to these casualties. I found letters he had written to his family, and one letter describes some of what he experienced:

> "Things here are looking bad. There's still a war going on and it's getting bigger. The VC and NVA have moved within striking range of my base and everyone's starting to worry since we really don't have any protection except ARVN which is like I said no protection. I hope they run out of supplies soon or we'll be in for some trouble.
>
> "We're starting to get casualties in from the field hospitals now, so we're going to be quite busy this month. I wish they would just get all the Americans out of here before it becomes a bloodbath. Everyone that has gone home on R & R has come back saying that the war was over as far as everyone in the States was concerned. I wish they could see the young GIs going out of here with no legs, arms, and eyes, not to mention the ones going home in the Box! 98 Days to go!"

How did my husband survive that? How did he maintain normalcy for thirty-plus years after he experienced what he encountered as a medic in the Vietnam War? I would like to think I had something to do with that. I would like to think my daughters had something to do with it as well. My brother-in-law once said Mike was the happiest after he met me. I know Mike loved us. I know he had trouble showing it. I also know that we all loved him and cared for him. He was a Vietnam vet, a war hero. My daughters and I should feel good that we were able to offer him some joyful moments, even though he may not have responded with joy.

I had forgotten the impact trauma has on the brain. It is a fact that the physiology of the human brain is altered once trauma occurs. Stress can create elevated cortisol levels in the brain, and when the stress is removed, the levels of cortisol dissipate. With prolonged stress, however, a large amount of cortisol remains in the brain, which can result in long-term changes in the brain structure and function. These changes lead to anxiety, depression, and post-traumatic stress disorder. This applies directly to our soldiers, who are in highly stressful war situations and are experiencing life-threatening and prolonged stress. My husband could not feel happy the way you and I feel happy. He had said that a number of times. "I don't feel happy." Vietnam did that to him. Vietnam caused him to take his life.

My daughters and I have grieved for this war hero. Our grief is small compared to his load. I know that now. He had no choice. He could not "do this" anymore. He had said those very words. He had tried as long as he could to appear "okay," but he had to continually escape through the bottle to keep that appearance up. When the bottle overtook him, he had no other escape.

What a strong man. He lasted many years longer than he probably desired. He did that for his family. If it had not been for us, he would have been a drunk on the side of the road many years earlier. He had said those words, and he knew them to be true. He would have joined his fellow soldiers who at this very moment are lying on the sides of roads all throughout our country, empty bottles in their war-torn hands, desperately wishing for more, and praying they can forget what they saw and touched in the jungles of Vietnam.

I wasn't married to Merlot. I was married to the Vietnam War and the devastation it caused for one soldier. He was only twenty years old when he enlisted. The average age for soldiers in that war was under twenty years—19.2 years has been reported by some sources. As a young man of twenty, he saw incomprehensible suffering brought on by the Vietnam War. Merlot was his only escape from the memories of that war. Others escaped with harder drugs and escaped from life itself. They live on the streets in California, Colorado, Florida, and many other states. They are homeless. My husband did not take that route initially, but he could not sustain the route he took. He could not maintain the appearance of normalcy. He just could not do it anymore. He succumbed to his demons, and he left us before he escaped from all of it.

The Vietnam War was unlike any other. We sent our young men out and exposed them to unspeakable horrors and then returned them home amidst a growing antiwar movement (which was in full swing in the late sixties and early seventies). We did not honor them upon their return, but instead ridiculed our Vietnam veterans and treated them with great disrespect and sometimes even with cruelty. Sometimes we flicked obscene gestures in their direction or shouted disparaging words into their haggard faces. Sometimes we spat on them. Sometimes we kicked them. I cannot begin to imagine their shock as they witnessed this homecoming after all they had been through. I cannot imagine how demoralized they must have felt.

Many veterans learned later that they could not discuss their service during that bloodshed war, and many learned to pretend the war had never existed for them. Many learned to compartmentalize their experience and numb themselves to any memory of it. How dare we do that to them? How dare we expect them to pretend all was well? How dare we not recognize their withdrawal and their numbness? We did not revere our warriors as we should have. Instead, we allowed them to set up residence on our streets with our homeless population, and we enabled them to become drug addicts and even to commit suicide. I think Oprah Winfrey said it first: Shame on us.

I look out over the valley from where I perch on the rock-strewn mountainside. Mount Nebo has so many special memories for me, and I bask in the sunshine and hug the memories to my healing heart. I loved this broken man, and I felt his presence here on Mount Nebo as I wrote the words that somehow lessen the blow that his undoing has done to me and to my daughters. I watch as a white, luminescent hang glider floats by, the wings glistening in the sun's rays. I see an eagle fly by and thank God with gratitude for all He has brought into my life in the past ten years.

This summer marks the eleven-year anniversary of my husband's leaving me, and I can only marvel at God's world as it lay at my feet. I see Petit Jean Mountain in the distance. I see the S-shaped curve of the Arkansas river as it winds through the valley, threading its way toward Dardanelle and the Lock and Dam. I look out to my left and see Lake Dardanelle with its pelican-faced, gaping-mouth shape as viewed from where I sit. I watch the hang glider make a maneuver and turn back toward me and then make another turn away from me. It reminds me of the butterfly that hovered in this very spot, when we released my ex-husband's ashes nearly ten years ago. I see the glider coast lazily back and forth, and I watch as it drifts higher and higher into the pale blueness of the sky. As it vanishes into the heavenly arc high above my head, I know it was there to remind me that he is at peace ... and now I am at peace.

POSTFACE

How many of us know military men and women who have returned to their homeland following the trauma of war and have exhibited symptoms of post-traumatic stress disorder? While the specific symptoms may vary from individual to individual, many returning service members display symptoms of distress after they have encountered the significant stressor of war. If the symptoms are a result of chemical reactions in the brain, how do they avoid this natural development? While some are likely to avoid it, I think many of our returning military are impacted to some extent.

Mike displayed symptoms of PTSD, and I am sure he made attempts to ignore any intrusive memories of his times in the medical hospital in Vietnam. I do recall in our early years of marriage, he occasionally cried out and awakened from a distressful dream, but he did not react physically, thank goodness. I was never in harm's way. While I never saw any evidence of his having intrusive thoughts or of his re-experiencing events that occurred in Vietnam, he did have a lot of anxiety.

I was taught that anxiety was a manifestation of an attempt to repress distressful memories, thoughts, or feelings. I am sure there are other explanations, but Mike was apparently very good at repressing unwanted memories, and he avoided talking about Vietnam at all costs. Over time, he became more withdrawn and eventually withdrew from his friends and from his loved ones, which coincided with his depressive symptoms becoming more noticeable. His drinking enabled him to further avoid any reminders of Vietnam and to numb him at those times when he felt uneasy or when he felt he did not belong in this world.

Many military individuals avoid talking about their war experiences and avoid activities that remind them of their war days. These individuals refuse to read books or see movies depicting war. They may not acknowledge any emotions associated with the trauma of war, and they may not allow their fear, their pain, or their guilt to surface. They may keep these feelings bottled up, and they may become numb to any reminders of their trauma. With the passage of time, they may become generally numb, and they may no longer react to life events, to people, or to any expressed emotion. They may withdraw from their friends and their loved ones, and they may isolate themselves from their family members. They may eventually resist participating in family life or in family outings or events.

When military personnel have PTSD, their staunch avoidance of activities that might remind them of their war experiences may become wearing and fatiguing, and they may become impatient, irritable, and easily angered. I did see Mike's irritability. He was easily annoyed, and he let you know when he was irritated. His tendency was to be rather passive, however, and it usually took a lot for him to react with anger. In addition, service members with PTSD may have a pessimistic outlook, and they may have difficulty feeling positive emotions. They may have psychosomatic complaints. Some may engage in maladaptive behaviors, and some may self-medicate. Many soldiers who returned from the Vietnam War have said, "I am not happy. I don't fit into this world. I don't belong in this world."

When military members are exposed to life-threatening events associated with wartimes, the severity of their distress symptoms may partially depend on how they view the events. If they go off to war with realistic views of themselves, clear understandings of right and wrong, views of the world as just or fair, and feelings of safety in their normal world, how does wartime and the change to battlefield scenery impact them? When soldiers fight in battles and participate in or witness actions contrary to their beliefs, how do they continue to see the world as just or normal? And how can they not lose sight of who they are when they do or see something they normally would not, such as kill or see personnel, civilians or even enemies wounded or killed? Or when they survive IED, mortar, and rocket attacks? How do they interpret their actions or the events when they suddenly shift from what they perceive as right to what they perceive as wrong? And how do they get through their guilt and second-guessing of their actions ("If I had acted sooner, my buddy would still be here.")? Understandably, stressful wartime events, when coupled with the violation of previously established beliefs or views, could produce an intensification in distress symptoms.

For medics, is it possible that the sense of self is violated when they do not do something they should have done? For example, when a dying soldier pleads for his life, and the medic is unable to save a life, how is that medic not tormented and ridden with irrevocable guilt?

The service member likely feels alone when either of these war situations occur. Both the soldier on the battlefield and the medic tending to the wounded could feel abandoned by the world when they find themselves in their respective, horrendous scenarios. Their trust in all that is good and honorable could be shaken, assuming they had that beforehand. They may no longer have feelings of safety, and their views of the world and what to expect from the world become altered. I do not understand how our deployed military come back to our "normal" world and become reintegrated without a lot of difficulty. It is not an easy process, evidently, as there are numerous articles and websites to assist the returning service member and their families. I have listed some of these articles in the resources section that follows.

Some returning service members have difficulties in relationships. While the returning spouses may be interested in the sexual relationship with their significant other, they may have difficulty feeling the intimacy and the closeness. The partner, of course, may sense the spouse's lack of emotional involvement and may question their love and ultimately question the relationship. The partner may feel increasingly hurt by the spouse's apparent emotional unavailability.

The U.S. Department of Veterans Affairs has a wealth of information on PTSD, its symptoms and its behavioral manifestations, as well as its impact on family members, and, specifically, the spouse. The information from the National Center for PTSD is found under Health Care on the VA website and is available to veterans, their family and friends, and the general public. One article in particular, "Partners of Veterans with PTSD: Common Problems" highlights the partner's reactions to the veteran's PTSD symptoms and behaviors and provides helpful suggestions for coping and for reducing the stress that is felt when living with a trauma survivor. This resource as well as others are noted in the resources section.

The military's plight and its suicide rate are major concerns. At the same time, we are seeing increasing evidence of emotional difficulties in our civilian population. A rise in complaints of anxiety and depression are reported in our youth and young adults as well as in all adult groups, and these issues cross all professions and all socioeconomic levels.

The suicide statistic is also on the rise for civilians. The American Foundation for Suicide Prevention reports suicide is the tenth leading cause of death in the United States. According to the foundation, veterans account for approximately twenty percent of all suicides. The majority are civilians. Each year, 44,965 Americans die by suicide. The actual number is estimated to be higher due to underreporting because of the stigma attached to suicide.

The World Health Organization (WHO) estimates that each year approximately one million people die from suicide, which represents a global mortality rate of sixteen people per one hundred thousand or one death every forty seconds. It is predicted that by 2020, the rate of death will increase to one every twenty seconds. These statistics are alarming and point to the need for a more comprehensive approach, one that involves all of us.

Multitudes of people have gone through tragic events that seemed insurmountable at the time. We are not alone. We all are a part of the same species, and we share our humanness, our vulnerabilities, and our societal responsibilities. We are all connected, and it is time we show our support, offer our love, and be there for each other. We must all unite and bring love into our world. We must put less focus on hate and haters and let love expand. If we don't, the mental health issues will skyrocket, and we will continue to see increasing numbers of suicide events as well as upsurges in school shootings, mass shootings, homicides, gang killings, and other acts of hate. Our society could see its undoing if we do not change our current path and make this world a truly better place for all of mankind. Let's focus on love.

***

To live is a luxury
I am living
And if I would only remember
that time is passing me by
I would appreciate my life more
and revel in its glory

RESOURCES

I have read many books and articles that have helped me during this journey. Part of these writings have stimulated my thinking and may be apparent in what I have stated within these pages. I would like to encourage anyone who is seeking answers and seeking inner peace to consider any of the following manuscripts and websites. While I hope you find these helpful, I cannot endorse or guarantee the efficacy of any particular resource.

Bach, Richard. *Illusions—The Adventures of a Reluctant Messiah.* New York: Delacorte Press/Eleanor Friede, Dell Publishing, Random House, 1977.

Deits, Bob. *Life after Loss: A Practical Guide to Renewing Your Life after Experiencing Major Loss, Fourth Edition.* Boston: Da Capo Lifelong Books, 2004.

Kingma, Daphne Rose. *Coming Apart: Why Relationships End and How to Live Through the Ending of Yours.* San Francisco: Conari Press-Red Wheel/Weiser, LLC, 2012.

Kovacs, Liberty, PhD, MFT. *Building a Reality-Based Relationship.* New York: I Universe, Inc., 2007.

Levang, Elizabeth, PhD. *When Men Grieve: Why Men Grieve Differently and How You Can Help.* Minneapolis: Fairview Press, 1998.

Moore, Beth. *The Patriarchs: Encountering The God Of Abraham, Isaac, and Jacob.* Nashville: LifeWay Press, 2005.

Norwood, Robin. *Women Who Love Too Much: When You Keep Wishing and Hoping He'll Change.* New York: Pocket Books, 1986.

Rothschild, Jennifer. *Walking By Faith: Lessons Learned in the Dark.* Nashville: LifeWay Press, 2003.

Rushnell, Squire. *When God Winks at You: How God Speaks Directly to You Through the Power of Coincidence.* New York: MJF Books, 2006.

Tolle, Eckhart. *The Power of Now: A Guide to Spiritual Enlightenment.* Vancouver: Namaste Publishing Inc., 1997.

Wolfelt, Alan D., PhD. *Understanding Grief: Helping Yourself Heal.* New York: Brunner-Routledge, 1992.

Walsch, Neale Donald. *Conversations with God: An Uncommon Dialogue.* New York: G.P. Putnam's Sons, 1996.

Walsh, Sheila. *Life Is Tough But God Is Faithful: How to See God's Love in Difficult Times.* Nashville: Thomas Nelson, Inc., 1999.

Daily Inspiration—Dr. Wayne Dyer
www.drwaynedyer.com/wayne-dyer-quotes/

Living Proof Ministries—Beth Moore
www.lproof.org
https://blog.lproof.org

Symptoms of Inner Peace ©1984 by Saskia Davis
www.symptomsofinnerpeace.net

Magazine articles and books for a better understanding of the Vietnam War and what the soldiers experienced:

Smith, Jack P. "Death in the Ia Drang Valley." The *Saturday Evening Post*, January 28, 1967.

Steinman, Ron. *The Soldiers' Story: Vietnam in Their Own Words.* New York: Fall River Press, 2011.

Sheehan, Neil. *A Bright Shining Lie: John Paul Vann and America in Vietnam.* New York: Random House, Inc., 1988.

Books and articles related to PTSD and Addictions/Alcoholism:

American Psychiatric Association. *Diagnostic and Statistical Manual of Mental Disorders, Fifth Edition.* Washington: APA, 2013.

Beattie, Melody. *Codependents' Guide to the Twelve Steps: How to Find the Right Program for You and Apply Each of the Twelve Steps to Your Own Issues.* New York: Simon and Schuster, 1990.

Ellers, Kevin, MDiv, Nancy Rikli, MS, and H. Norman Wright, MRE, MA. *Grief Following Trauma.* Ellicott City: International Critical Incident Stress Foundation Inc., 2006.

Keller, John E. *Alcohol—A Family Affair—Help for Families in Which There is Alcohol Misuse.* San Diego: The Kroc Foundation. Operation Cork.

Lange, Gary, PhD, MFT, NCGC. "Addictions 'Light Up' the Brain." *The National Psychologist.* May/June 2011, page 21.

Mitchell, Jeffrey T., PhD, CTS. *Advanced Group Crisis Intervention: Strategies and Tactics for Complex Situations – Participant Manual, 3rd Edition.* Ellicott City: International Critical Incident Stress Foundation, Inc., 2006.

Pisano, Mark C., EdD, NCSP. "Military Deployment: How School Psychologists Can Help." *Communique, The Newspaper of the National Association of School Psychologists,* November 2011, pages 21-22.

⤳⤳

Resources for service members and/or their families:

"Partners of Veterans with PTSD: Common Problems," The U.S. Department of Veterans Affairs, Health Care, National Center for PTSD

AboutFace—a website where Veterans, their family members and
    clinicians talk about turning life around with PTSD treatment

"Here's What You Need to Know About Reintegration"
    https://www.military.com/spouse/military-deployment/
    reintegration/returning-to-home-life-after-deployment.html

"Returning home: What we know about the reintegration of deployed
    service members into their families and communities," The
    National Council on Family Relations. www.ncfr.org/ncfr-
    report/focus/military-families/returning-home

"Returning Home From Deployment" https://www.militaryonesource.
    mil/military-life-cycle/deployment/returning-home-from-
    deployment

"5 Rules for the Best Possible Reintegration / Military Spouse" https://
    militaryspouse.com/relationships/5-rules-for-the-best-possible-
    reintegration/

～つ～つ

National Suicide Prevention Lifeline
also servicing VA Suicide Hotline:

1-800-273-8255

www.speakingofsuicide.com/resources/

ACKNOWLEDGMENTS

Mike's brother, John, and his cousin permitted my stay at the Mount Nebo cabin whenever I asked, and I thank them for that writing time on the mountain. I appreciate my extended family and all their support; they allowed me to write at the cabin without interruption when I visited that beautiful area.

I am not sure if I would have thought of using my poetry in *Married to Merlot*, but when my friend Don Israel sent my poems to me, I immediately saw the parallels and decided to insert them where they were most compatible. I appreciate Don's thoughtfulness and wisdom in suggesting I have all those poems before publishing.

I thank my high school buddy Ann Wiedower Renfroe for her permission to print the poem "Solitude" she and I wrote in 1970 on a car trip to Florida. My college pal Paulette Locke Johnson and I coauthored the poem "Love Can Be Lonely" in 1971, and I was granted permission by her sister, Margaret Moore, to use it for this publication. Paulette was a dear friend we all lost to ALS in 2009. I will always hold her in my heart.

My nephew David Freyaldenhoven served in the Regular Army and Army National Guard and has seen his share of distressed fellow service members. I am grateful for his support and encouragement as well as his input on the postface regarding the impact of PTSD on the military. David was deployed three times, and I thank him for his service and dedication to our country.

A college buddy Roger Dale, who served our country during the Vietnam War, steered me to the research on white phosphorus when he told me Mike had treated service members who had been exposed to it. I appreciate Roger's input which provides a harsh reminder of the agony endured by some of our military, as well as by the medical staff who treated them.

I thank Tootie Beck Nicholson for her encouraging comments and for her thoughtful input on certain highly personal passages in the manuscript. I have tender feelings for her mother, my Aunt Louise, who kept telling me she wanted to read my book. I am thankful I sent her the manuscript in 2016, as she left this world in January 2018 before I started the final edit. I appreciate her positive response, and I miss her and our telephone conversations.

Linda Reed was a great support, and we were in each other's lives at the right time. She had her own tragic loss several months after mine, and we spent many moments holding each other up and giving praise to our Maker. She encouraged me to write the story, and I am grateful to her for allowing me to talk about my intentions which in turn helped this book take form.

A special thank you goes to three of my readers: Frances Starnes, my dear friend and college roommate, for her continuous support and elevating feedback; Jacquie Byram Reed, my dancing buddy, for her positive input and encouraging words; and Gloria Henry, my adventuresome friend, who affirmed my hope that my book would be helpful to others. I also appreciate her daughter, Jordan, and her words of wisdom during my grieving period: "It has to work through you."

I appreciate two of my readers and dear friends Lorrie Cosgrove and Vivian Pinner Watson who reinforced my belief that I might be able to help others who find themselves in difficult relationships and tragic situations. Another dear friend Michelle McDonald graciously read my manuscript at the peak of her busyness, and I am thankful for her and for our connection.

I thank two other readers: John for his openness and Becky for shedding light on specific incidents. I appreciate Becky's suggestions and input on the edited manuscript.

I thank all others who were supportive and who encouraged me during this time: Cindy Richetti, Dawn and Rachel Lytle, Jane Weden, Charlie and Samm Morgan, Tom and Mary Peugh, Jodi Johnson, Joan Bauer, Barb Traylor, Susan Korb, BJ Martin Wiegmann, Kathleen Furness, Rita Garlanger, Hope Hanna, Ruthanne Stabler, Diane Eymer, Nancy Ulerick, Diana Stewart, Tom Peterson, Valerie Tanner, Stacey O'Brien, Erica Hague, Phyllis Ingram, Karen Thurlow, Phyllis Crotty, Debbie Cymbaluk, Susan Wadsworth, Libby Stout, Nikki Perry, Lisa Armele-Dalton, Elaine Edwards, Laurel Coon, Judith Thayer, Kelly Whitaker, Wanda Peterson, Lynelle Jackson, and Tori Strahan. I am sure I have missed a few, but all were important to me.

My dear, talented sister Carol Watson designed and painted the beautiful cover image. Carol was also a reader, and I am grateful for her feedback, especially her comments on my representation of family members.

Dr. Kathleen Lewis, PhD was a significant influence, and I gratefully accepted her awareness and knowledge of the Vietnam veteran's plight, her insights, and her compassion. She made suggestions as I was writing my memoir, and I appreciate her contributions.

My heartfelt thanks to the Palms Presbyterian Church in Jacksonville Beach, Florida, and to the pastor, Dr. Tom Walker. I quoted some of the passages from Mike's uplifting funeral sermon, and I thank Dr. Walker for his permission to use those portions. Carol DiGiusto, associate pastor, who met with my family the day after Mike's death to discuss the funeral service, later said to me, "It is a story that has to be told."

Debbie Gomer, author of *The By-Your-Side Cancer Guide: Empowered, Proactive, Prepared,* had suggestions that helped start me on the path to publishing. I wish her luck in her writing endeavors. We both attended publishing and blogging workshops by Sharon Y. Cobb, professional screenwriter and workshop instructor at the University of North Florida. Sharon provided a wealth of information and started me on the path from writing to publishing.

I can never thank my editor enough for her infinite wisdom, clear vision, and unrivaled talent. Deborrah Hoag, The Right Editor, and I were destined to meet, and I have enjoyed her as much as I have been dazzled by her thoughts, ideas, editing abilities, and beautiful red hair.

I thank Fran Keiser, Sagaponack Books & Design, for her mentorship during the pre-publishing months. I appreciate her suggestions, boundless knowledge, and extraordinary design capability.

I am forever grateful to my mother for her wisdom and for her spoken words when I was writing and feeling joy. "That is because your spirit is joyful when you are doing what you are supposed to be doing." I once described the man I would meet to her and told her he would be kind, considerate, smart, funny, and he would adore me, as I would adore him. She did not tell me then, but she did not think there were men like that (other than her sons). I met Jim, and she told me she was wrong. I miss her, and she will be in my heart forever.

I am thankful for both of my sons-in-law. My eldest's husband, a successful corporate leader, surprised me with a gift of the first purchased domain name. My youngest daughter's husband, a gifted musician with The New Starts Now, stepped out with his music despite his fears and anxieties and inspired me to release my own anxieties and shed my uncomfortableness.

My heartfelt thanks and all my love go to my three dear daughters, true women of exceptional strength. They have been on this journey from their beginning, and they are venturing out on their own paths and learning their own lessons. I think they did give up on my publishing, and I thank the youngest for pushing me toward the finish. I think they now realize "things happen for a reason," and it is not our timeline but our Creator's.

A special thank you to my best friend, Jim, who encourages my writing and who is my greatest supporter. He has provided continuous encouragement, praise, and unconditional love as well as many delicious meals during the final pre-publishing days. He has proven that yes, indeed, "there are men like that."

ABOUT THE AUTHOR

Martha Louise is a retired school psychologist and former mental health therapist. She credits her psychology background and education as the catalyst that prompted her to write her self-help memoir with its message of hope. Martha currently resides in Florida. Her three daughters live in Illinois. For additional information, visit her website:

www.MarthaLouise.net

Made in the USA
Columbia, SC
29 May 2019